PACIFIC OCEAN

Oahu

HAWAIIAN ISLANDS

Wake

Johnston

MARSHALL ISLANDS

P O L Y N E S I A

Pohnpei

Kosrae

KIRIBATI

Howland
Baker

EQUATOR

NAURU

PHOENIX ISLANDS

LINE ISLANDS

ND

SOLOMON ISLANDS

ELLICE ISLANDS

SANTA CRUZ ISLANDS

SAMOA

A N E S I A

VANUATU
(NEW HEBRIDES)

FIJI ISLANDS

0	STATUTE MILES		1,000
0	KILOMETERS		1,600

Island Groups of the Pacific

Prehistoric Architecture in Micronesia

PREHISTORIC ARCHITECTURE IN MICRONESIA

by William N. Morgan
with photographs by Newton Morgan
assisted by Dylan Morgan

KEGAN PAUL INTERNATIONAL, LONDON

ISBN 07103 03580

This edition published in 1989 by Kegan Paul International
PO Box 256, London WC1B 3SW
Distributed by
The Canterbury Press Pty Ltd
2/7 Rushdale Street
Scoresby, Victoria 3179
Australia

Frontispiece:
A portal flanked by walls of stacked prismatic
basalt leads into the residential compound of
Lurun in the ancient island city of Leluh,
Kosrae.

CONTENTS

Beyond the walls of Fanana/Sremuta's west corner lie the remains of the central canal that once served numerous boat landings in Leluh, Kosrae.

PREFACE

During the many centuries before Western contact, the people of Micronesia adapted themselves to their remote island environments with increasing success. Largely isolated from foreign influences, they developed an architecture uniquely suited to their cultures. Their richly diverse and inventive architecture evolved from a very fundamental level of human creativity. Unlike the Western architects of today, who necessarily work with a sometimes bewildering array of synthetic information, the ancient Micronesian builders created their monuments in direct and intimate contact with the natural systems of their environment. A distinct sense of immediacy, of the direct interaction between viewer and place, pervades the prehistoric architecture of Micronesia.

The study of prehistoric architecture presents an opportunity to deepen our understanding of creative human instincts and to expand our awareness of architecture. Since prehistoric people left no written explanation of their intentions, if any, regarding architectural symbolism, style, or meaning, we the observers are free to focus our attention on such fundamentals as order and pattern. We clearly do not know whether or not aesthetics motivated the ancient builders in selecting their sites, placing their structures, or shaping their spaces. Nonetheless, prehistoric architecture presents contemporary observers with ideas about the built environment that previously lay beyond our experience.

The sites presented in this study were selected primarily because they had been recorded relatively accurately and were distinguished examples illustrating the unique architectural characteristics of particular islands or groups. A deliberate attempt is made to treat each island equally rather than lavish more attention on one or two locations and all but ignore the others. In the final analysis, the site selection represents my preference; consequently, it is subject to the alternative views of other observers.

My first encounter with the prehistoric architecture of Micronesia occurred in 1954. While serving in the United States Navy, I was stationed for nineteen months in Guam.

There I saw numerous *latte* foundations (stone columns and capstones) but could find no reliable source of information about the unusual structures. During a chance visit to the neighboring island of Tinian, an elderly Micronesian told me of an immense *latte* in the jungle. Following his directions, I found the ruins of the extraordinary House of Taga with two of its original twelve columns still standing. The tops of the capstones were some sixteen feet above ground level. While photographing and measuring several of the fallen megaliths, I noticed that some shafts seemed to exhibit pronounced entasis, a slightly convex curve compensating for the illusion of concavity.

Late one night in Guam I entered a bar for a nightcap. Sitting next to me was a naval aviator whom I did not know. He said he routinely flew aerial reconnaissance missions over the islands of Micronesia, primarily looking for ships fishing illegally in the islands' territorial waters. An unusual incident had occurred earlier that day during a flight over an island that began with the letter *P*. Unfortunately, I did not recall whether he said Palau or Pohnpei—the two islands are separated by a distance of some sixteen hundred miles. From a high altitude the aviator saw what appeared to be a Venice-like city built on a shallow reef along the island's shore. His aircraft descended for closer inspection.

Stone walls surrounded innumerable rectangular islets bigger than football fields, and a network of canals and seawalls extended from the open Pacific to dense mangrove swamps along the shore. Since the mysterious city obviously was not a Second World War structure or a more recent installation, the aviator did not photograph it although his mission involved aerial photography. At this point I wrongly assumed that the stranger was testing my credibility with an outlandish tale. I asked him what he was drinking and how long he had been in the bar and suggested that the next time he should photograph any mysterious cities or pink elephants he might see.

Not until more than thirty years later did I realize that the aviator, whom I have not seen again, had described accurately some of the extraordinary remains of Nan Madol on Pohnpei. The ancient center is a magnificent example of prehistoric Micronesian architecture. To the best of my knowledge no mention of the remarkable work has existed heretofore in the literature of architectural history. One of the reasons for this study is to bring the ancient monuments to the attention of persons interested in the world's past achievements, with the view of stimulating fresh and meaningful possibilities for the future.

Upon resuming my studies in architecture at the Harvard Graduate School of Design, I sought information on *latte* stone structures and other possible monuments in the Marianas and the Carolines. Not knowing where to look, I found nothing. My distinguished professor of architectural history, the late Siegfried Gideon, examined my House of Taga photographs and sketches. He concluded that he had no idea of its origins and suggested that I explore the subject further if the opportunity ever arose.

Some thirty years later I happened to see an article about early migrations of people to various island groups of the Pacific. In the article, published by the National Geographic Society (Stuart, 1983), a brief reference to Micronesia mentioned an ancient ceremonial center named Nan Madol on Pohnpei and there was a small illustration of the House of Taga *latte* on Tinian. The aviator's tale and my recollection of *latte* stones in the Marianas immediately came to mind. I searched again through an encyclopedia, where I found a vague reference to sculpted hills in Palau and continuing archaeological research.

Now more than ever interested in the origins and extent of ancient architecture in the South Seas, I sought the advice of Professor Stephen Williams at the Peabody Museum of Harvard University, who had assisted me in the past. Having no familiarity with current archaeological activity in Micronesia, he referred me to Dr. Richard Gould of Brown University. Dr. Gould recently had been in Hawaii and fortunately knew exactly where to find the information I sought.

Moreover, he put me in contact with a former student of his at the University of Hawaii, Joyce E. Bath, who at that time was preparing her doctoral dissertation on Pohnpeian prehistory. Without Dr. Bath's patient cooperation, this study never would have been possible.

After visiting various sites on the islands in 1984 and reviewing the information available, I decided to prepare a study of prehistoric architecture based on five distinct island groups. The architectural ideas of each group are presented in their respective cultural and geographical contexts. The first two sections, the Palau Archipelago and the Yap Islands, introduce contrasting examples of prehistoric architecture in western Micronesia. The third and fourth sections present Pohnpei and Kosrae, respectively. The remarkable stone cities of Nan Madol and Leluh illustrate the ancient monuments of central Micronesia. The last of the five study areas is the section on the Marianas, about which least is known at present. The four better known subjects are examined first with the view of understanding more thoroughly the range of reasonable possibilities for prehistoric architecture in the Marianas.

Certain omissions from the study require mention at this point. First, the reader may wonder why major island groups, such as Truk Lagoon, are not discussed. The reason is that I elected to concentrate as thoroughly as space permits on a few examples rather than including more island groups in less detail. The ancient and extensive stone wall enclosure of Fauba on Tol island and the stone platforms of Moen are excellent and worthy examples of Truk's enduring prehistoric architecture. Also missing are presentations of traditional architecture on the low coral islands of eastern Micronesia: the Marshalls, Kiribati (formerly the Gilberts), and Nauru. For instance, illustrations are lacking for a *maneaba*, a traditional meeting house in Kiribati. A very impressive example of this building type is the *maneaba* of Tarawa. The reader is requested to accept the study on the basis of its several thoroughly presented examples and to seek additional information from other sources.

METHODOLOGY

". . . pay close attention to what we regard as untutored people and how they approach their problems, how they approached them in the past, and how they still approach them. . . . quite often people naturally do things when left to their devices, do things very well, and solve an awful lot of problems that architects tend to forget."

—PAUL RUDOLPH,
on vernacular architecture
(Warfield, 1983)

I began this study of prehistoric architecture in Micronesia in 1983 by assembling available information and identifying additional sources of data. Dr. Joyce Bath of the University of Hawaii was particularly helpful in obtaining copies of valuable documents from the Hamilton Library and from the Bernice P. Bishop Museum in Honolulu. After I spent four months reviewing information on various sites, the overall plan for conducting the study evolved.

Monumental remains and relatively sound documentation seemed to exist on five major islands and groups: Pohnpei, Kosrae, Yap, Palau, and the Marianas presented a rich diversity of solutions to similar architectural problems. Before visiting the sites, however, I made a concerted effort to develop a comprehensive overview of existing information so that my field activities could concentrate on missing information. Unpublished basic research, such as Hans G. Hornbostel's documentation of Marianas *latte* sites during the 1920s, proved invaluable. Many research projects in Micronesia presently are nearing completion or recently have been completed. The often unpublished results of this research are another highly valuable resource.

The Bernice P. Bishop Museum's library is a rich repository of information on many of the prehistoric monuments in Micronesia, such as English translations for the German reports of the South Sea Expedition from 1908 to 1910. Lee S. Motteler generously assisted with reproductions of photographs and maps selected from the Bishop Museum's extensive resource files. Interviews with Dr. Patrick V. Kirch, Dr. Patrick C. McCoy, and other scholars at the Bishop Museum broadened the scope of the study and sharpened its focus.

The problems of interpreting the prehistoric monuments deserve special and continuing emphasis. Because this study primarily concerns architecture, the text often contains extensive architectural details and precise site descriptions. In many cases weighty issues of interpretation also are involved; these engage archaeologists and anthropologists in ongoing investigations. The issues cannot be ignored. For example, the nature of the chiefdom society that built Nan Madol is the subject of a variety of interpretations by scholars. Readers who may be more deeply interested in problems of interpretation are invited to refer to the authorities cited in the text and the sources listed in the bibliography.

During April and May of 1984 I visited each of the five major sites. Shortly after arriving on Pohnpei my party established its base camp on Nahnningi Island. The island is located in the lagoon near Nan Madol, where we spent the daylight hours for the next several days. Unfortunately, the Pohnpei historic preservation officer, Pensile Lawrence, was on vacation at the time of our visit. Drs. J. Stephen Athens and Joyce E. Bath took time from their archaeological surveying to show us many of the islets of Nan Madol, to discuss prehistoric architecture at length, and to recommend additional reading on the subject.

Our hosts arranged for a Pohnpeian whose name was Ansber to act as our guide. One morning Dr. William S. Ayres of the University of Oregon showed us Pahnwi, where his archaeological team was working. He discussed details of several islets with which he was particularly familiar. Our party thoroughly photographed architectural features on four of the major islets, sketched typical architectural details, and recorded measurements. We noted construction systems of wood-framed Pohnpeian structures, such as the cookhouse on Nahnningi and the airport terminal where traditional cord bindings join log posts and beams.

On Kosrae the historic preservation officer, Teddy John, graciously guided us through the ruins of the ancient stone city of Leluh. He and his assistant, Perlin, helped us by cleaning vegetation from architectural features that we wished to record. Mr. John provided maps of the island, plans of the compounds, English translations of the accounts of Ernst Sarfert and Paul Hambruch, and numerous other documents on the prehistoric ruins.

In Leluh's public library we examined and photographed a model of an ancient Kosraean wood house. Mr. John called to our attention the traditional cord bindings that connect the posts, beams, and rafters of the Community Development Office. Together we discussed means of restoring and preserving the architectural remains at Leluh and methods of removing silt and debris from the canals. Several weeks later in Hawaii, I discussed ancient Leluh at length with Dr. Ross Cordy, the leading authority on the site. Dr. Cordy has provided great and continuing assistance to this study.

Andrew P. Kugfas, the historic preservation officer on Yap, provided extensive information on the traditional architecture of the island group. He also supplied several maps, an English translation of Wilhelm Mueller's report for the South Sea Expedition, and information on Micronesian canoe building and navigation. Mr. Kugfas also informed us of Yapese building traditions and construction processes that continue to be used today in much the same way they were used in precontact times. Of all the major islands of Micronesia, Yap is perhaps the most conservative and the least affected by Western contact.

The architect of the structures in Bechiyal was also the village chief, John Tamag, or Tamageoron. He granted us an interview and permitted us to photograph and measure the traditional community buildings. Dr. Rosalind L. Hunter-Anderson, a leading authority on Yapese prehistory, provided us with extensive information relevant to our study on a number of occasions. The accurate map of Bechiyal was prepared by Michiko Intoh, a student at the University of Otago who provided us with a copy of her survey.

Our work on Palau was assisted by the historic preservation officer, Moses Sam, who headed the Division of Cultural Affairs. Particularly helpful members of the division were Vince Blaiyok and archaeological surveyors Walter Metes and Delemel Mobel. Mr. Blaiyok explained details of the *bai* (men's clubhouse or community house) at Irrai where young men were learning traditional Palauan building skills. Mr. Sam arranged a vehicle and guide for sites accessible overland and a boat and crew for visits to coastal Melekeok, Ulong Island, and Ngchemiangel Bay.

Kempis Mad, a project researcher at the Palau National Museum, provided an English translation of Augustin Kramer's report for the South Sea Expedition, books by Douglas Osborne and Roland and Maryanne Force, and other documents. The chairman of cultural affairs in Melekeok, Mongami Elechuus, guided our tour of his village and explained the legends of the stone sculptures there. David M. Snyder of the Southern Illinois University Center for Archaeological Investigation repeatedly assisted our research effort on Palau.

Dr. Michael W. Graves of the University of Guam advised us on Marianas *latte* sites. He brought to our attention two important sites on Rota, the quarry at As Nieves and the exceptionally large Mochong site. Jay Bright, property manager for Tomás Mendiola, conducted an informative tour of the Mochong site. Drs. Marjorie G. Driver and Dirk Ballendorf of the Micronesian Area Research Center and Dr. Hiro Kurashina of the University of Guam's Department of Anthropology also provided valuable information and advice. Alejandro B. Lizama, chief technician to the territorial archaeologist, provided information and drawings suggesting a reconstructed *latte* house.

Additional information on *latte* sites of the Marianas was supplied by Dr. Scott Russell, the deputy historic preservation officer of the Commonwealth of the Northern Mariana Islands. Dr. Graeme Ward of the Australian Institute of Aboriginal Studies made available accurate copies of his crew's well-documented survey of the Mochong site. The final drawings were prepared by Gordon Claridge, who was a member of the Mochong field survey party.

Douglas K. Mukai and Ed Matsumra of the R. M Towill Corporation in Honolulu prepared an accurate photogrammetric survey of the beautiful hill terraces southeast of Ngchemiangel Bay on Babeldaob. Dr. Thomas F. King of the Advisory Council on Historic Preservation in Washington, D.C., provided information and documents describing prehistoric sites on certain islands of Truk. Shortly after our return from Micronesia, Dr. Arthur A. Saxe of Ohio University visited our office and discussed his research on greater Nan Madol and its environs.

During each of our five major island visits a series of architectural photographs was recorded by my elder son, Newton, with the assistance of my younger son, Dylan. Their many hours of painstaking work on each subject proved to be of critical importance in the preparation of this study. Many of the accurate drawings presented here were traced from photographs of walls and other architectural features recorded in the field. The precise descriptions of the text also rely in many instances on carefully recorded photographs.

Each of the five sections of the study was composed within a flexible format designed to emphasize the unique features of each particular island or group. An early attempt to prepare all drawings at comparable scales proved awkward and was abandoned. For example, comparing the city plan of Leluh to modestly scaled Bechiyal Village or to a vast network of hill terraces on Babeldaob would have required serious and unnecessary compromises of scale and detail. Consequently, each section is presented at a scale appropriate to its particular architectural features.

Certain conventions were adopted early in the process of drawing preparation. Where possible the direction of north in a plan is toward the top of the page; north arrows indicate precise orientations. Scale in elevations, sections, and perspectives usually is indicated by human scale figures five feet six inches tall, the assumed height of a typical adult male in prehistoric Micronesia. Final drawings were prepared with ink lines on mylar film. Drawn about 2.7 times as large as the illustrations published in this volume, the drawings were reduced in the same proportions in order to maintain consistent line weights.

Each section of the study was prepared in sequence, depending on several considerations. Kosrae's chapter was undertaken first because thorough current data were available. The preliminary text and copies of pencil drawings were sent to Dr. Ross Cordy for review. While awaiting his response the section on Yap was begun. When Dr. Cordy's review comments were received, the text and drawings were modified accordingly and final ink drawings were prepared. A similar process was used in each of the subsequent sections.

Dr. Rosalind L. Hunter-Anderson reviewed the section on Yap; David M. Snyder, on Palau; Dr. J. Stephen Athens, on Nan Madol; and Dr. Michael W. Graves, on the Marianas. Each scholar has conducted extensive recent field research on the respective site. The Marianas section was prepared last due to the relative lack of information on the probable appearance of prehistoric *latte* houses there. Three sections of the study required substantial corrections after their initial reviews; in these cases, second reviews were necessary to assure accuracy.

MICRONESIAN LANGUAGE NOTES

When Magellan arrived in 1521, at least twelve distinct languages and many dialects were spoken in Micronesia. For the most part, they still are spoken. During the last century the languages of Micronesia have been a subject of increasing interest. In the early 1970s the Trust Territory of the Pacific Islands, in cooperation with the University of Hawaii, sponsored a number of intensive linguistic studies, the most comprehensive until that time.

The dictionaries listed in the bibliography are products of that effort. Readers who may be interested in the pronunciations, definitions, and uses of Micronesian words and phrases are invited to consult the bibliographic entries of Rehg and Sohl (1983) for Pohnpeian; Lee (1987) for Kosraean; Topping, Ogo, and Dungca (1975) for Chamorro; McManus, Josephs, and Emesiochel (1976) for Palauan; and Jensen (1977) for Yapese.

Relatively small numbers of people are fluent in Micronesian languages. Perhaps six thousand people speak Kosraean, and possibly fifteen thousand use Pohnpeian. With so few people speaking a given language within a comparatively limited geographic area, linguistic conventions are relatively easy to discuss and agree upon. Maintaining the vocabulary, grammar, and pronunciation of languages spoken by such small populations stands in dramatic contrast to the linguistic conventions required for the 585 million users of Mandarin Chinese, or for the 275 million native speakers of English who are spread over several continents (Woolf, 1973:20a).

The Pohnpeian language serves to illustrate the linguistic diversity of the islands. A nuclear Micronesian member of the larger Austronesian family of languages, Pohnpeian is spoken by the natives of Pohnpei and its two satellite atolls, Pakin and Ant. The language has two major dialects: the Kiti dialect used by the inhabitants of Kiti province, and the northern, or main, dialect. The languages spoken on nearby Ngatic, Pingelap, and Mokil seem to be closely related to Pohnpeian. Other nuclear Micronesian languages are Kosraean, Trukic, Gilbertese, Marshallese, and probably Nauruan.

Alternate spellings for words with the same meaning occur frequently in Pohnpeian. Precise definitions of Pohnpeian words often lack equivalents in English. The meaning of Pohnpeian words also may be changed by sentence context or through modification by associated words. Affixes, prefixes, suffixes, and reduplication permit thousands of new words to be created in Pohnpeian.

Succeeding Spanish, German, Japanese, and United States administrations also have influenced Micronesian languages. An illustration of foreign influence is the word *ampangia,* meaning "umpire" in English but borrowed into Pohnpeian through Japanese (Rehg and Sohl, 1983:xiv).

Like Pohnpeian, Kosraean is a nuclear Micronesian language within the larger family of Austronesian languages. Also like Pohnpeian, Kosraean is a unique language with its own lexicon and grammar. Many foreign words, particularly Japanese and English, have been incorporated into the Kosraean sound system and vocabulary. Affixes, prefixes, and suffixes present opportunities to create thousands of new words in Kosraean just as they do in Pohnpeian.

Unlike the nuclear Micronesian languages of Truk, Pohnpei, and Kosrae, the languages of western Micronesia probably had different origins. Scholars believe that the early settlers of the Marianas, Palau, and probably Yap came from the direction of the Philippines, Halmahera, or the Celebes (Sulawesi). Their languages bear affinities with those of the islands of southeast Asia. While Yapese, Palauan, and Chamorro have their own vocabularies and grammars, cognates appear in their languages occasionally. The Palauan word *bai,* for example, seems phonetically related to the Yapese word *pebaey,* and both words mean "clubhouse" or "community meeting house."

After centuries of massive foreign influence the present-day people of the Mariana Islands are no longer pure-blooded Chamorro. However, the language and cultural traditions of the ancient people have been preserved to a significant extent. The Chamorro language still is spoken and understood on Guam, Rota, Tinian, Saipan, and elsewhere in the Marianas.

In view of Yap's extensive trade and centuries of contact with many of the tiny islands of the central Carolines, it seems likely that the Yapese language has been influenced at least to some extent by nuclear Micronesian dialects. For further information on Yapese and other Micronesian languages, the reader is referred to the bibliographic references listed at the end of this volume.

INTRODUCTION

"... great architecture is at the very origins of humanity. ... it is the immediate product of human instinct. ... Geometry is the measure of the measure of the mind."
—Le CORBUSIER
(1926:54)

The 8-foot-high stone column and capstone from the Mepo site probably once supported a traditional frame house.

Almost lost in the vastness of the Pacific Ocean are the tiny islands, the remarkable people, and the ancient architecture of Micronesia. The methods used to construct prehistoric monuments, as well as their materials, sizes, functions, and designs, vary widely from one island group to the next. Prismatic basalt and coral native to Pohnpei and Kosrae were used by resourceful builders to create the dramatic stone cities of Nan Madol and Leluh, respectively. Beautifully terraced hills with sculpted earthen crowns abound on twenty-six-mile-long Babeldaob Island in the Palau Archipelago. Carefully fitted stone platforms with hexagonal plans form the bases of meeting houses, residences, and other ornamented structures of wood in the Yap Islands. The enigmatic *latte* stone columns and capitals of the Marianas apparently once served as the foundations for wood houses raised above the ground, sometimes as high as sixteen feet. This study examines some of the best recorded examples of prehistoric architecture on five of the major island groups in Micronesia.

The islands of Micronesia lie in the Western Pacific near the equator, east of the Philippines and north of Melanesia. They include the Marianas, the Carolines, the Marshalls, Kiribati, and Nauru. The total land area of the islands is some 708 square miles, a very small area compared to the 3 million square miles of water in Micronesia. For each square mile of land there are well more than 4,200 square miles of sea. The distance from Tobi Island southwest of Palau to Arorae in Kiribati is about 3,150 miles, some 500 miles greater than the distance from Boston to San Francisco. The population of Micronesia in 1986, excluding the mixed population of Guam, was estimated to be perhaps 135,000 people with an annual growth rate in the range of 1 to 3 percent.

The largest of the world's oceans, the Pacific covers almost one-third of the planet and contains almost one-half of its water. South of Guam the Pacific plunges to a depth of 35,810 feet in the Marianas Trench, the ocean's deepest abyss. The relatively very small islands of Micronesia, ranging in size from 215-square-mile Guam to bare specks

of coral reefs, probably were among the last habitable areas on earth to be occupied by human beings.

Quite likely the earliest settlers to arrive in Micronesia brought with them ideas about architecture from their homelands. In time populations increased, people occasionally migrated between islands, and traders exchanged goods and, presumably, ideas. Thus the ancient architecture of Micronesia might have been expected to evolve with a relatively uniform and limited vocabulary of architectural design and planning ideas. However, precisely the opposite is the case. Given generally similar technologies and materials, the ancient builders of Micronesia developed an exceptionally broad range of approaches to architecture.

For the purpose of this study, the term "prehistory" refers to times antedating written history. While "architecture" often refers to the art or science of building, here the term alludes specifically to structures whose designs move well beyond the functional necessities of shelter. Architecture expresses the choices, preferences, and predilections of the people who create it. In short, it is a reflection of the human spirit. This study celebrates the distinguished architecture of ancient Micronesia and the remarkable islanders who created it.

ISLAND TYPES

Palau, Yap, and the Marianas have high volcanic islands that rest on the ocean's floor and rise to peaks above sea level. Geologically related to continental Asia, these islands frequently contain andesite. The islands on the continental shelf west of the andesite line are old and weathered compared to the more recent and rugged islands to the east, such as Pohnpei and Kosrae. The only area of current volcanic activity in Micronesia is located in the northern Marianas.

By far most of Micronesia's more than one thousand islands are coral rather than volcanic. All of the Marianas and Kiribati, and many of the Carolines, are coral atolls. Both classic reefs and raised coral islands are found in Micronesia. Classic reefs (Darwin, 1901) result from the growth of coral around the perimeters of subsiding volcanic islands that later disappear below sea level. The reefs continue to grow, and some eventually become islands averaging up to eight feet in height and several miles in length. Raised coral islands were formed on volcanic bases that reversed the pattern of subsidence and now rise fifty feet or more above sea level.

The often hilly and sometimes mountainous volcanic islands usually have fresh water streams, valleys suitable for cultivation, and stone useful in making tools. Varying widely in size, topography, and richness of soils, the volcanic islands offer greater diversity in plant materials and ecological zones than do the low coral islands where little or no soils are found.

ENVIRONMENT

The tropical maritime climate of Micronesia usually has temperatures averaging in the eighties throughout the year, with generally high humidity and rainfall. The climate in the western Caroline Islands and the Mariana Islands is much more seasonal than in the central and eastern Caroline Islands. Seasonal tradewinds tend to prevail from November through April or May. The typhoon season usually extends from June to November. About 180 inches of rain, the highest in Micronesia, falls annually on Pohnpei and the central Carolines. Yearly rainfall decreases to about 75 inches in the Marianas and the northern Marshalls and to less than 40 inches in southern Kiribati. The quantity of rain in Nauru fluctuates from as little as 15 inches to as much as 170 inches annually.

Typhoons pose a particular threat to the Carolines and Marianas. The tropical storms usually are much more powerful and potentially destructive than the Atlantic Ocean hurricanes that annually threaten the eastern United States. Some of the typhoons originate in the southern Marshalls, but the majority develop in the central Carolines. The storms often move westerly along the island chain before veering to the northwest and passing near Ulithi and Yap or through the southern Marianas. High winds, mountainous seas, and air-borne salt water can contaminate fresh water sources and damage vegetation to the extent that recovery may require six or seven years, an unmitigated disaster for coral atolls.

The most important subsistence crops in Micronesia traditionally were bananas, breadfruit, taro (*Colocasia, Cyrtosperma,* and other aroids), coconuts, sweet potatoes on Yap, and, on high islands, yams. Significant differences in agricultural practices between islands probably relate to climatic and environmental factors. For example, breadfruit is the most important staple on Pohnpei, while Kosrae emphasizes swamp taro, and the Mariana Islands probably utilized primarily cycad nuts (*fadang,* Athens, 1986*a*: 24–25).

Animal life tended to be very limited, although wild birds occasionally were caught and eaten and fruit bats were hunted on the larger islands of the Carolines and the Marianas. By far the most important sources of protein in the diet were the abundant fish, mollusks, and sea turtles harvested from the rich lagoons and seas surrounding the islands.

EARLY SETTLERS

The people of Micronesia are of Asian origin. Archaeological and linguistic evidence suggests that people originally entered Micronesia at different times from two distinctly separate directions. The first group seems to have migrated to the Marianas, Palau, and possibly Yap from the direction of the islands of southeast Asia, perhaps the Philippines, Halmahera, or the Celebes (Sulawesi). The first settlers in Micronesia may have been the people who arrived in the Marianas, possibly about 1300 B.C.

A second group of settlers is believed to have migrated later to central and eastern Micronesia from eastern Melanesia, possibly the area of the Bismarck Archipelago, Vanautu (the New Hebrides), or Fiji, with a probable link to Polynesia. The languages spoken on these islands, called nuclear Micronesian, are distinctly different from the languages of western Micronesia. Settlers are believed to have arrived in Pohnpei, Kosrae, and most of the major islands of the

Carolines sometime between perhaps 500 B.C. and the beginning of the Christian era.

Subsequently, canoes are believed to have continued arriving from outside Micronesia, either intentionally or inadvertently, in much the same way that the original settlers arrived. As populations increased in Micronesia, internal migrations apparently occurred. For example, the people of Tobi Island southwest of Palau are said to have come from Ulithi Atoll, some 750 miles to the northeast. This type of movement apparently served to diffuse ideas and material items throughout Micronesia.

At the time of Magellan's arrival in 1521, the first Western contact with Micronesia, no fewer than twelve distinct languages were spoken in the islands. The widest geographic distribution of dialects occurred in the coral atolls of the central Carolines and Marshalls. The people living in the low islands of Micronesia had highly developed canoe building and navigational skills, virtual necessities for survival on islands so vulnerable to typhoons. They became superb fishermen and consummate navigators. Lacking local sources of stone, the inventive artisans fashioned adzes and other tools from shell, coral, bone, and wood. The low islanders sometimes traveled hundreds of miles in outrigger canoes to conduct trade and exchange ideas.

By contrast, the languages and ideas of the high islanders had comparatively restricted distributions. They rarely took their canoes beyond the sight of their own coastlines. Living in relatively well protected and rich environments, the high islanders often were less widely traveled than the atoll dwellers, who conducted trade over large areas of Micronesia. Perhaps the unique architectural characteristics traditionally associated with individual high islands groups were due in large part to the inward-looking nature of their indigenous societies.

The people of Yap, Palau, the Marianas, and other western Micronesian islands today continue to cultivate *Areca* palms that yield the traditional stimulant "betel nut." The nuts are chewed with a mixture of locally produced powdered lime and citrus juice. The ingredients combine to form a dark reddish juice that stains the chewer's teeth. Stains found on the remains of human teeth in ancient burial sites attest to the antiquity of betel nut chewing in western Micronesia.

A distinctive ceremonial beverage is used widely in the islands of eastern Micronesia. Called *sakau* on Pohnpei and *saka* (also *suhka*) on Kosrae, the drink is similar to *kava* in Polynesia. The beverage is prepared by pulverizing the root of a species of pepper plant (*Macropiper methysticum*) on a flat stone, mixing the residue with water, and squeezing the liquid through the soft, fibrous inner bark of the hibiscus tree. The beverage then is placed in a coconut shell and passed ritually from person to person. The effect is intoxicating. Like betel nut chewing in western Micronesia, *sakau* drinking in central and eastern Micronesia apparently was a common practice in ancient times and continues to be popular today.

TECHNOLOGY

The prehistoric architecture of Micronesia demonstrates an exceptionally high level of ingenuity and technological ability. Another impressive example of technological achievement by the islanders was the building of graceful outrigger canoes. Their carefully proportioned and finely hewn hulls, often exceeding 40 feet in length, were lashed tightly together with coconut husk fibers. The hulls were carved with controlled asymmetry for improved maneuverability.

The canoes were rigged with single, triangular sails of plaited matting. The lateen sails were extended by a long spar slung to a low mast. The canoe's direction of movement could be reversed by moving the spar from one end of the double-ended hull to the other, while keeping the outrigger to windward. The Micronesian outriggers differed markedly from the double-hull catamarans of Polynesia. Sailing canoes up to 100 feet long were used in Palau and the Marshall Islands, while those in the Carolines were at most some 60 feet long. Built without plans or metal tools and fastenings, the canoes were powered only by wind, currents, and paddles. Yet the ancient shipwrights and navigators accomplished passages of many hundreds of miles, sometimes to islands that they may not have known were there.

Today the natives of the remote islands of the central Carolines, such as Pulawat and Satawal, continue to build ocean-voyaging canoes and to sail them according to millennium-old traditions. The accomplishments of their forefathers were greater and earlier than those of the Vikings. They colonized the remote islands of the vast Pacific, "a feat comparable to colonizing the frontiers of outer space in our time" (Malone, 1983 : 13).

Lacking compasses, sextants, or charts for guidance, Micronesian navigators relied on their own understanding of the seas. Sea birds, such as frigates, boobies, and terns, indicate the direction to nearby islands. During the heat of the day clouds tend to form over the warm land masses of islands, indicating the existence of land often well beyond the horizon. Certain types of fish are associated with reefs and lagoons while others are pelagic. At night the navigators steered by the stars that rose and set unerringly (Stuart, 1983 : 327). Ocean swells provided the Micronesian navigators with another type of information. Sometimes swells roll on for thousands of miles, setting up secondary patterns when waves bounce back from islands. By feeling the pattern of a reflected swell, a navigator can fix his position and sail directly into the swell to reach the island.

The Marshall Islanders invented a type of chart consisting of a geometric arrangement of sticks and shells that represented currents, swells, and islands. Once at sea, however, the mariners relied entirely on their own memories and senses to accomplish their remarkable feats of navigation. Memorized charts recording stars' names, seamarks, and other navigational information have been passed down through the generations. Students of navigation begin memorizing charts when they are about six years old; few complete the course. The process of memorization involves the repetition of rhythmic verses about each chart, a procedure recalling the melodious sounds of canoe building. Similar chants accompany traditional house building in Micronesia.

FOREIGN CONTACT

No evidence exists for significant foreign influences in prehistoric Micronesia. The ancient ideas and achievements associated with the islands seem to have been produced entirely by the indigenous people before the time of Western contact.

Magellan's arrival in the Marianas in 1521 marks the beginning of the historic era in Micronesia and signals the commencement of foreign influence in the islands. The Marianas were the first islands to feel the brunt of Westernization. The people living on the islands were Chamorros, a Micronesian group about whom relatively little is known. By 1710, after several decades of epidemics, warfare, and disastrous typhoons, almost no Chamorros lived on any island other than Guam, where only 3,439 natives remained. The survivors are estimated to have numbered fewer than one-tenth of the precontact population (Spoehr, 1954).

Although periodic contact occurred with Palau during the sixteenth and seventeenth centuries, it was not until 1783 that the archipelago began to be opened up to the West. Kosrae remained relatively isolated until 1824, and some four years later Pohnpei initiated sustained contact with the West. Yap, perhaps the island group least affected by foreign influences, did not begin to trade with the West until 1843. Depopulation due to foreign diseases and other factors generally occurred throughout Micronesia, but nowhere was the destruction of a native culture more complete than in the Marianas, where no pure Chamorros survive today.

Spain maintained at least nominal control of Micronesia, except Kiribati, from Magellan's time until the conclusion of the Spanish-American War. At that time the United States occupied Guam, and Germany bought the remainder of the Marianas, Carolines, and Marshalls. On the eve of the First World War, Japan occupied Germany's former South Sea possessions. Following the Second World War, the United States began its administration of most of the islands under the mandate of a United Nations trusteeship.

In the late 1970s many Micronesian islanders began to exercise their sovereign rights to become self-governing entities in close association with the United States. The islands north of Guam elected to form the Commonwealth of the Northern Mariana Islands in a status with the United States similar to that of Puerto Rico. Palau and its neighbors became the independent republic of Belau, while Yap, Pohnpei, Truk, Kosrae, and their neighbors comprised the sovereign Federated States of Micronesia. The Gilberts, formerly a British possession, joined most of the Phoenix and Line Islands to form the republic of Kiribati.

Since the late 1970s archaeologists and other scientists from the United States have greatly intensified their research in Micronesian prehistory. Many studies have been funded by the United States in the interest of historic preservation. The new and struggling island governments encourage research with the view of developing their nascent tourist industries, while preserving their people's authentic cultural traditions.

The intensification of the investigation of Micronesian prehistory has been a boon to this study. Much of the information presented here was not available a decade ago. With this background in mind, the following sections present detailed examples of ancient architecture in Palau, Yap, Pohnpei, Kosrae, and the Marianas with emphasis on Guam, Tinian, and Rota.

Yenasr Islet lies on the coral reef north of Leluh. To the left is the main island of Kosrae; to the right, the Pacific Ocean.

1. PALAU

Among the foremost achievements of prehistoric architecture in Micronesia are Palau's monumental sculpted hills, megalithic stone carvings, and elaborately decorated structures of wood placed on piers above elevated stone platforms. During the centuries preceding European contact the Palauan people successfully exploited the substantial resources of their island environment, evolving in the process their distinctive architectural tradition. The preliminary overview of prehistoric architecture in Palau presented here is based primarily on existing ethnographic and archaeological data and on my observations of the architectural remains themselves. Future research in Palauan prehistory may be expected to expand our present understanding beyond its current limitations.

The Palau (also Belau and Pelew) archipelago lies in the southwesternmost corner of Micronesia, 550 miles east of the Philippines and 410 miles north of New Guinea. The archipelago consists of some 250 islands in a group that stretches about 95 miles in a northeast to southwest direction between the Philippine Sea and the Pacific Ocean. Near the center of the Palau group is 154-square-mile Babeldaob (also Babelthaup), the largest island of the archipelago. Second only to Guam in size among the islands of Micronesia, 27-mile-long Babeldaob accounts for 80 percent of Palau's land area. Other main islands of the group are Koror (also Oreor), Peleliu, and Angaur to the south of Babeldaob and Kayangel to the north.

The highest point of land in the archipelago is a 713-foot-high hill on Babeldaob, about one-third the height of Mount Finkol on Kosrae. Like Yap, Palau is relatively ancient in geological terms. Its volcanic formations are old and weathered compared to the newer and more rugged islands of Kosrae and Pohnpei. The present-day administrative and commercial center is Koror, but many of Palau's 14,000 people reside in coastal villages that also were inhabited in prehistoric times.

The islands of Palau vary widely in size and appearance. The largest were formed by

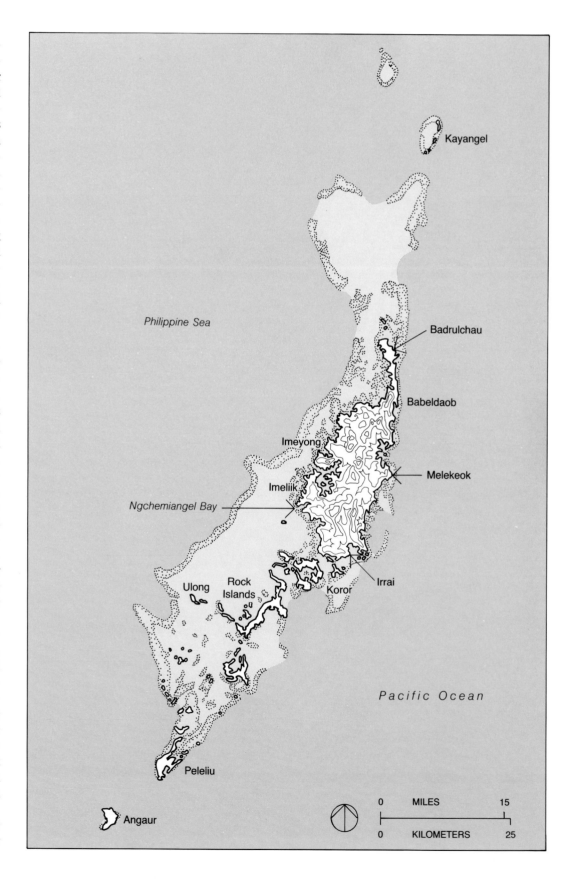

volcanic activity and are composed of basalt and andesite. Most of the other islands are coralline limestone reefs, some uplifted as much as 600 feet. A few, such as Kayangel, are classic coral atolls. Coral reefs surround much of the archipelago, extending offshore as far as 18 miles to the west. Although Palau lies outside the Pacific's main typhoon belt, some ten typhoons have struck the island group during the last century.

THE PEOPLE OF PALAU

At some unknown time in the past the first settlers arrived in Palau, perhaps by inadvertent drift voyages. The archipelago is known to have received drift voyages from the Celebes and Halmahera in Indonesia and from Mindanao in the Philippines. These areas also may have been the origins of the first Palauans. Peter Bellwood (1979a) suggests extensive contact between Palau and Melanesia, particularly New Guinea and the Admiralty Islands, as evidenced by such cultural traits as nose piercing and female tattooing. The ornate wooden structures of Indonesia, with steep thatched roofs and elevated wood platforms, such as those at Tana Toradja in Sulawesi, suggest parallels with the traditional architecture of Palau.

Following the initial occupation of the entire archipelago, a number of large villages were established in the rock islands. Activity in the villages seems to have reached a peak between A.D. 1200 and 1400. Subsequently, the rock islands were abandoned. Terrace construction on the volcanic islands apparently was underway by 500 and continued until perhaps 1700, with major activity between 1000 and 1400. Some terraces continue today to serve as garden plots. Although some volcanic island villages date from as early as the twelfth century, most of them were established after 1600.

At the time of Western contact the Palauans did not have dogs, but they did have fowls and, probably, pigs. Pigs were unknown elsewhere in Micronesia. Although fruit bats are native to Palau, other mammals are rare. Reptiles are numerous, including the ubiquitous gecko, two species of marine crocodiles, and the large monitor liz-

ard. More important as a food source for Palauans are hundreds of species of edible mollusks and some 1,500 types of fish that abound within the fringing reefs. The subsistence economy of Palau today is based, as it probably was prehistorically, on the cultivation of taro (both *Colocasia* and *Cyrtosperma*), bananas, breadfruit, papayas, and coconuts. Figs, bamboo shoots, and Malay apples are gathered wild (Osborne, 1966). The bountiful food resources of Palau supported a prehistoric population in the range of perhaps at most 40,000 and provided a basis for the development of traditional Palauan architecture.

Apparently once accomplished mariners, the Palauans in time confined their activities to the waters of their home islands and largely abandoned their voyaging skills. At the time of contact, however, Yapese mariners periodically visited Palau. Palau was a major source of circular limestone disks that were valued by the Yapese. Under a trade arrangement with the chief of Koror, the Yapese quarried their stone valuables in Palau's rock islands and ferried their cargos back to Yap on rafts or outrigger canoes. The round-trip voyage involved navigating the waters of the open Pacific for a distance of over 500 miles.

Traditional Palauan villages were organized according to clan ranking. The four highest ranking clans were called the "corner posts" of the village. The traditional "corner post" villages of Palau are understood commonly to have been Koror, Melekeok, Imeyong, and Imeliik (also Aimelik).

Early European observers noted clubs in Palauan villages. The village council assigned men's clubs such tasks as cleaning paths, fishing, or thatching village structures. Every village had a women's council and women's clubs, organized like the men's but generally lacking the impressive buildings that men's clubs had. Smaller villages apparently formed alliances clustered around larger or more powerful villages. Individual villages within an alliance may have been assigned special functions, such as making pottery, producing food, supplying warriors, or prefabricating wood structures.

European Contact

The first European to visit Palau may have been the English privateer Sir Francis Drake, in 1579 (Lessa, 1975). In 1710 the Spanish explorer Francisco Padilla stayed briefly in the archipelago. Palau was sighted on various occasions during the next several decades.

In 1783 the 300-ton English packet *Antelope*, under the command of Capt. Henry Wilson, struck the reef west of Ulong and foundered. The crew was able to salvage much from the wreckage and with the assistance of the *ibedul*, the powerful chief of Koror, they built a new ship in the course of several months (Keate, 1789). Upon his departure from Palau, Captain Wilson presented his surplus tools to the *ibedul*, presumably in appreciation of the chief's assistance. In the process of building the ship Palauan craftsmen may have learned new techniques in wood construction, such as mortise-and-tenon joinery, and methods of working with metal tools unknown before European contact.

In 1871 Jan S. Kubary, the first ethnologist to visit Palau, found the most sophisticated wood structures in all of Micronesia. The extent to which European tools and techniques may have been employed in constructing the edifices recorded by Kubary is unknown. It seems most probable, however, that the underlying concepts of traditional Palauan architecture originated within the island chain itself.

The wreck of the *Antelope* generally is accepted as the beginning of Palau's recorded history. During the nineteenth century foreign influence increased with the coming of the trepang industry to Palau. Unlike the Marianas, Palau was little influenced by Spain until 1885 when Jesuit missionaries began to introduce the alphabet and Christianity to the islands. In 1899 Spain sold its Micronesian possessions, except Guam, to Germany. By 1900 Palau's population apparently had declined to fewer than 4,000, perhaps only a tenth of the precontact population. Quite possibly the cause was recently introduced diseases. In connection with the

Monumental sculpted hills rise majestically above the dense forests southeast of Ngchemiangel Bay. The view shown here was taken with a telephoto lens from the north-northeast in May of 1984.

comprehensive South Sea Expedition survey of 1908–1910, the German ethnographer Augustin Kramer recorded valuable data on Palau.

Financial difficulties and the outbreak of the First World War forced Germany to sell her Micronesian possessions to Japan in 1914. Fortified to serve as a Japanese stronghold during the Second World War, the archipelago was bombarded by American forces, who invaded Peleliu and Angaur in 1944. A UN mandate in 1947 placed Palau under the trusteeship of the United States. Recently, Palau asserted its sovereignty as an independent republic in a compact of free association with the United States.

THE SCULPTED HILLS OF BABELDAOB

Perhaps the most spectacular monuments of prehistoric architecture in Palau are terraced earthworks sculpted from natural hill formations. The most numerous and impressive of the sculpted hills are found on Babeldaob. As one moves along the island's coasts by boat, sculpted hill complexes appear constantly. It seems in places that, if the intervening areas of forest and jungle were removed, the terraces might be interconnected and extend for miles in a single composition. "It is probable that many of the terraces form larger systems and that further races form larger systems and that further

analysis will integrate several seemingly discrete terraced areas into a single system" (Gumerman, Snyder, and Masse, 1981:15).

In this discussion of prehistoric Palauan architecture, a four-part site designation system will be used. The system presently is being implemented by scholars studying the island group. For example, B:IM−2:7 stands for Belau (Palau), Imeliik State, area 2, site 7. This designation system appears in the text, drawings, and captions for illustrations in this section. Place names are those given on the 1983 U.S. Geological Survey topographic maps for the archipelago. Palauan terms throughout this study are italicized and spelled according to the *Palauan-*

English Dictionary by Edwin G. McManus et al. (1976).

The term "crown and brim," which refers to the shape of a hat when the terraces are viewed from eye level, frequently occurs in discussions of Palauan earthworks. Douglas Osborne (1966) has presented a thorough discussion and illustration of this arrangement. The "crown" usually is a truncated pyramid formed by cutting earth away from a natural feature or by building up earth fill. The brim frequently slopes inward slightly toward the base of the crown, forming a shallow basin that retains rainwater. Depressions often occur in the crown as well. Brims sometimes slope upward toward their ends.

The term "footcatcher" refers to a deep trench or ditch excavated across one or more terraces, perhaps for the purpose of obstructing movement along the terraces. However, the footcatchers of B:IM-11 seem to have served as ramps for access to upper levels. Footcatchers also may have acted as storm drains. On rare occasions earth walls were constructed across terraces, perhaps as boundaries or for defensive purposes.

Several types of terraces occur in Palauan earthworks in addition to the distinctive crowns and brims that frequently are the culminating features of sculpted hills. Stepped terraces have level surfaces that often range from 30 to 60 feet in width and relatively

steep terrace faces that sometimes rise 15 feet or more in height. Backsloping terraces are higher at their outer edges, perhaps for the purpose of erosion control and water retention. They seem to be agricultural in nature (Lucking, 1984). Slope terraces, which are lower at their outer edges, are the most common and the least spectacular of Palauan terraces.

Of all the sculpted hills I saw in Palau, none were more beautiful than those of Ngchemiangel Bay on Babeldaob's west coast. Whether approached from land or sea, the magnificent complexes envelop the horizon. The sometimes steeply sloped terrace faces are covered with grasses that ap-

In this reconstructed view from the north-northeast the truncated crown of B:IM-2:7 rises some 317 feet above sea level, dominating the skyline southeast of Ngchemiangel Bay. To the right is the domical crown of 190-foot-high B:IM−6:1.

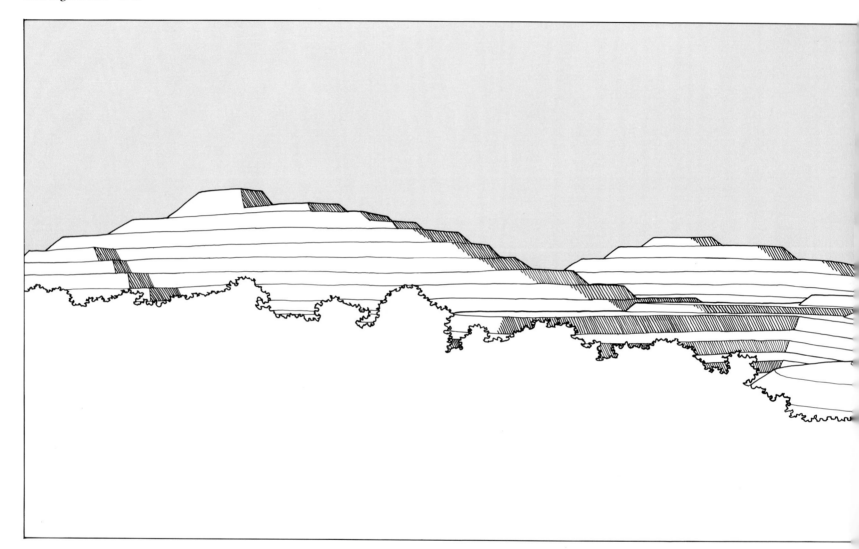

pear to change in color from red and green to yellow and blue, depending on the light, shadow, and time of day.

The examples of prehistoric Palauan terraces presented here are located on a hill system that forms the southeast wall of Ngchemiangel Bay. The sculpted earthworks form a crescent around the bay, terminating in a peninsula to the west. Today mangrove swamps around the peninsula extend outward from the shore more than 600 feet in some places. Some fifteen stream beds along the perimeter of the peninsula convey storm water runoff into the adjacent bay and lagoon.

The aerial photograph presented here shows clearly several extensive terrace complexes in a 1-mile-wide area southeast of Ngchemiangel Bay. North is toward the upper right-hand corner of the photograph. The reconstructed site plan suggests the possible original configuration of the impressive terraces to assist the reader in visualizing the scope and complexity of the ancient earthworks.

The site plan is based on a photogrammetric survey prepared especially for this study by the R. M. Towill Corporation of Honolulu in 1984. Douglas K. Mukai, manager of photogrammetry, and Ed Matsumra, production supervisor, prepared the photogrammetric survey by using overlapping 9 × 9-inch aerial survey photographs 4/83/6-3 and 4/83/6-4. The survey was drawn at a scale of 1 inch equals 200 feet and covered an area of approximately 4,800 × 7,200 feet. Contour intervals were 5 feet in open areas and 10 feet in vegetated areas. Features appearing to be terraces, based only on topographic features in the photographs, were shown in red. Terrace edges were shown at their actual elevations rather than on 5-foot contours.

The idealized plan presented here was prepared by overlaying a transparent Mylar print of the survey on a black-and-white print of aerial photograph 4/83/6-3, both at a scale of 1 inch equals 200 feet. Terrace

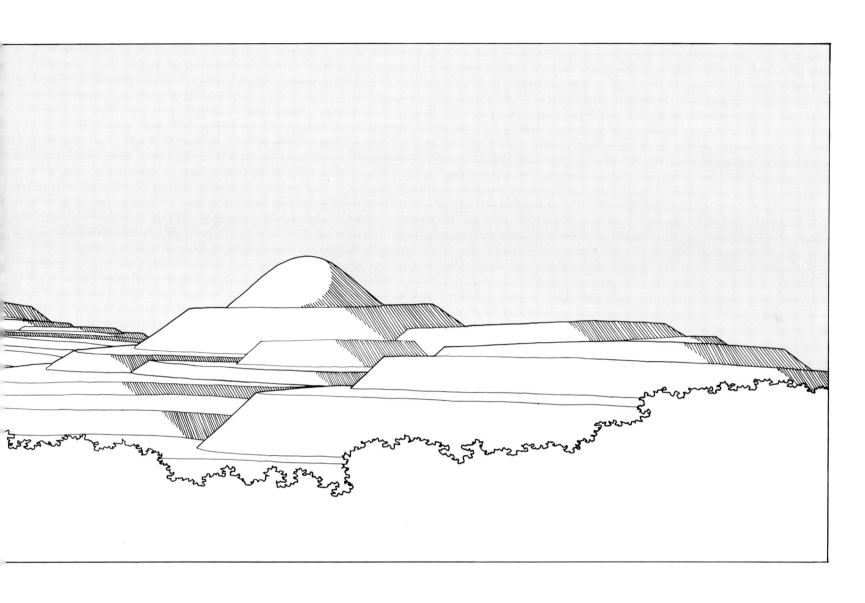

lines were drawn solely on the basis of sharp drops in elevation as they appeared in the aerial photograph, in the survey, and in eye-level photographs from various angles. It is entirely possible that some of the suggested artificial terraces actually are natural features, and that some terraces exist where none is shown on the drawing. The reconstructed drawing seeks to express the overall character of the terraces rather than define and identify each terrace individually.

Following the aerial and plan views is a ground-level photograph of the monuments taken from the north-northeast by Newton Morgan in 1984: a reconstructed drawing suggests the possible original configuration

of the earthworks before erosion occurred. The small white rectangles appearing to the left in the aerial photograph are corrugated metal roofs of the community center, residences, and other structures of present-day Elechui Village. The roads and paths appearing in the photograph may follow traditional routes.

The extensive mangrove swamps now present along the shoreline probably were much smaller or nonexistent at the time of original terrace building. Forests generally cover the valleys and lower reaches of the hill system. The bold lines appearing in the site plan represent the centerlines of stream beds that serve to convey water away during

often torrential rainstorms. Knee- to waist-high hilo grass entirely covered the terrace complexes during my visit in 1984.

Three seemingly interrelated terrace complexes that appear in the aerial photograph were designated B:IM-6:1, B:IM-2:7, and B:IM-2:17. Douglas Osborne's (1966) earlier study of Palauan prehistory referred to the same sites as B-9, B-10, and B-12, respectively. To avoid confusion, only the current designations will be used in this discussion.

The highest of the three terrace complexes, and the most dominant feature on the skyline, is B:IM-2:7, which appears near the lower right center of the aerial

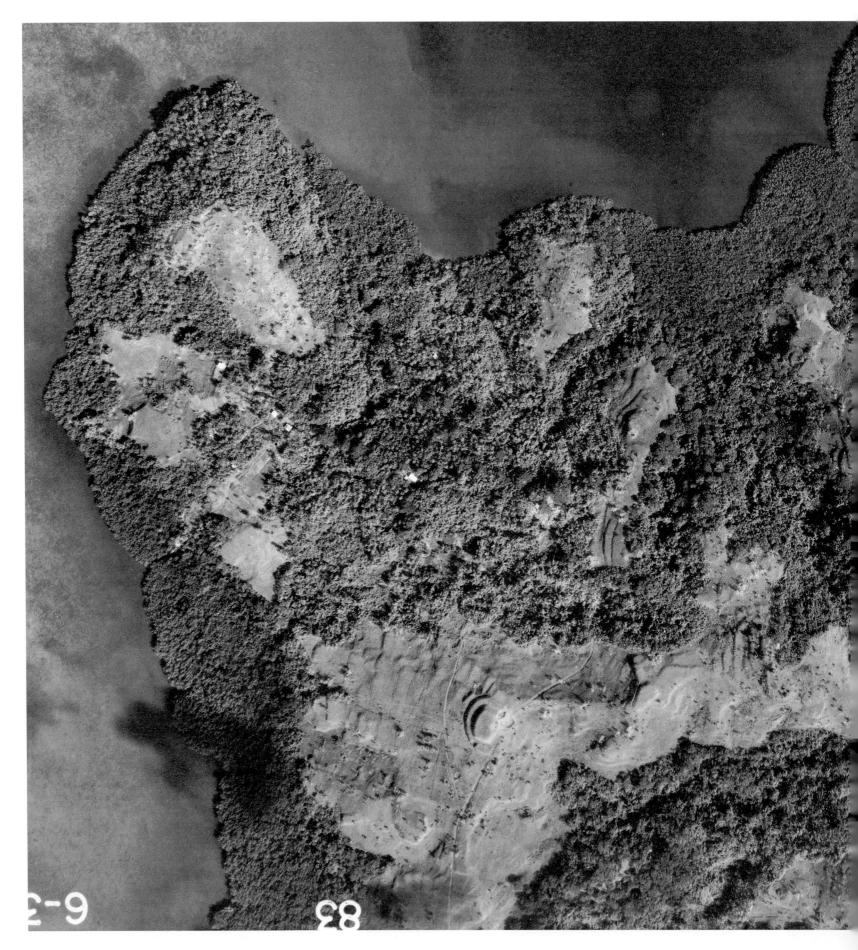

A complex of prehistoric sculpted hills appears clearly in this aerial photograph taken southeast of Ngchemiangel Bay on Babeldaob's west coast.

photograph. The top of the symmetrical truncated pyramid crowning the summit rises some 317 feet above sea level. The terrace's eastern side descends at a maximum slope of approximately 26 degrees into a valley filled with trees and vegetation. The platform of the summit measures about 40 × 60 feet and is at most 25 feet high. On the northeast and southwest sides, the truncate slopes downward at an angle of very nearly 45 degrees, a remarkable slope for an earthwork that for centuries has survived the erosional forces of wind, rain, and tropical sun. No depression occurs in the platform of B:IM-2:7, a feature often found in the crowns of Palau's sculpted hills. The truncated crown rests on an irregular brim terrace some 15 feet high that measures in plan at most 200 × 330 feet.

The isolated hill mass of B:IM-2:7 stands in dramatic profile against the skyline to the left in the eye-level photograph. From the well-defined crown and brim four major terraces descend toward the northwest in approximately 15-foot-high steps. The terraces average about 55 feet in width and are somewhat eroded. From this point the terraces rise again to a secondary platform, designated B:IM-2:8. It has an elevation of 280 feet, some 37 feet lower than the main crown. The less distinctively formed secondary hill mass appears near the center of the eye-level photograph and 500 feet to the northwest of B:IM-2:7's crown in the aerial photograph.

About 2,400 feet north of B:IM-2:7 is the crown of another spectacular hill complex overlooking Ngchemiangel Bay, 190-foot-high B:IM-6:1. Although its crown lies more than 125 feet below its lofty neighbor, B:IM-6:1 also stands distinctly isolated from other terrace complexes and clearly maintains its unique identity. Apparently, its crown was never completed, and, thus, its domical profile is unlike the truncated pyramids of most Palauan hill crowns.

The brim terrace of B:IM-6:1 measures about 100 × 300 feet, almost the size of a football field. The dome and its descending step terraces appear to the right in the ground-level photograph. Because the pho-

9

A reconstructed site plan suggests the original configuration of the impressive terraces southeast of Ngchemiangel Bay.

tograph was taken from the north-northeast with a 105-mm telescopic lense, the hill systems seem to be closer together than they actually are. Not visible between B:IM-6:1 and B:IM-2:7 is a deep valley densely covered with trees.

On the second terrace down to the northwest of B:IM-6:1 are two footcatchers about 10 to 13 feet deep. The footcatchers roughly align with similar features in the third terrace down and seem to form earthen ramps through the steep terrace faces, perhaps for the purpose of facilitating access to the upper levels of the hill complex. The footcatchers of B:IM-6:1 may have been used to assist in the construction of the terraces and crown. Perhaps the footcatchers would have been reconfigured upon completion of the upper earthworks.

A third distinctive hill system southeast of Ngchemiangel Bay is 176-foot-high B:IM-2:17, little more than half the height of majestic B:IM-2:7 some 2,400 feet to the northeast. The shore of the peninsula lies about 1,000 feet to the southwest. B:IM-2:17 is an impressive feature as one approaches from the lagoon, particularly in the morning light when the west slopes of the earthworks are in shadow.

The 75 × 125-foot crown of B:IM-6:1 rises about 20 feet above the brim terrace. From the 15-foot-high brim a series of broad and weathered terraces, some exceeding 150 feet in width, step down in 5- to 10-foot increments toward the southwest. Like the terraces, the risers seem relatively gentle, lacking the dramatic steepness of the higher hill systems farther inshore. To the northeast of B:IM-2:17 two terraces, 211 and 264 feet high, respectively, step up as they approach B:IM-2:7. The 264-foot-high complex is designated B:IM-2:6.

Observations on Palauan Terraces

The sculpting of earth to serve the purposes of people has occurred in broadly separated geographical areas of the world at widely varying times. Examples range from the leveling of modest garden plots to the reshaping of mountains to serve as architectural monuments, such as the ancient

Ngchemiangel Bay

B:IM-2:9
elevation 160 ft.

B:IM-2:11
elevation 116 ft.

B:IM-2:10
elevation 167

B:IM-2:17
elevation 176 ft.

Ngertachebeab Bay

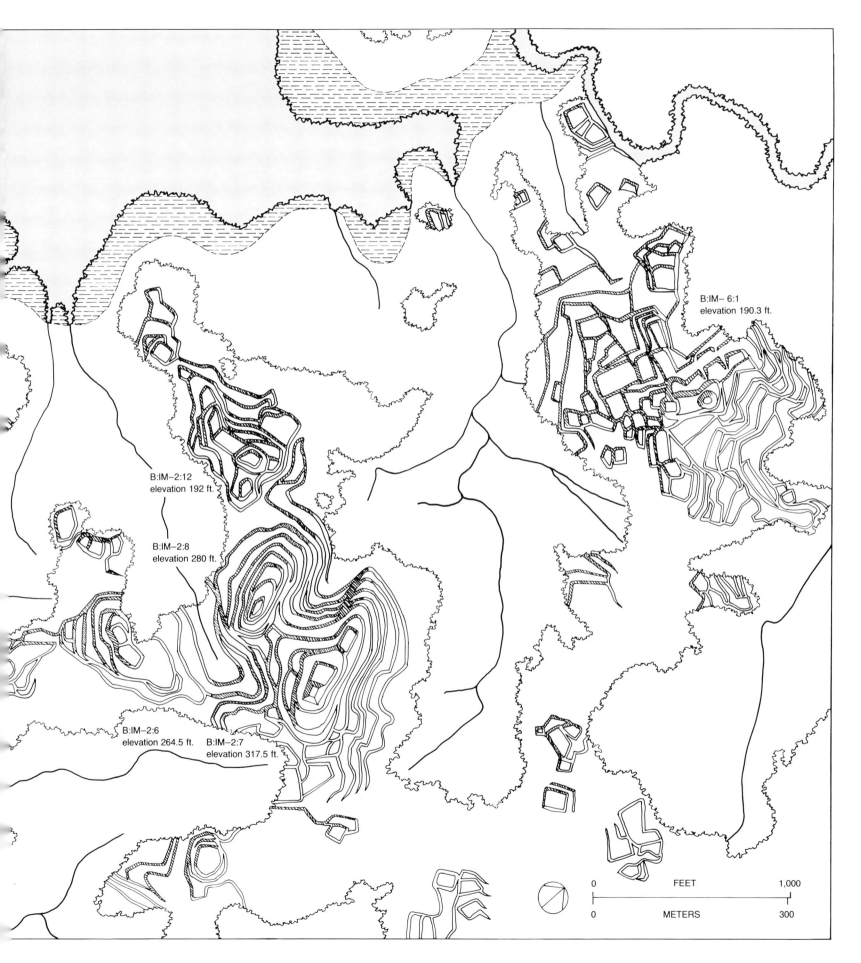

B:IM–6:1
elevation 190.3 ft.

B:IM–2:12
elevation 192 ft.

B:IM–2:8
elevation 280 ft.

B:IM–2:6
elevation 264.5 ft.

B:IM–2:7
elevation 317.5 ft.

0   FEET   1,000

0   METERS   300

Temple of the Sun at Pachacamac on the Pacific coast of Peru. While the often immense terrace complexes of Palau seem to have been created primarily for agricultural purposes, the extraordinary sculptures have a strongly architectural presence in the visual environment of the archipelago.

On the whole Palauan terraces seem more organized than the agricultural terraces of the Maori of New Zealand to which they bear no relation (Bellwood, 1979a). Lacking upland water sources, the earthworks of Palau did not rely upon irrigation systems like the more highly organized, often stone-faced terrace systems of Luzon and Java. From a distance the truncated earthen sculptures on Babeldaob reminded me of certain prehistoric monuments in the eastern United States, such as Monk's Mound at Cahokia and the truncated pyramids of Etowah and Moundville (Morgan, 1980).

Construction of Palau's huge terraces seems to have begun by the fifth century A.D., reached a peak perhaps between 1000 and 1400, and ceased by perhaps 1600. The major, systematic use, construction, and maintenance of the terraces were abandoned well before European contact. Some of the terraces continue to be used today on a modest scale as individual garden plots. Obviously, the villages, stone pathways, and platforms constructed on top of the terraces were later additions.

Palau's terraces and stoneworks seem to have resulted from a combination of private and public efforts. Agricultural terraces apparently were created as they were needed rather than all at one time. Family units working on small farms were the likely builders of low, gently sloping terraces. Elaborate crowns and brims probably were made by larger community groups. These earthworks were not necessarily related directly to agriculture (Osborne, 1979).

Families or larger kin groups probably also built private dwellings and their associated platforms. Public works apparently included roads, public platforms, docks, wharfs, and megalithic structures, such as the colonnades of Badrulchau. It seems likely that public projects were carried out by club

members at the request of village councils or chiefs (Osborne, 1979).

Several theories have been put forward concerning the possible uses of the terraces. In view of the substantial effort required to shape the extensive hill systems, the reason for building them presumably was strongly compelling. The general absence of habitational debris suggests the terraces were not used for prolonged occupation. Water retention by brimmed, backsloping, or flat terraces suggests agriculture, perhaps the cultivation of an upland (*Colocasia*) species of taro. Crowns and brims suggest possible defensive uses, such as temporary refuges in times of civil unrest.

Terrace construction primarily was a matter of reshaping natural hill formations. Fill was used to level and extend terraces following the elevations of natural contours, to augment crowns, and to form embankments. Brims less than 5 feet high usually were carved from sterile soils. Soil concretions in fill material suggest possible erosion control. I would suggest that pottery debris in sufficient quantities also may have assisted in erosion control in Palau. Shells or pottery debris mixed with soil assisted in controlling erosion in some of the prehistoric earthworks of the southeastern United States, such as the Sapelo shell rings of coastal Georgia.

Recent research has discounted the possibility that topsoils were removed to reach fertile subsoils (Lucking, 1984). Terracing originally may have been a method of increasing agricultural production while reducing dependence on swamp agriculture that is susceptible to drought, salt water intrusion due to typhoons, and insect infestations. Terracing also may represent a method of improving production of hillslope agriculture while reducing erosion. Increasing populations could have been an important factor in agricultural intensification. As was the case elsewhere in Oceania, competitive feasting between rival districts may have required improved production systems in agriculture (Spriggs, 1980).

The abandonment of major terrace building occurred long before contact and subse-

quent reduction of population in Palau. The shift in emphasis away from sculpting hills may have been caused by the increasing difficulty of maintaining the fertility of naturally infertile soils. Typical of leeched soils in the tropics, the terraces' latosols require long fallow periods under forest cover or the introduction of organic matter at regular intervals to make them usable for agriculture. Changes in political structures, civil unrest, or migrations could have disrupted terrace maintenance. Another reason for abandoning upland terrace building could have been the increase in swamp agriculture for higher yields of crops, such as the *Cyrtosperma* species of taro, with less labor. At the time of Western contact terraces continued to be part of a larger settlement pattern incorporating villages and nearby agricultural plots.

An unusual aspect of Palauan terraces is their lack of mention in oral histories and ethnographic accounts. At the time of contact they were "reminders of the past." In his diary entry of 29 June 1864, Andrew Cheyne (1866) wrote: "All the hills of the Pelew Islands that are clear of timber are terraced and crowned with a square fort, having a deep and wide ditch around it." He was the first to term them "crown and brim" structures and speculated that they were used for defensive purposes.

Augustin Kramer (1917:239) observed, "I have seen similar formations on the east coast of New Ireland." Kramer recognized that the sculpted hills of Palau are artificial constructions and noted that depressions are formed in the surfaces of crowns. He observed that some terraces had stone platforms and pathways and that bonfires on the crowns could be used for island-wide signaling.

Karl Semper (1873) spent ten months in Palau in 1862 and 1863. Although he carefully recorded scientific and cultural information on Palau, he made no mention at all of the extraordinary sculpted hills. This seems quite unusual, particularly since Semper spent most of his time on Babeldaob, where the largest number of the impressive monuments is located.

Regardless of the absence of ethnographic

data concerning the magnificent terrace complexes, they fortunately continue to stand today as records of distinguished and impressive achievements in prehistoric Palau.

THE STONE SCULPTURES OF MELEKEOK

A group of nine ancient stone sculptures, locally known as "Great Faces," are located in Melekeok on the east coast of Babeldaob. One of the traditional four corner post villages of Palau, Melekeok was a powerful village at the time of the wreck of the *Antelope.* A series of impressive terraces west of the village was surveyed by Douglas Osborne (1966 and 1979), who noted that the village also contained stone platforms, boat landings, and sculpted megaliths.

Melekeok is notable for its sandy beaches with occasional rock outcroppings. Along most of the coastline of Babeldaob mangrove swamps line the shore and extend into the lagoon for hundreds of feet in places. I approached the village by boat from the south end of the island. Three or four hill complexes were visible from the boat at any single time. They typically consisted of six to eight terraces. Along this section of the coast the reef is closer to shore and the lagoon is more shallow than along the west coast of Babeldaob.

The boat came ashore on a sandy beach lined with numerous coconut palms. Members of our party waded a couple of steps through the surf and proceeded across the narrow beach to nearby Ngermelech Village, one of five settlements in Melekeok. In the immediate vicinity I counted eight single-story houses elevated about 2 feet above grade; we were told that the present population of Melekeok exceeded 300. After a brief wait we were greeted by the chairman of cultural affairs for Melekeok, Mongami Elechuus. He guided us along a path leading south from the village and parallel to the shore. Passing through a stand of banana trees, breadfruit, lime, and areca and coconut palms, we came upon the site of the famous stone sculptures.

In all, the site originally contained nine

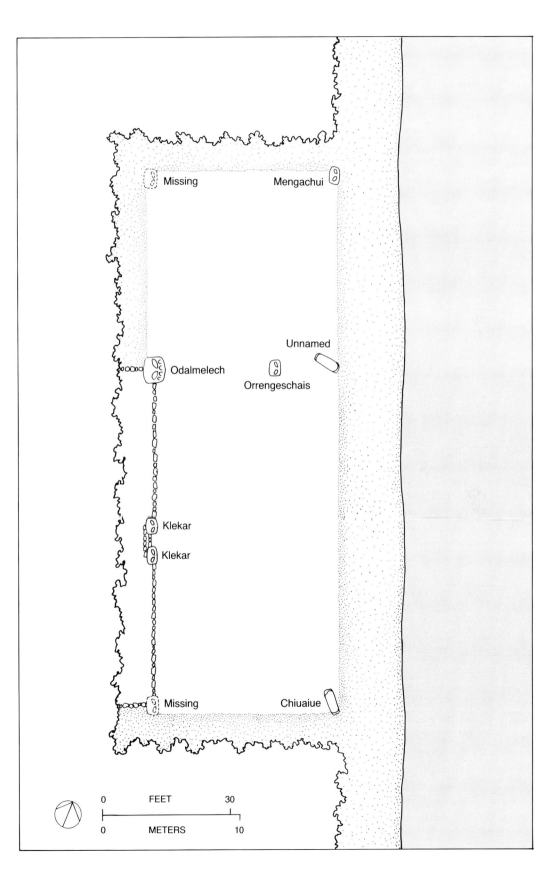

The megalith of Odalmelech measures 8 feet in height, 5.7 feet in width, and 3.5 feet in thickness.

carved megaliths ranging from 3.3 to 8 feet in height. Unfortunately, two of the sculptures were moved to another location in the village during the Japanese administration and their original positions have been lost. Arranged basically in two rows parallel to the nearby beach, the standing stone sculptures stare mutely toward the sea. The easterly row consists of three megaliths about 15 feet from the shore. Three more stone sculptures lie in the westerly row about 45 feet inshore. The ninth megalith of the group is situated slightly northeast of the plan's center.

Judging from the locations of upright stone backrests on elevated platforms, and repeated references to four corner posts in traditional Palauan architecture, I would hazard the guess that the two missing megaliths originally may have stood at or near the north and south ends of the westerly row. If so, they would form the corners of an approximately 45 × 123-foot rectangular composition. The sketch plan of the Melekeok stone sculptures presented here illustrates the arrangement as it appeared in 1984. Douglas Osborne (1979) suggested that some of Melekeok's stone sculptures probably have been moved from their original positions in the group.

The largest of the carved megaliths lies just north of the westerly row's center. The gigantic stone measures 8 feet in height above grade, 5.7 feet in width, and 3.5 feet in thickness. Osborne's (1979) photograph of the megalith with its base excavated suggests that the stone extended downward into the earth perhaps 15 inches.

The upright sculpture rests on the edge of a stone platform about 2 feet high and tilts back slightly to the west. Even in its eroded state the grimacing face inspires a sense of awe. Locally called Odalmelech, the anthropomorphic stone carving is illustrated in the photographs presented here. This was the most precisely carved stone sculpture that I saw in Palau.

Legend says that Odalmelech, the god of Ngermelech Village in Melekeok, "and his councilmen set out to lay a huge stone work over the village ground. That night, they

started bringing in huge reef stones for the project, but the work was only partially completed when dawn approached. Odalmelech, seeing that his cohorts could not accomplish the project before daylight, called his crew together and told them of the shame of being caught working in the morning sun. So he ordered his crew to carve all their faces on the monoliths and place them to eternally face the rising sun" (Palau, 1981:15).

The smaller carved megalith due east of Odalmelech is named Orrengeschais. The andesite column measures 4 feet in height above grade and is about 2 feet in diameter. Chairman Mongami Elechuus explained that the name combines the Palauan words "hearing" and "news." Perhaps long ago Orrengeschais was the news carrier and spreader of Melekeok.

In the northeast corner of the group is Mengachui, meaning "eating" and "hair." The name is believed to suggest cutting hair, perhaps a reference to a type of Palauan barber shop. Hair eating is a common metaphor in Palau with a variety of connotations, including some very specifically sexual. Mengachui is similar in size to Orrengeschais.

The megalith at the southeast corner of the group lies on the ground. Named Chiuaiue, or "sleeping" in Palauan, the stone is believed to have stood erect originally before being pushed over long ago, perhaps by European adventurers. The stone measures some 8.9 feet in length, 3.8 feet in width, and at most 2.3 feet in thickness. The name and meaning of the middle stone in the easterly row are unknown. Like Chiuaiue, this megalith is in a horizontal position although originally it may have stood erect.

The two stone faces south of Odalmelech are named Klekar, or "guard." Standing 6 feet apart at the edge of an ancient stone platform, they maintain their silent vigils at the entry stairs. These stones are about 3.3 feet high, 2.1 feet wide, and 1.3 feet thick. The two sculptures now missing from the group were said to have been moved by a Japanese teacher. They were reported to have served as gateposts for the teacher's house, but ought to be returned to their original site. One of the missing stones was Obadebusch, meaning "carry" and "horn." The name seems to refer to blowing a shell horn to summon villagers for news.

Two noteworthy aspects of Melekeok's stone sculptures are the precision with which the stones are placed in relation to each other and the symbolism that is associated with each individual monument. The relation of each element to the overall composition and the inherent meaning in each element seem to be recurrent concepts in traditional Palauan architecture. One may wonder what meaning, if any, the Palauans associate with new relationships when the sculptures are relocated. Expression of symbolic meaning and the relationship of symbols are fundamental concerns of Western architecture. Perhaps the prehistoric builders of Palau had similar concerns.

Bellwood (1979a: 287) observed that the anthropomorphic stone carvings of Babeldaob, such as the 2-foot-high one at Aimeong, resemble a similar andesite head carving on Unea Island off the northwest coast of New Britain. This may be another possible instance of Palauan parallels with western Melanesia. The noted megalithic sculptures of Easter Island in Polynesia, some 8,000 miles east-southeast of Palau, apparently are unrelated to the anthropomorphic stone carvings of Babeldaob. While megalithic sculptures have been found elsewhere in Oceania, the huge carvings of Palau are unique in Micronesia.

THE MEGALITHS OF BADRULCHAU

The largest and most impressive assemblage of megaliths on Palau is located at Badrulchau (also Bairulchau and Badrulau). The site lies near the north end of Babeldaob and is designated B : NE-4 : 4. It is considered to be the location of the first *bai*, a men's clubhouse or community house in Palau. The Badrulchau *bai* differs significantly from the present-day Palauan *bai* and may offer a valuable insight into the evolution of prehistoric architecture in the island group. Douglas Osborne (1966 and 1979) has recorded the site thoroughly.

Badrulchau contains a total of fifty-two megaliths. Of these, twenty-five are arranged in a 180-foot-long colonnade, the site's dominant feature. Southeast of the major colonnade is a smaller colonnade having twelve stones. About 100 feet northwest of the larger colonnade is an earth pyramid measuring some 60 feet on each side and rising at most 25 feet to its apex. The pyramid was carved out of a natural earth formation rather than being built up as are many Palauan pyramids. The site also has a plaza containing two monoliths and six carved "Great Faces." The sculptured megaliths are similar to those of Melekeok, although somewhat smaller and less impressive.

A reconstructed plan and section for Badrulchau's larger colonnade is presented here. The idealized reconstruction is based on Osborne's (1979) site map showing the conditions existing in 1968. It seems likely that thirty-six upright stone columns were planned originally, and that the structure was never completed. Of the twenty-five megaliths presently in the larger colonnade, two are only fragmentary remnants. Other columns may have been relocated to nearby villages in recent centuries to serve new functions, a common practice in Palau.

The Badrulchau colonnades, the legendary origin of *bai* building in Palau, seem unfinished. Many of the standing columns are badly weathered or fractured, some are leaning, and others have been overturned, perhaps by one or more earthquakes. In the larger colonnade the megaliths rise from 3 to 10 feet above present grade, but changes in grade since original construction suggest intended heights of perhaps 6 to 7 feet. The columns range in width and depth from 1.8 to 4.2 feet, but most are about 2 × 3 feet in section. They extend several feet into the ground, indicating an original length of about 10 feet for each column. The columns taper from their tops to their bases and generally taper to a point below grade. The tops of the outer columns align horizontally, perhaps to support a level superstructure.

A most unusual feature of Badrulchau's larger colonnade is the longitudinal grooving of all column tops with only one excep-

tion. The grooves range from 7 to 9 inches in depth and seem to have been intended to receive horizontal wood beams parallel to the centerline of the structure. Present-day Palauan *bai* have a series of transverse wood beams resting on low stone supports, but they never have longitudinal wood beams resting on tall stone columns. The grooves apparently were formed by pecking out two parallel grooves and then breaking away or knocking out the ridges between the grooves. This technique was easily within the technological skills of ancient Palauan stone workers.

The material for the megaliths of Badrulchau is an andesite conglomerate. Nearby sources for this type of stone are found along the coasts of Babeldaob. Andesite conglomerate is relatively easily worked when it is wet, a fact that the prehistoric Palauans apparently knew. Bamboo rafts reasonably could have transported the column stones from the quarries to the coast near Badrulchau.

In plan the larger colonnade may have consisted of three parallel rows of perhaps twelve columns each, a total of thirty-six. The parallel rows are some 12.5 feet apart, indicating a plan width of 25 feet. The maximum distance between the northernmost and southernmost columns is 180 feet, suggesting twelve columns spaced about 16.4 feet apart. This spacing is typical for the presently standing columns of the larger colonnade.

The purpose of Badrulchau's center row of columns seems to have been to support superimposed wood posts below the longitudinal ridge beam of a hipped roof. Slightly higher than the perimeter columns, the tops of the center columns may have been shaped to receive roof posts. Center posts clearly are not used in present-day *bai* in Palau, but they are found in Yap.

Douglas Osborne (1979) proposes, and I agree, that the Badrulchau colonnade probably represents an early version of the traditional Palauan *bai*. Subsequently, new architectural ideas may have arrived in Palau, possibly from Indonesia. Perhaps the idea of a structure without center posts never found its way to Yap or failed to impress the conservative Yapese if it did reach their island group.

Another unusual feature of the Badrulchau *bai* is its apparently intended floor on grade. Present-day Palauan *bai* have wood platforms raised several feet above grade. The height of the roof edge in the Badrulchau structure clearly suggests that a raised floor originally was not contemplated. Here again a parallel appears with Yapese structures built on stone-paved platforms with low roof edges. The Badrulchau *bai* is located on a hillside, suggesting that a level floor of earth may have been intended, possibly with a ditch upslope to control rainwater running down the hillside.

A remaining architectural problem with the larger colonnade at Badrulchau is its extraordinary length of 180 feet, well more than twice the length of traditional large wood structures in Micronesia. The plan of the *bai* at Irrai Village is on the order of 20 × 68 feet, an area of about 1,760 square feet. A single structure at Badrulchau suggests a 25 × 180-foot plan containing some 4,500 square feet, more than two and a half times the size of the Irrai structure. It seems more likely that Badrulchau may represent two 82-foot-long buildings containing about 2,050 square feet each, or perhaps three 50 feet long with 1,250 square feet areas.

The idea of two or three structures exactly aligned in a row is unprecedented in the known traditional architectural planning of Palau. The three *bai* that once stood together on the same platform in Irrai were parallel to each other, not aligned end to end. Neither are end-to-end alignments of buildings found in Yap, although this arrangement is sometimes found in the *latte* houses of the Marianas, such as those at the Tachognya and Taga sites on Tinian. Even so, the alignments are not as precise as those of Badrulchau. It would be incautious to assume any relationship between the prehistoric sites of Palau and those of the Marianas.

The meaning of the enigmatic *bai* at Badrulchau presently is not clearly known, and may never be. Nonetheless, the presence of this early structure in the evolution of prehistoric architecture in Palau may assist us in more fully appreciating the changes in ideas that seem to have occurred in the island group before Western contact.

IRRAI VILLAGE

Irrai (also Airai) Village is located on the south end of Babeldaob, about 10.5 miles southwest of Melekeok and 7.5 miles southeast of the sculpted hills overlooking Ngchemiangel Bay. One of several paramount villages of prehistoric Palau, Irrai contains stone platforms, pathways, boat landings, and terraced hill slopes in and around the village. The site lies on rolling hills on a peninsula extending into Irrai Bay. It is bordered by streams and hills to the north and west and by bluffs to the south and east. Prehistoric terraces on the hills inshore may have been part of the village originally.

The reconstructed village plan presented here is based primarily on the survey published by Gumerman, Snyder, and Masse (1981), with the exception of several features shown on Kramer's (1917) map. Kramer recorded much less extensive mangrove swamps along the peninsula's shore and noted that the village extended beyond the westerly stream. His map showed a causeway interconnecting the reef south of the peninsula with the mainland, and more extensive stone bulkheads and paving in the vicinity of the southerly boat landing.

Today the site is dominated by dense vegetation and trees, including coconut, areca palm, breadfruit, and almond. Wet (*Cyrtosperma*) and dry (*Colocasia*) taro, tapioca, and bananas are cultivated in occasional garden plots systematically grouped in approximately rectangular areas. Numerous sherds and artifacts of shell, coral, and stone have been found in several areas of the site, indicating prolonged human occupation (Gumerman, Snyder, and Masse, 1981).

An approximately 3,117-foot-long network of stone pathways, all perhaps originally interconnected, gives access to most of Irrai's elevated stone platforms. The major north-south pathway measures some 1,427 feet in length; the longest east-west path, about 886 feet. At the intersection of the

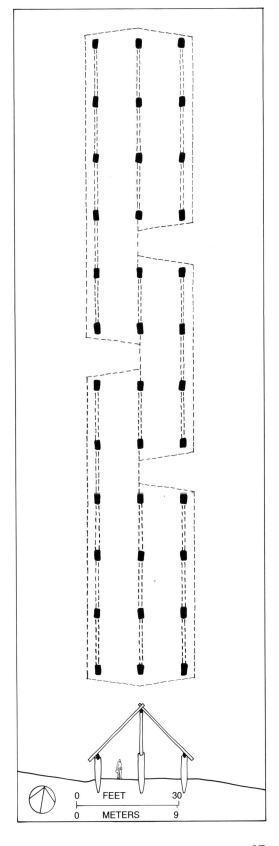

Irrai Village plan (after Kramer, 1919, and
Gumerman, Snyder, and Masse, 1981).

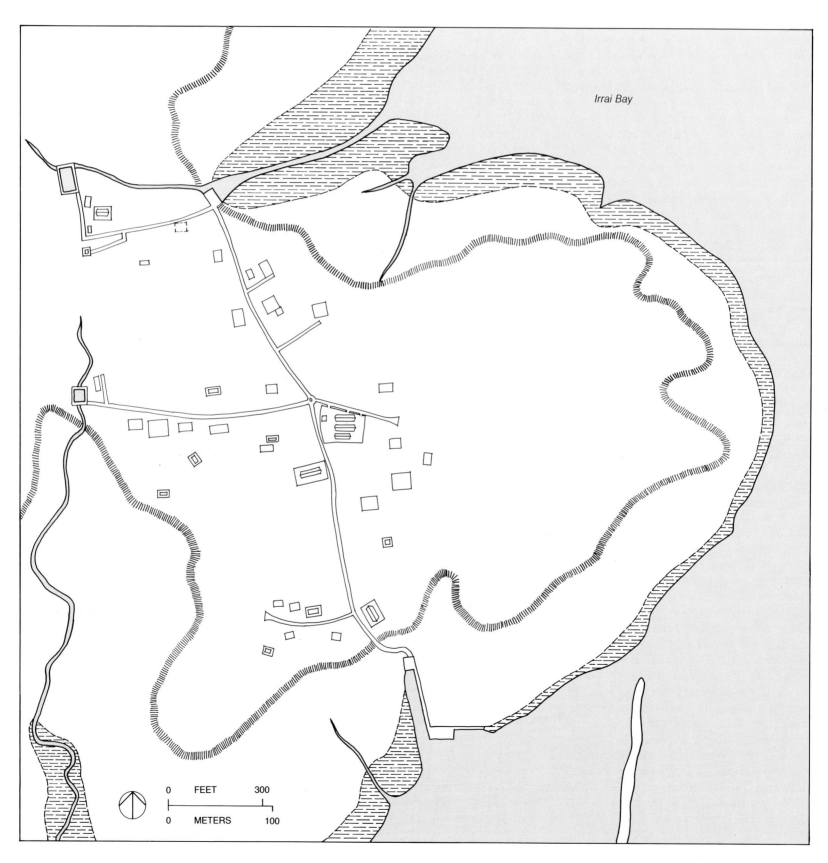

Irrai Bay

FEET
0   300

METERS
0   100

main paths is a 1-foot-high circular tier of stones 13 feet in diameter. Serving as a resting place today, the circular platform apparently did not exist at the time of Kramer's visit.

The cobbled surface of the pathways ranges from 5 to 10 feet in width and consists of a single layer of stones with drainageways on one or both sides. Three of the pathways terminate in broadened platforms of stone. The approximately level stone paths cut through higher terrain and are elevated on fill in low-lying areas. Just south of the platform of the *bai* the main path passes through a deep cut in the terraced hillslope. Apparently made during the German administration about 1905, the cut permitted the funeral procession of an important person to proceed from the boat landing to the village without struggling over the hill.

The site plan of Irrai Village shows forty-three rectangular stone platforms ranging in size from about 150 square feet to 12,000 square feet. Some of the platforms are a single stone high, while others exceed 3 feet in height. Eight platforms had two additional levels of stones in the shape of stepped pyramids. One three-tiered platform was noted.

Eighteen platforms contained one to seven stone graves, each consisting of long, narrow walls of stones forming a crypt within the platform. Stone uprights were found on eleven platforms. Some uprights served as "backrests" while others were carved into statues that are connected with stories and legends (Osborne, 1966). Combinations of tiers, graves, and uprights indicate the complexity of activities that focused on the platforms.

At least four of the platforms in Irrai Village once may have contained *bai*. The 300-year-old Bai-ra-Irrai is built on the platform southeast of the major paths' intersection. Generally arranged orthogonally with respect to nearby pathways, most of the platforms originally were used for domestic purposes. Modifications to platforms commemorate important events in the lives of clan members.

The channel north of Irrai leads from the bay through dense mangrove swamps to a stone-paved boat landing. Stone pathways connect the landing with the domestic centers of the village. Still in good condition during Kramer's (1919) visit, the landing in 1984 was only a remnant although it apparently still was used occasionally. The stream passing north of the landing leads west to the women's bathing area.

The approximately 59 × 89-foot women's bath is enclosed by walls of earth some 6 to 10 feet high. Stones line the inner surfaces of the walls. The stream flows through the rectangular reservoir and cleanses it during rainstorms. The major path leading west from the village center terminates at the men's bathing area. Cleansed by the westerly stream, the roughly 49 × 52-foot men's bath is bounded by a stone-lined wall of earth similar to the enclosure of the women's bath.

Near the bluff defining the western edge of Irrai lies a cemetery on a slightly raised mound of earth. The cemetery contains at least twenty graves, each generally oriented in an east-west direction. Each grave measures about 1.7 × 6.7 feet and is lined on both sides with four to eight coral slabs that project above grade. Similar coral slabs are placed at the ends of the graves. No covering slabs or cap stones are used. The major use of the cemetery apparently predated the German administration (Gumerman, Snyder, and Masse, 1981).

The major path leading south from the village center terminates in Irrai's main boat landing. A 200-foot-long stone quay interconnects two stone-paved landing areas, one on the shore of the bay and the other farther inshore and accessible by way of a channel lined with mangrove swamps to the west. Still in good condition and very much in use, the dock probably was rebuilt during the Japanese adminstration. The original village system of Irrai probably also included agricultural terraces inshore to the northwest.

At the time of Western contact several regional centers of power existed in Palau. Sometimes called "chiefdoms," they actively competed against one another for power and prestige. Each region seems to have been dominated by a paramount chief's village allied with varying numbers of lower-ranked villages. Because Irrai was a paramount chief's village, it appears to have had more numerous and prestigious architectural features than did lower-ranked villages.

The Irrai Bai Platform

Near the center of Irrai is a stone platform containing the recently restored Bai-ra-Irrai. Two lesser *bai* once stood immediately to the south. The term *bai* means village meeting house, guest house, or community house and includes the stone platform on which the building stands. The *bai* is the nucleus of administrative power for the village. From within the *bai* decisions are made on the construction of features surrounding the *bai*, including the stone pathways, platforms, boat landings, bathing areas, garden plots, cemeteries, and all other elements essential to village life (Sam, 1984).

The basis of the reconstructed drawing presented here is a survey and report by James Carucci (1983) and the map prepared by Augustin Kramer (1919). Omitted from the presentation are the present-day flagpole, a concrete water tank installed below grade during the Japanese administration, three stones associated with a recent cooking hearth, and a large area that presently is not paved but was part of the platform at the time of Kramer's map. The stone pathway west of the platform did not exist when Kramer visited the site. His map shows the path crossing the platform proper, immediately west of the three *bai*.

Two major stone pathways located immediately to the north and west of the platform give access to the domestic centers of the village. The approximately 10-foot-wide paths are paved with basaltic stone and some coral. Somewhat elevated above adjacent grade, they are flanked by drainage ways on both sides. Three stairways give access to the platform from the north pathway.

Containing an area of approximately 12,000 square feet, the platform of the *bai* measures at most 111 feet north-south by 136 feet east-west. Although the platform appears to be level, it actually slopes downward 2 feet from its southeast corner, where it is level with the adjacent grade, to the northwest corner, where it is more than 2 feet higher than the north path. The platform's stone alignments suggest more than one phase of construction.

Of the three *bai* shown on Kramer's map, only the north structure existed at the time of my visit in 1984. The open area immediately to the south had a surface of clay soil with scattered rubble from which the original stone paving had been removed, probably during the Japanese administration. South of the extant *bai*, and parallel to it, probably once stood the Ngerdubech Bai and the Medechibelau Bai. Kramer noted that both of these buildings were in dilapidated condition at the time of his visit.

The largest and most important of the three *bai* probably always was the existing structure. Fortunately, it continues to be used today for political and clan meetings. Clan heads and village elders have assigned seating areas within the *bai* according to their ranks.

The middle structure, the Ngerdubech Bai, probably was somewhat smaller than the north *bai*, although it too is believed to have had eight main floor beams (*bad*) and two fire pits (*chab*). The Ngerdubech Bai seems to have been a more common place for storage of everyday items and cooking. It might be thought of as the "commissary" for the group (Carucci, 1983).

The southernmost and smallest of the three structures probably was the Medechibelau Bai, a special building used to house village men who were chosen to be instructed in religious dance. Called *meai*, the men were sequestered within the *bai* during their period of instruction (Carucci, 1983). Unlike the two neighboring structures, the Medechibelau Bai apparently had two stories and is believed to have had only 5 or 6 floor beams with perhaps a single fire pit. Kramer (1926) reported that two-story *bai* in Palau were called "goutang."

The module for constructing the *bai* reportedly was a span, the distance on an adult from fingertip to fingertip with arms outstretched, about 6 feet. Coral rubble

foundations support stone hearths of the *bai*. The reconstructed drawings presented here suggest that the northern *bai* stands on a roughly 20 × 72-foot podium, and that the southern buildings perhaps occupied an approximately 44 × 65-foot podium. Both podia were elevated about 1.7 feet above the main platform. The *bai* podia contain an area of some 4,888 square feet, about 36 percent of the main platform's area. The areas immediately below the wood structures traditionally remained unpaved.

Near the west edge of the platform is a 16-foot-square paving about 2 feet high called the "Platform of Seventy Stones." In the center of the paving stands a 1.7-foot-high stone upright. In all, the *bai* platform contains a total of fifteen stone uprights ranging from 1.1 to 4.3 feet high. Of these, four are at the corners of the existing *bai*, four are at the corners of the main platform, and the remainder generally are near the perimeter of the platform, where they may have served as backrests for seated persons.

The present-day condition of the stone platform and wooden structure of the Bai-ra-Irrai, like many of the ancient sites that I visited in Micronesia, is threatened by the uncontrolled growth of large trees whose roots burst apart remaining stone structures, by erosion due to heavy rainfall and lack of maintenance, and by swarming insects and termites that relentlessly attack buildings of wood. In the interest of preserving the invaluable and irreplaceable cultural heritage of Micronesia, effective measures are needed to protect the monuments from gradual destruction.

Traditionally, the structures were maintained by the people who used them according to the social order of each village. In many cases the impact of Western culture has disrupted traditional political and social systems in Micronesia, thus removing the original means of preserving the remarkable prehistoric architecture.

The Bai-ra-Irrai

The Bai-ra-Irrai is a spectacular example of traditional Palauan art and architecture, the most highly decorated structure that I

saw in Micronesia. The design of the *bai* relies on symmetry, repetition, and symbolism to achieve its architectural expression. The slightly upward curved ends of the *bai* reminded me somewhat of the graceful hull of a Palauan canoe. Constructed entirely of local materials, the structure is bound and fitted together entirely without the use of nails, screws, or pegs.

Once commonly found in the island group, only two *bai* existed at the time of my visit: the Bai-ra-Irrai and an octagonal house or temple with a *bai* for spirits built in 1978 on Peleliu, an island some 34 miles southwest of Irrai. A third *bai* was built near the museum in Koror in 1969, but, unfortunately, it burned down in 1978 due to faulty electrical wiring installed to facilitate evening meetings. Traditional *bai* used a type of lantern or a fire pit for illumination.

The closest constructional relatives of the Palauan *bai* perhaps may be the heavy plank-and-beam clubhouses of the islands of Malaysia and Indonesia, although research thus far is inconclusive (Osborne, 1969). Also unclear is the extent to which Western tools and construction techniques may have influenced Palauan architecture since the wreck of the *Antelope* more than two centuries ago. It seems quite likely that the wood structures seen by the earliest European visitors to Palau were less sophisticated than the present-day Bai-ra-Irrai.

The drawings of the *bai* presented here are based on my own observations and photographs, several drawings provided by the Division of Cultural Affairs of the Republic of Palau, and the foundation survey by James Carucci (1983). The numbers shown in the longitudinal section refer to the sequence of erection for roof components. These are discussed later in this section.

Originally constructed perhaps three hundred years ago, the Bai-ra-Irrai was being refurbished at the time of my visit. Deteriorating wood members were being replaced and the original decorations were newly painted. The work was being done by young Palauans learning traditional craftsmen's skills. Even though most parts of the *bai* have been replaced over the centuries, some

The 12,000-square-foot stone platform near the center of Irrai Village was once the site of three important *bai* (after Kramer, 1919, and Carucci, 1983).

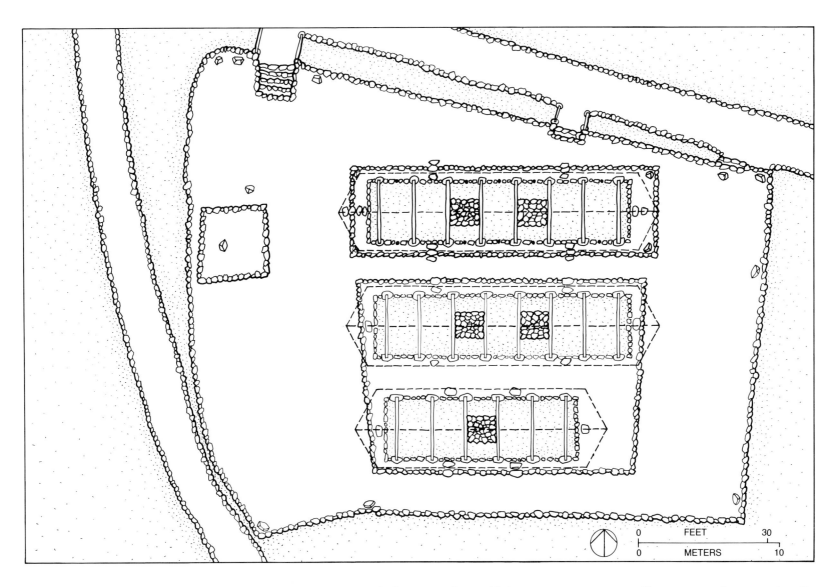

of the components probably date from the original structure.

Approaching the *bai* from the main east path near the village center, I found the ornately decorated structure on its handsome stone podium and platform. Overall, the *bai* measured about 20 × 68 feet in plan, an area of some 1,360 square feet. The gabled ends rose approximately 37.5 feet above the stone platform and projected 9 feet beyond the main structure, developing an overall length of some 86 feet along the roof's ridge.

Vince Blaiyok, the Division of Cultural Affairs representative for the *bai*, explained certain features of the structure that are not readily apparent. He pointed out that the

roof stringer lashings easily could be released to permit each side of the roof to slide down to the stone platform during very high winds. Additional typhoon precautions included lashing the upper structure of the *bai* with ropes to the bases of nearby trees.

Lowering the roof would reduce uplift and horizontal wind resistance high in the structure, thus substantially reducing the vulnerability of the *bai* to damage from typhoons. Vince spoke of the roof planes as a mariner would speak of sails, another possible nautical parallel to the structure of a *bai*. Easily removable roofs apparently are not a recent innovation in Palau. Kramer (1926) referred to mischief making by ob-

streperous village men who occasionally dislodged the roofs of their unsuspecting, lower-ranked neighbors.

At the four corners of the podium, called the "sidewalk of the bai," were upright stone backrests assigned to the four ranking clan heads and village elders. The main floor of the structure was elevated some 4 feet above the podium. Each end projected about 2.5 feet beyond the end floor beam, reminding me of the bow of a canoe thrusting beyond the crest of a wave.

The main structure rests on sixteen foundation stones in two parallel rows of eight each. The eight main floor beams that span the 20-foot width of the *bai* rest on founda-

Bai-ra-Irrai, longitudinal section and plan.

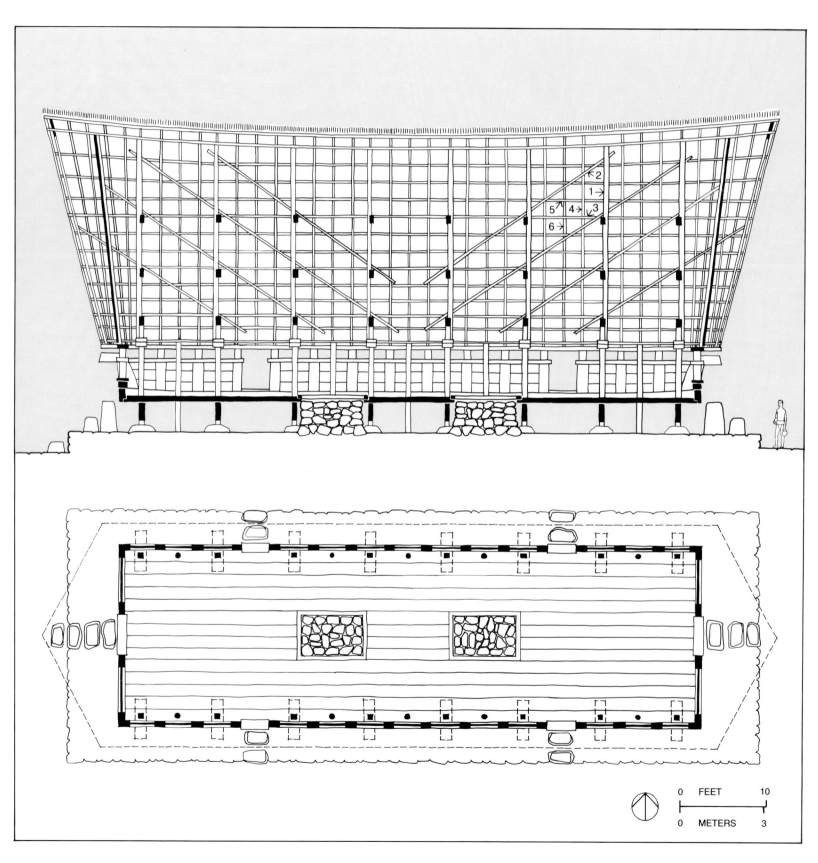

tion stones at both ends. The approximately 8 × 30-inch beams are hewn from *ukall* logs with adzes (*chebakl*), the traditional woodworking implement of Micronesia. The craftsmen of Palau are able to wield their adzes with exceptional skill and speed and can quickly reduce timbers to rectangular planks or beams with seemingly little effort.

The blade of the adze is at right angles to the handle and usually is wielded efficiently with one hand. By contrast, the axe blade is in line with the handle and typically requires two hands to wield. Larger adze blades, perhaps 3 inches wide, are used for rough carpentry. Blades 1.5 to 2 inches wide are used to shape more complex sill and plate joints (Osborne, 1969). A variety of chisels, gouges, drills, and other implements of shell and stone were available to the traditional carpenters of Palau. Saws, hammers, and nails were unknown in prehistoric Micronesia.

Six portals provide access into the *bai*, one at each end and two on either side. Stepping stones at each portal assist ascent to the elevated floor of the *bai*. The side portals are slightly more than 3 feet wide and 4 feet high. Both end portals are about 4 feet square. The roof gables extend outward beyond the walls of the *bai*, affording protection from the rain at the entries.

Many taboos are associated with the threshold (*iis*) of each doorway. Traditionally, a man without rank was not allowed to cross it, nor was anyone allowed to touch it. On the underside of the lintel above each portal, the image of a bat with outstretched wings was carved and painted. Vince Blaiyok explained that the bat symbol was derived from an old legend. At present it is interpreted as an admonition to bow one's head when entering.

Within the *bai* is a single large room about 19 × 67 feet in size. The uninterrupted space is illuminated by daylight from the portals and from a 1-foot-high horizontal opening that runs continuously around the structure between the top of the 4-foot-high wainscot and the underside of the roof. The floor consists of large planks, perhaps 6 × 18 inches in cross section, of naturally polished hardwood called *dort*. Two stone hearths, each measuring about 5 × 8 feet, are placed in the floor on either side of the center bay. Coral rubble fill supports the hearths from grade. Uncluttered by furnishings or partitions, the great hall is worthy of the dignified group of chiefs and elders who gather there (Owen, 1969).

The perimeter side walls consist of wide horizontal boards spanning between sixteen wall posts, two flanking each interior column. A continuous sill ("gorsegobl," Kramer, 1926), interrrupted only at the portals, terminates the wall 4 feet above the floor. Resting on a continuous base (*uchutum*), all of the components of the wall are fitted together with mortise-and-tenon joints. Dovetail joints are used elsewhere in the structure. The door posts ("gad," Kramer, 1926) and four corner posts (*saus*) are of particular symbolic importance in the *bai*.

The interior columns of the *bai* bear on the ends of the floor beams directly above the sixteen foundation stones. Each pair of columns stands free of the adjacent wall and rises vertically about 8 feet to support the lowest of three horizontal roof ties. Some 6 feet above the floor an unbroken lintel (*chellabed*) rests on the wall posts and supports the roof on both sides of the *bai*.

Between the hewn, rectangular columns are unfinished wood posts, one in each bay

A two-story *bai* in Ngarageluk (after Kubary 1895: pl. 32). Kubary photographed a similar structure, the Medechibelau Bai, which once stood south of Bai-ra-Irrai.

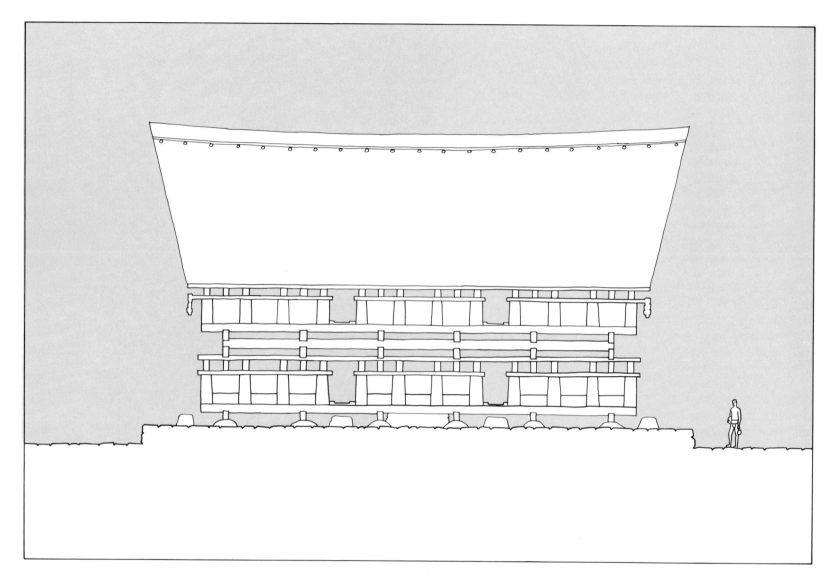

except at the side portals, where they would obstruct entry. The posts are placed in 3- to 4-foot-deep holes in the podium between the foundation stones and extend continuously to the underside of the roof structure. Apparently the ten intermediate posts serve to tie the entire structure together and resist horizontal wind forces that could have caused the *bai* to slide off its foundation stones during a typhoon.

A very unusual method is employed to tie together the columns, lintels, and roof beams. Carefully fitted horizontal wood members, each about 4 feet long, serve to lock the members together. Called *rekoi*, they are shown about 6 feet above the floor in the section presented here. Their ends curve upward toward the interior of the *bai* to serve as shelves for rolled-up sleeping mats. A hole drilled through the *rekoi* permits the column to penetrate it and continue vertically. The outer end of the *rekoi* is notched to receive the main roof beam (*orengodel*) on top, and the wall lintel (*chellabed*) on the bottom. This intricate system for interlocking structural members is unprecedented in Micronesia, or anywhere else to my knowledge.

As soon as the main roof beams (1 in the longitudinal section drawing) were erected, diagonal braces (2) were installed on both sides of the roof pointing upward toward the gable ends. Next the primary roof purlins (3) and rafters (4) were lashed in place, completing the main structure. A network of secondary purlins (5) and rafters (6) was installed to receive the roof's nipa palm thatch. The sequence of erection described here is based on my own observations, on the account of Kramer (1926), and on the report of Osborne (1969), who observed the actual construction of a *bai* in Palau.

An unusual construction feature of the traditional *bai* was prefabrication of the main structure in one location for final erection in another: "The purchasing village completes floor and thatch. The builders will paint and fill the carvings with white kaolin at their new location, and the gable sections will be

24

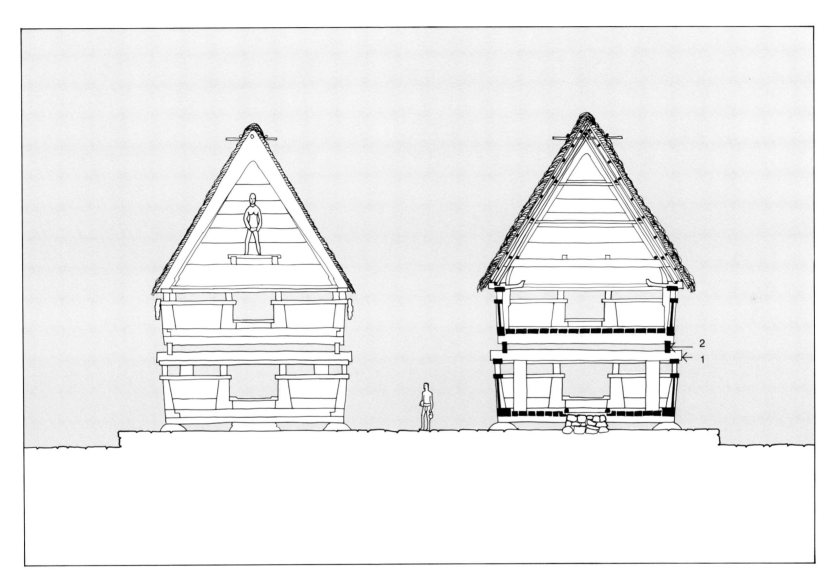

carved and painted and erected as the thatch is lashed on" (Osborne, 1969:19). The size of the *bai* to be prefabricated usually was noted by the number of floor beams, ten being the maximum number observed.

Two-Story Bai

A two-story *bai* once stood about 35 feet south of the Bai-ra-Irrai. Precise descriptions of the original edifice, the Medechibelau Bai, are lacking. It seems probable, however, that the two-story *bai* at Irrai may have resembled the "goutang" in Ngarageluk recorded by Kubary (1895:pl. 32). According to Kramer (1926:264), two-story *bai* on Palau "were not too rare. I myself

saw one in [Irrai] in 1907, although it was in a very poor state of preservation." Kramer found two-story *bai* at six locations in Palau and noted that they probably were dedicated to the god (*chelid*) Medechibelau. He suggested that "goutang" were constructed more for their impressiveness than for practical purposes.

Kramer observed that in many places the important god Medechibelau was worshipped by the head chiefs and the priests. The village leaders inhabited the richest and most beautiful houses; "among them are the two story dwellings" ("sop," Kramer, 1926: 225). Like the "goutang," the two-story houses were beautiful and very impressive.

Buildings with more than one story are not found elsewhere in Micronesia, although spaces beneath elevated platforms, such as the *latte* houses of the Marianas, often were paved and perhaps served as women's work areas.

The reconstruction presented here is based on Kubary's Plate 32, a photograph published by Kramer showing the "goutang" at Irrai in 1907, and observations by Carucci (1983). For ease of comparison the drawings of the building are at the same scale as those of the Bai-ra-Irrai. The human figure shown standing on the ground is about 5.5 feet high, the assumed height of a typical Palauan. The figure shown standing in the

Decorations of the *bai:* colorful symbols recall the mythical Palauan money bird, stylized *Tridacna* shell with accentuated hinge, and rooster summoning daybreak; female demigod recalls the importance of women in Palauan society, legendary bat appears above entry portals, and spider god symbolizes natural childbirth in Palau.

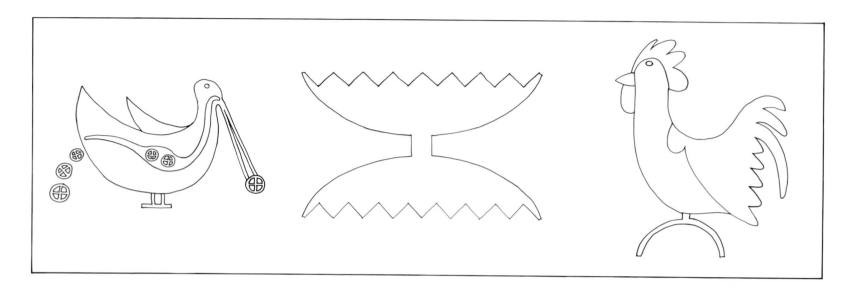

gable is larger than life-size; part of the artwork of the *bai,* it represents a woman.

Both floors of the "goutang" measure about 20 × 51 feet, an area of perhaps 1,020 square feet. Compared to the Bai-ra-Irrai, the two-story *bai* may have been somewhat lower in overall height. It probably had only six main floor beams and a single fire pit on its lower floor. The lower floor was elevated only about 2 feet above its stone podium. The headroom clearance of the structure's lower floor was barely sufficient for a typical Palauan adult to stand erect.

The slope of the roof was lower than the slope of the main *bai,* but both buildings had six entry portals, one at each end and two on each side. The two-story *bai* also had six entry portals on its second floor corresponding to the lower-level arrangement. The second-floor thresholds were some 12.5 feet above the podium. Presumably, they were accessible from the exterior by means of ladders.

A very unusual structural feature of the "goutang" is the duplication of the support for the second floor. If the lower-floor columns had extended 2 feet higher, the transverse beams (1 in the transverse section) that obstruct the lower-floor headroom could have been eliminated, and the longitudinal beams (2) along both sides of the structure would not have been required. In both ele-

vation and section, the two structures are technically redundant but aesthetically important. If the builders wished to add weight to resist wind pressures, heavier framing components would have served the purpose without obstructing headroom by adding redundant beams. Apparently, the traditional architecture of Palauan two-story *bai* was inspired more by preferences for beauty and impressiveness than by engineering efficiency or functional expediency. Undoubtedly, the "goutang" is one of the most extraordinary examples of prehistoric architecture in Micronesia.

Decorations of the Bai-ra-Irrai

The photograph of the Bai-ra-Irrai's west elevation illustrates the extensive and colorful decorations of the structure's gabled end. Symbolic in meaning, the ornamentations depict particular events and ideas that are important to the people of Irrai. The symbols reflect the village's traditions rather than the preference or imagination of the artist who creates them. The colors used are yellow ochre (*cheduu*), red (*orriich*), black (*chas*), and white (*cherou*). Blue, green, brown, and other colors are not traditional and therefore are not employed. Subjected to the intense tropical sun of Palau, the pigmentations fade comparatively quickly and require periodic refurbishment over the lifetime of the *bai.*

Across the base of the *bai* near the elevated floor line is a frieze that contains two rows of black crosses inscribed in circles on a background of white. These are symbols of Palauan money, emphasizing the concept of wealth that is deeply entrenched in the society. On the face of the portal's threshold are five curved yellow ochre symbols with serrated edges and accentuated hinges. They represent *Tridacna* (*kim*) shells, an important source of protein food and of material for adze and gouge blades. These bivalves are found in the waters that surround Palau.

On the corner posts and portal jambs are inscribed four perky roosters, all facing to the observer's left and seen from the side. The portal jambs represent two of the four leading women (*ourrot*) of Irrai. The corner posts (*saus*) of the *bai* stand for the village's four important clans, their leaders being the nucleus of the governing body of Irrai. "The remaining posts are dedicated to lesser clans and individuals. Those honored by the posts of the *bai* were also subject to rewards as well as obligations in the functions of the community. Though in a state of fluctuation and modernization, chieftainship and the hierarchical system associated with this social structure coexist in a modified version in present day Palau" (Owen, 1969:22).

The rooster is a common symbol in Palau, of which the following legend from Badrul-

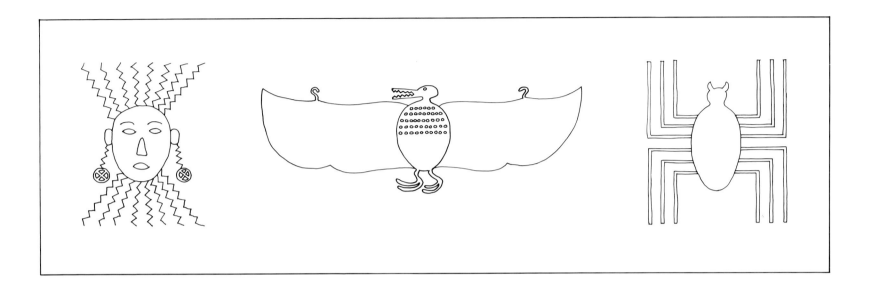

chau is an example. According to the legend, the mighty god Uchel Kebesadel practiced "magic by charring some coconut husk fiber and tossing it into the air, upon which the rooster appeared. Techadrengel [a lesser god] heard the rooster crow and on the seventh cry of the cock he thrust out the sun, which he had previously carved, and daylight flooded the islands. Since the gods worked exclusively in the dark of night the light put an abrupt stop to their work" (Owen, 1969:24). Thus, the structure of Badrulchau was never completed. Similar legends surround the stone sculptures of Melekeok and other prehistoric sites in Palau, all referring to the legend of the rooster summoning daybreak.

On the window sill above the roosters is a decorative band of *Tridacna* symbols showing pairs of serrated shells rendered in black on white backgrounds. On the faces of the white-painted window sills projecting toward the viewer are stylized Palauan money birds. The fowls consume, digest, and excrete money, another of the ubiquitous references to the traditional importance of wealth in Palau. Flanking the portal are stylized images of demigods with money earrings, referring to the dedication of these parts to ranking women.

On the underside of the portal's lintel is carved and incised the representation of a giant black bat, the subject of another famous Palauan legend. It is said that long ago the giant bat of Idepeluochel, a jungle area of Babeldaob, "was endowed with an unappeasable appetite for two sweetmeats, one made of Indian almond and the other of grated coconut. Upon detecting these foods in the *bai* at Angaur, the southernmost main island of Palau, the bat flew there. Thrashing its membranous wings it crushed the building and flew off with the confections. Horrified but defiant, the Angaurese planned to destroy this creature and so set spear like projections in their new *bai*. They set some sweetmeats there to lure the bat, which came, and by this masterly plan became impaled" (Owen, 1969:24).

Across the base of the gable is a band of stylized human faces rendered in yellow ochre and outlined in white. The eyes, nose, mouth, and money earrings of each face are black. Beneath the projecting roof planes are sloping end plates painted yellow ochre and decorated with *Tridacna* shell symbols in black. The triangular peak of the roof displays a stylized demigod with money earrings on a red-painted background. On the sloping faces of the gable below the projecting roof are white-painted borders with black zigzagging lines and pendant money earrings. The meaning of the zigzag lines is unknown.

The gable infill consists of twelve horizontal boards of equal widths but diminishing lengths. They are surmounted by a triangle bearing the representation of a butterfly fish, the Palauan symbol of greatest beauty. Each board is painted white and has a jagged black border at its base. The lowest band, about 17 feet long and slightly more than 1 foot high, presents a legend depicting a heroic event related to the history of Irrai. The depiction is in the form of a pictograph whose subject has, just as have all the decorative symbols of the *bai*, been chosen by the village chiefs and titled elders (*rubak*). Traditional Palauan pictographs are unique works of art and represent a number of scenes that varies from one to twenty, depending on the length of board and the content of the story.

In all, ten pictographs, or story boards, appear on the west gable of the Bai-ra-Irrai. Realistic figures of six sharks and seven surgeonfish appear on the second and third boards, respectively, from the bottom. On the other ten story boards are stylized representations of animated human figures, canoes, stone foundations, houses, trees, and other objects familiar to Palauans. Here zigzag lines represent conversation.

The shapes of human heads are stylized and elongated with buns of hair frequently pinned with long bamboo combs. The vivid

The colorfully decorated gable of the Bai-ra-Irrai rises some 37 feet above its stone-paved platform.

compositions are not studied. Their styles, though somewhat untutored and simple in line, convey powerful feelings of action and intent with unmistakable directness. Traditional Palauan views are taken from the side or front of the subject. Perspective drawing was not used in the archipelago.

The interior of the *bai* also was highly decorated with colors and symbols similar to the embellishments of the exterior. Horizontal tie beams depict heroic legends like the story boards of the gables. On the undersides of each projecting matholder (*rekoi*) is painted and incised the stylized symbol of a huge spider. The figure is rendered in black on a white background. "It recalls the story of the famous spider-god who taught Palauan women natural childbirth, as previously infants were released from the womb by cutting the mother's abdomen" (Owen, 1969:25).

SUMMARY

The distinctive prehistoric architecture of Palau survives today in the form of beautifully sculpted hill complexes, megalithic sculptures representing human faces, and extensive stone pavings, pathways, boat landings, and graves of ancient villages. While terraced hills and sculpted megaliths are not found elsewhere in Micronesia, ancient stone pavings and structures also exist in the villages of the Yap Islands, Pohnpei, Kosrae, and elsewhere in the South Seas.

The magnificent sculpted hills of Palau, such as those southeast of Ngchemiangel Bay, sometimes stretch for miles across the skyline of Babeldaob. The lower terraces seem to have served agricultural purposes, while truncated earthen pyramids crowned many of the sculpted hilltops. The culminating features of the hilltops apparently were constructed by groups of village workers, perhaps to serve as community refuges in times of civil unrest or other purposes not presently known.

Megalithic sculptures, such as the anthropomorphic stone carvings of Melekeok and other ancient villages, are among the most distinguished achievements of Palau. The sculptures are associated with traditional Palauan legends of great significance to the islanders. Locally called "Great Faces," each carving apparently has a name and specific symbolic association. The sculptures exhibit varying degrees of artistry, suggesting that they were carved by different sculptors at different times. Anthropomorphic stone carvings also have been found on Easter Island in Polynesia, on Unea Island in Melanesia, and elsewhere in Oceania.

Unlike Nan Madol on Pohnpei and Leluh on Kosrae, Palau had no single administrative or religious center. Alliances of smaller villages with paramount villages established the basis of social order and architectural expression in Palau. Village *bai* were the focus of village life and the most important of traditional buildings in the island group. Unlike the meeting houses (*pebaey*) of Yap, the *bai* of Palau had column-free interiors and wood platforms elevated above grade.

Although the *latte* houses of the Marianas apparently also had elevated wood platforms, the stone supports of traditional Palauan structures were comparatively low. Capstones on columns, such as those of the Chamorros, were not used in Palau. *Latte* houses often were aligned end to end rather than side by side, as was the case of the three *bai* in the center of Irrai Village.

The remarkable megaliths of Badrulchau seem to afford an insight into the evolution of prehistoric architecture without parallel elsewhere in Micronesia. While many questions still remain unanswered about the exact configuration of the remarkable Badrulchau *bai*, it seems likely that the earliest meeting houses in Palau may have had floors on grade, central column supports, and primary wood framing in the longitudinal direction. Present-day *bai* differ markedly from these earlier ideas, perhaps the result of new influences arriving from other areas of Oceania long before Western contact.

The two-story buildings of Palau are unique in Micronesia, although areas on grade below wood platforms serve domestic purposes in some island groups. The intricate joinery of wood structures, such as the Bai-ra-Irrai, demonstrates a level of technological achievement not found on Yap, Pohnpei, Kosrae, or elsewhere in Micronesia. The highly sophisticated craftsmanship of traditional Palauan architecture may be to some extent the result of foreign influences, beginning with the wreck of the *Antelope* in 1783. Nonetheless, the prehistoric architecture of Palau is among the most distinguished of ancient Micronesia.

2. THE YAP ISLANDS

Western influence has had less impact on traditional Yapese architecture than on the architecture of Palau, the Marianas, Pohnpei, and Kosrae. The Yapese in several places have continued their architectural traditions with relatively little change since the first European contact with Micronesia during Magellan's circumnavigation of the globe in the early 1520s. As with the other islands of Micronesia, the prehistory of Yap is very imperfectly known. The following presentation is a preliminary synthesis of what presently is known, with the view of understanding more clearly the achievements of prehistoric architecture in Micronesia.

Yap is a compact group of four major and six minor islands. The major islands are Rumung and Map toward the north, Gagil-Tomil near the center, and the large island of Yap toward the south and west. The narrow waterway separating Gagil-Tomil from Yap is a canal that the Germans employed Yapese to dig in 1901 to facilitate navigation in the island group. The distance from the north tip of Rumung to the south tip of Yap is about fifteen miles. The present-day town of Colonia is located on a protected harbor within the reef along the southeast coast of Yap Island. The Yapese generally have confined foreigners to Colonia while maintaining their traditional society elsewhere in the island group.

One of the smallest of Micronesia's major high islands, Yap presently has a land area of 30.6 square miles. Some of the coastal areas may be the result of land fill in historic times. The area within the reef, the major source of protein food for the islanders, is 49.8 square miles. At some points the reef lies more than a mile from the shore.

Yap's closest neighbors are Ngulu Atoll, 55 miles to the southwest, and Ulithi Atoll, 100 miles to the northeast. Palau lies 280 miles to the southwest; Guam, 530 miles to the northeast; and Truk, 950 miles to the east. On the average, three typhoons every two years occur in this area of the Pacific Ocean, but most of them pass to the north of the Yap Island complex.

Like Palau and the Mariana Islands, Yap lies along the edge of a tectonic plate that geologically separates the basin of the Philippine Sea from the Pacific Ocean. Volcanic activity frequently occurs along the edge of the plate. Compared geologically to Pohnpei and Kosrae, Yap is relatively old and weathered. Its highest point of land is 607-foot-high Mount Matade, less than one-third the height of Mount Finkol on Kosrae.

Schist outcroppings, metamorphic rock formations that originally were volcanic, occur in many areas of Yap. These provided the stones for building Yap's many elevated platforms, house foundations, streets, causeways, grave facings, bulkheads, and piers. Coral heads from the lagoon also were used. Overlying much of the island is an impermeable clay soil that ranges in color from yellow to red to brown. Brightly colored clays traditionally have served as pigments for paint, stains, and dyes on Yap. Clay also was essential to pottery making on the island.

Poor soils are characteristic of most of Yap's inland areas, although the majority of the coastal areas are quite fertile. Here numerous fresh water streams flow down to the sea and breach the reef in seven places. Natural ventilation and protection from the sun and rain appear to have been major determinants of form in traditional Yapese architecture.

The earliest people on Yap, like those on Palau and the Marianas, apparently came from the vicinity of the Philippine Islands or eastern Indonesia. They may have arrived sometime around 1,000 B.C., perhaps by inadvertent drift voyages. Thus far, the earliest radiocarbon date for Yap is within 80 years of 360 B.C. (Takayama, 1982), but it seems likely that the island was inhabited well before that time.

The Yapese developed numerous villages along the coasts where they cultivated taro (mostly *Cyrtosperma*, giant swamp taro), yams, Tahitian chestnuts, mangoes, citrus, and sugarcane, as well as coconut and papaya trees. Inshore they raised yams and sweet potatoes. The reefs yielded mollusks and over two hundred species of fish. No large animals were found originally on Yap. Foreigners later introduced dogs and pigs, while native to the island were sea turtles, fruit bats, and several species of reptiles, including large monitor lizards that grow up to ten feet in length.

Like the people of Palau and the Marianas, the Yapese commonly chew betel nuts seasoned with lime and pepper leaf. The ceremonial drink called *saka* on Kosrae and *sakau* on Pohnpei was unknown to the prehistoric people of western Micronesia. The distinctive language of the Yapese seems more closely related to the languages of the Palauans and the Chamorros of the Marianas than to those of the people who live in Truk, Pohnpei, and Kosrae. Within Yap itself dialects vary to a considerable degree from one part of the island complex to another.

LANDOWNERSHIP AND RANKING

The traditional roles of Yapese men seem to have been fishing, gathering coconuts and betel nuts, clearing land, and building houses and canoes. Women probably tended gardens and did most of the cooking. The men wore loincloths of woven banana fiber; the women, voluminous skirts of various shredded leaves.

Yapese society was divided according to age and sex into groups of old men, old women, adult men, adult women, and young women and children. Each of the five groups had its food cooked in a separate pot over a different fire in a separate cookhouse. The society was further divided into patrilineal and matrilineal kinship groupings (Alkire, 1977).

Every plot of land and lagoon area on Yap is named and ranked according to patrilineal descent. Villages are divided into two to five wards, each headed by the senior male living on the highest-ranked land within the ward. The Yapese society is ranked according to a complex system of caste related to landownership and class based on alliances. Higher-ranking land could be acquired by marriage, adoption, inheritance, service, or warfare. Social ranking encouraged stability and discouraged adventurism. More complete information on Yap's complex social and political systems may be found in the references to Hunter-Anderson (1983).

The Yap Islands.

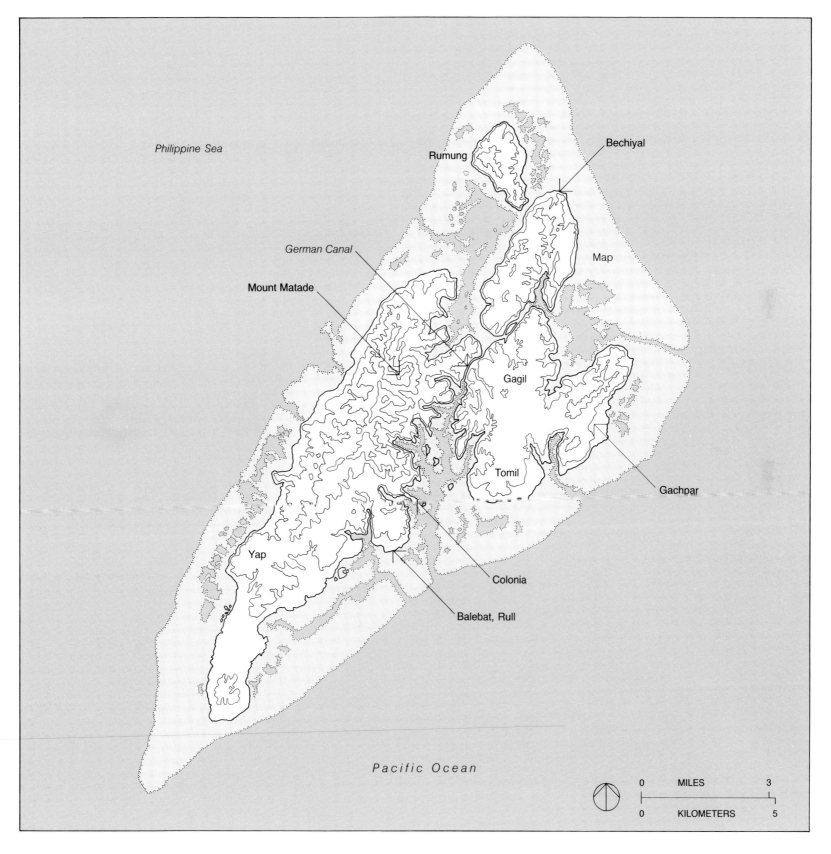

Philippine Sea

Rumung

Bechiyal

German Canal

Map

Mount Matade

Gagil

Tomil

Gachpar

Yap

Colonia

Balebat, Rull

Pacific Ocean

MILES

0   3

KILOMETERS

0   5

The environs of Bechiyal Village.

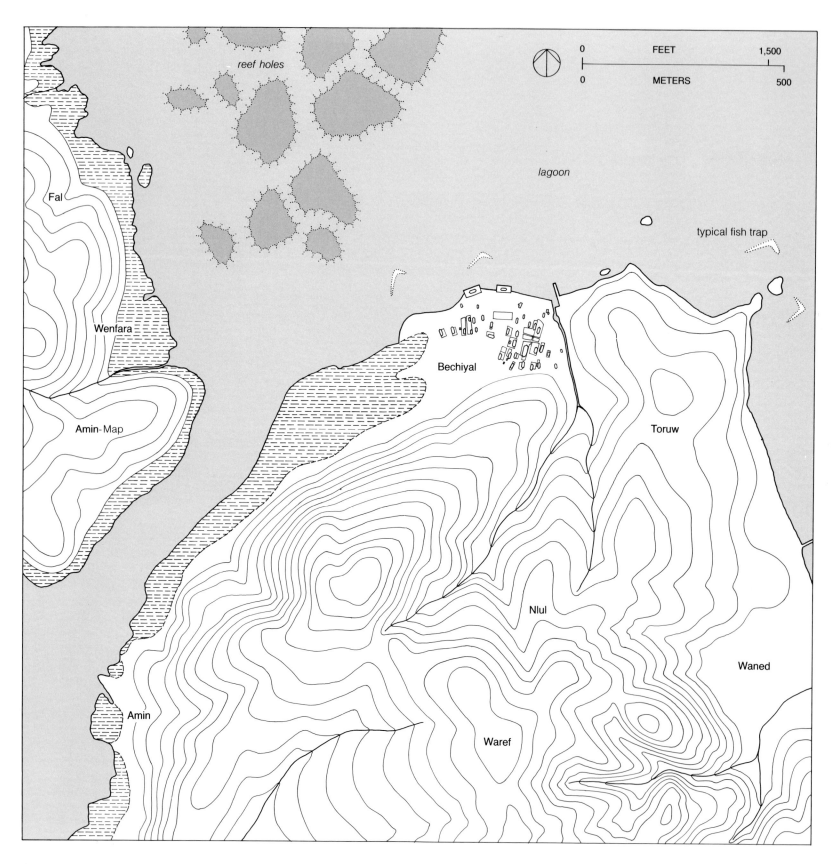

The basic organizational unit of Yap is the *tabinaw,* or "household estate." The stone platform of the highest-ranked house on an estate is called the "central foundation." In it "reside the ancestral spirits who have lived on the land, to whom the members of the group pray, from whom children come, and after whom parents name children" (Lingenfelter, 1975:24). All authority, political rights, and landownership are vested in the central foundation. The people who reside on the household estate only speak for the central foundation. The basic organization of traditional Yapese society is directly expressed in the elevated stone platforms of its *tabinaw.*

ALLIANCES AND TRADE

The 129 villages of Yap today are grouped in ten municipalities, although traditionally there were twelve. The two most powerful polities, Gagil toward the north and Rull toward the south, were the focus of rival alliances. Rumung and Map aligned themselves with Gagil, while the southern municipalities usually were allies of Rull. Between these two Tomil, which apparently was highly respected by the rival alliances, could shift its allegiance and influence the balance of power. Its magicians were said to be the most powerful on Yap, and some of its areas are reputed to be the most sacred in the island group.

The Gagil alliance extended its sphere of economic, ritual, and social ties from Ulithi in the west to Namonuito, 900 miles to the east. The many islands of the central atolls were linked to Yap by a unifying exchange system called *sawei* (Alkire, 1977:49–52). This area of influence is sometimes referred to as the "Gagil Sphere" (Lessa, 1956). According to William Alkire, the people on these islands believed that the Yapese possessed superior magic and control of the supernatural—without annual tribute the Yapese could destroy the low islands with violent storms and typhoons.

Until the beginning of the twentieth century, outrigger canoes annually set out from Namonuito for the long voyage to Yap. Canoes from other islands joined the growing fleet as it sailed westward, bearing tribute, such as woven fabric skirts, loincloths, sennit twine, and shell valuables. Command of the fleet shifted as it approached Yap because the atolls closer to Yap were higher ranked. Upon arrival, appropriate tribute was given to the chief of Gachpar (also Gatchepar), the highest-ranking village in Gagil. Other gifts were presented to the Yapese chiefs who owned the respective out islands. The chiefs, who considered themselves the "fathers" of their out island "children," usually reciprocated with gifts of turmeric or food.

The Rull alliance conducted trade with Palau for such items as pearl shell and the round stones used on Yap for money. These were quarried by Yapese in the aragonite/calcite mines controlled by the chief of Koror. The circular stone money traditionally was transported across the 280 miles of open sea to Yap by canoes or rafts. During the late nineteenth century an enterprising American trader, Capt. David Dean O'Keefe, developed a flourishing trade on Yap. He used his ships to import large quantities of stone money, mostly from Palau but partly from Guam.

POPULATION AND FOREIGN CONTACT

Mariners sighted Yap during the sixteenth, seventeenth, and eighteenth centuries, but very little foreign contact occurred until Andrew Cheyne's two-month stay on Yap in 1843. He recorded details of construction and plans of village meeting places. The maximum population of the island before foreign contact may have been in the range of about 27,000 persons (Hunter-Anderson, 1983). This represents a density of perhaps 882 persons per square mile, high for neolithic societies but not unusual for Micronesia.

During the late nineteenth century, trading increased substantially. Particularly prized were bêche-de-mer, or trepang, a type of sea cucumber valued by the Chinese, and copra, dried coconut meat. The foreign traders brought with them virulent epidemics, most notably influenza, syphilis, and dysentery. Because of the foreign diseases, a serious population decline began in the island group toward the middle of the nineteenth century.

The first colonial administration (1885–1899) was Spanish. At the end of the nineteenth century the population was estimated to have been only about 8,000 Yapese. By the end of the German administration of 1899–1914, the population had declined to perhaps 6,000. At the outbreak of the First World War, Japan occupied Yap and other former German possessions in Micronesia. By 1945 the population of Yap reached its lowest point of about 3,000 native islanders. During the United States administration the population of the Yap Islands increased to 9,630 by 1981, a density of some 315 persons per square mile.

THE ENVIRONS OF BECHIYAL VILLAGE

Bechiyal Village (also Bechiel or Bechyal) is located on the north end of Map Island overlooking a broad, shallow bay that is somewhat protected by Rumung Island to the northwest. Traditionally, the reef was divided into parcels as carefully as the village land, each parcel being ranked according to the *tabinaw* that owned it. Stone or bamboo fish traps were built on some parcels within the reef. Trolling and fishing with nets, spears, hooks, and lines were regulated carefully to a point seaward from the reef where the islands no longer could be seen. Fishing rights beyond this point in the deep sea were controlled by Gachpar in Gagil district.

Five basic types of stone fish traps apparently came to be constructed in prehistoric Yap as population increases brought increasing demands for food on the island's limited resources. Arrow traps usually were built near the shore or close to deep holes in the reef, and V-shaped lagoon traps were built away from the shore. These traps probably yielded bountiful catches that were taken to the villages owning the traps for distribution. Lesser yields may have been produced for individual families by piled-rock traps built in coral-free areas near the middle of the lagoon, by V-shaped reef-crest traps, and by rectangular surround traps, perhaps holding ponds, such as those found in Tomil harbor (Hunter-Anderson, 1981).

Arrow traps consist of stone walls arranged like arrows pointing toward the sea. The long shaft of the trap prohibits fish from moving parallel to the beach. The arrow tips are elongated rectangular chambers formed by parallel stone walls. Bamboo weirs at the ends of the chambers receive the fish as the tide ebbs. Larger fish tend to swim toward deeper water when confronted by a barrier. As low tide approaches, fish are concentrated inside the tips of the arrow-shaped trap, where they are vulnerable to spearing or can be scooped up with hand nets. Fish traps of stone require continuing maintenance. Rapidly growing coral formations, sand accumulations, and storms may render fish traps ineffective or destroy them entirely unless they are attended periodically. During my visit to Bechiyal Village the villagers were preparing to rebuild their stone arrow trap.

In Yapese, Map means "overflowing," a reference to the island's rich soils and abundant crops. For example, some of the best yams and betel nuts (areca palm) in all of Yap are grown on Map. Twelve contiguous villages ring the island's shores, and four more are situated inshore at the heads of streams. Map extends its hegemony to Amin-Map Village on the southernmost tip of Rumung Island, just across a shallow, 450-foot-wide reef passage west of Bechiyal.

A regional group of traditionally associated villages on the north end of Map consists of Bechiyal, Toruw, Waned, and Wacholab, together with the low-caste inshore villages of Nlul and Waref. By rank, Bechiyal is superior to Nlul, its southerly neighbor, but inferior to Toruw to the southeast. In turn, Toruw is subordinate to Gachpar on Gagil. Amin Village borders Bechiyal to the southwest. Workers from nearby Rumung Island have assisted in reconstructing several traditional structures in Bechiyal in recent years.

The ecological zones of Bechiyal are in many respects typical of those of many other coastal villages on Yap. Bechiyal's sandy beach, however, is unusual. Most of the

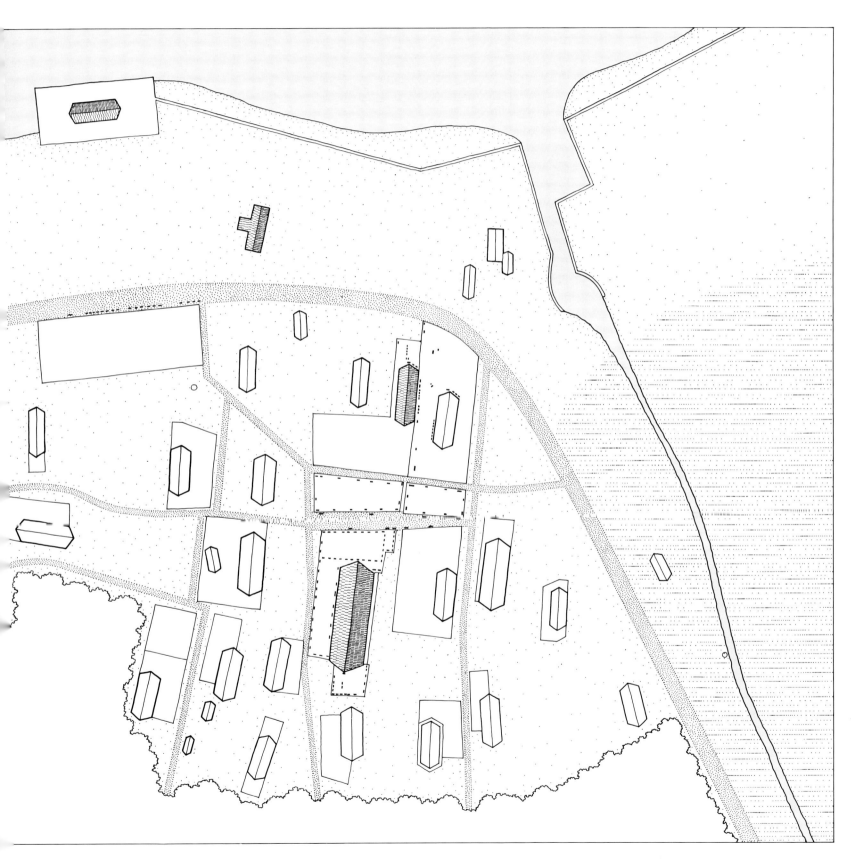

From south to north, the Bechiyal Village plan shows the shaded roofs of the present-day *pebaey, tabinaw, sipal,* and *faluw* (based on a survey by Intoh, 1984*a*).

coastal areas of the island are rocky or have dense mangrove swamps, and sea grass often grows close to shore near mangrove swamps. Toward the center of the lagoon the bottom generally is covered with algae and sand. Coral grows on both sides of the outer reef. Different zones of the reef yield different types of mollusks and fish. More prosperous villages on Yap often built stone piers out into the lagoon for the use of canoes at low tide. In 1910 Wilhelm Mueller (1917) observed a village pier that exceeded 1,180 feet in length.

Inshore from the high-tide line is a sandy coastal plain where coconut palms abound. This is a well-drained area suitable for dwellings. Farther inshore taro patches often are found in low-lying depressions where water levels can be regulated. On the fertile hillsides grow gardens, coconut palms, bananas, papayas, breadfruit, areca palms, Tahitian chestnuts, and forests. Hillside gardens on northern Map are laid out in rectangular plots that resemble village plans. Grassy savannas, pandanus, ferns, and occasional sweet potato terraces commonly are found on hillcrests and on the uplands inshore.

On the ridge crest between Bechiyal and Toruw are typical sweet potato gardens consisting of two-tiered stepped pyramids of clayey soil. The platform of one of these gardens is 8 feet wide. Its sides step down in 2-foot increments and form a continuous lower terrace that is 2 feet wide. Sweet potato cuttings are propagated in fertile soil placed on the well-drained terrace platforms. Sections of the terrace not under cultivation are covered by a native grass that grows to shoulder height.

Village borders in Map are defined from the shoreline to the hills by ridge crests, pathways, fences, or tree rows. The highest elevation in Bechiyal is the 240-foot-high hill south of the village. The inshore village of Nlul lies at the head of a stream that flows through Bechiyal and into the sea. A traditional footbridge that spans the stream consists of two coconut logs about 12 inches in diameter and some 20 feet in length. They rest on stone foundations on opposite banks of the stream. Between the coconut logs

and parallel to them lie three large bamboo poles, each about 5 inches in diameter. The bamboos form the walking surface of the bridge, flanked by coconut logs that serve as curbs. The bamboos are springy under foot as one crosses the bridge. Traditionally, bamboo stands were cultivated on hillsides near streams and springs. Bamboo was used to build houses, canoes, and implements as well as bridges, and in some areas bamboo tubes were used to divert water from streams or rocky pools that served as baths.

Inshore areas well away from villages were the sites of cemeteries, menstrual houses, wood lots, playgrounds, battlegrounds, and a network of pathways with occasional sitting platforms. The paths were often stone paved and sometimes drained by ditches on one or both sides. Apparently, the preferred location for a battleground was on land that was not suitable for any other purpose and that was well away from buildings and gardens that might be damaged needlessly.

Battles on Yap seem to have been frequently a matter of posturing by opposing groups. Their outcomes could be decided by damaging a canoe, by injuring an adversary, by one side's having more people present than the other side, or by an occurrence interpreted as an omen. The purpose of warfare on Yap seems to have been a matter of changing boundaries, redressing perceived insults, or testing alliances rather than genocide, property destruction, or environmental disruption.

Graves often were grouped in clusters that contained from several dozen to as many as 150 burials. Tombs varied in size and form. Those of important people often were three-tiered, stepped pyramids of earth faced with stone. Infants who died in childbirth were wrapped in mats and buried in unmarked graves near a village menstrual house where babies were born. A typical menstrual house was smaller than most residences but larger than cookhouses. In higher-ranking villages, traditionally, the menstrual house was built on a hexagonal stone foundation and had a rectangular stone sitting platform nearby for visitors (Hunter-Anderson, 1983).

Bechiyal Village Plan

Bechiyal Village is arranged according to topography in a gridiron plan along the shoreline, a typical Yapese village arrangement. All of the major structures are built on hexagonal stone platforms elevated 3 to 4 feet above the adjacent paving. The platforms, called *dayif*, are placed on rectangular stone seating terraces called *wunbey*. The latter are about 2 feet high. Upright stones are set into the seating terraces to serve as backrests for important participants in ceremonies. Dwellings in continuous rows flank the stone-paved paths. Widened, unpaved spaces between the seating terraces of meeting houses serve as dance areas (*malal*). All of the stone paving is grey schist.

Projecting out from the shore is the young men's house, called *faluw*. A low stone bulkhead extends along the shore from the *faluw* to the stream. In the sandy coastal area nearby is the shed (*sipal*) where the canoe is stored when not in use. Beneath the coconut palms along the beach, nets are dried and equipment is stored on several small wooden platforms. A short distance from the beach is a cookhouse, an open-sided house used for lounging and dining, and a shower house.

Near the center of the village is the residence, or *tabinaw*, of the village chief, John Tamag (Tamageoron). As in all of the village structures except the *faluw*, the long axis of the *tabinaw* is oriented perpendicular to the beach. Immediately south of the chief's house is Bechiyal's largest structure, the old men's meeting house, called the *pebaey*. Seating platforms with backrests adjoin the *pebaey* and overlook the dance area.

Traditionally, a residential unit, or *tabinaw*, consisted of the main residence with its attached *wunbey*, one or more additional residences, small structures for cooking, sleeping, and storage, gardens, and a refuse disposal area. Separate cookhouses (*ta'ang*) were required for the husband, his wife and small children, and other family members according to their ages, sexes, and ranks. Bamboo fences sometimes enclosed the *tabinaw* and its associated structures to provide privacy from the rest of the village (Mueller,

Bechiyal *pebaey,* plan.

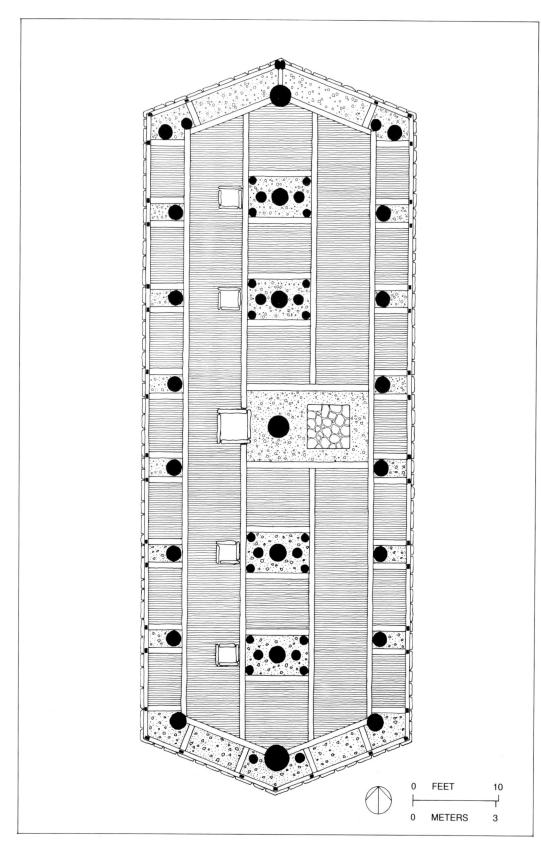

0 FEET 10

0 METERS 3

1917). Other areas in the village were set aside for small cooking and sleeping houses where young women stayed during the first year of puberty or longer and sacred areas, called *teliu,* where magicians performed rituals.

The village plan shown here is based on a recent survey by Michiko Intoh (1984). It locates a total of thirty-four *tabinaw* platforms, seven cookhouses, three wells, two dancing areas, two *faluw,* a *teliu,* numerous *wunbey,* platforms, the *pebaey, sipal,* and associated structures. Taro patches, fruit trees, and gardens grow farther inshore and along the stream that flows into the lagoon. The major village path continues southeast to Toruw and southwest to Amin.

At the time of my visit the population of Bechiyal was ten persons who were members of two families. Most of the stone foundations had no wooden structures. It appears that in the past Bechiyal may have had as many as two hundred residents (Kugfas, 1984). Although the island's population has been rising steadily since its low point forty years ago, some young people who formerly would have lived in the village now find Colonia more attractive. Fortunately, other young people prefer to remain in the villages of Map and Rumung where they carry on Yapese traditions in farming, fishing, and arts and crafts. The traditional structures of Bechiyal presently are being restored to serve as an authentic visitors' center.

The Yapese word for master craftsman is *salop.* The *salop* for architecture in Bechiyal also happens to be the chief, John Tamag. He is chief by virtue of inheritance from his father's side of the family. As a *salop,* he is a respected member of a small professional group on Yap. Here the landowner who wishes to build a house acts as the general contractor, and the *salop* is brought in (Kugfas, 1984).

The stylistic preferences of John Tamag appear in the particular angles of house ends, types of stone facings, and sculptural decorations, such as those in the *pebaey.* Most of the characteristics of Yapese architecture are determined by tradition according to building type. In the village of Toruw, Tamag's influ-

Intricate bindings join posts, beams, and rafters in traditional Yapese structures. Colorful decorations are tendered in red, yellow ochre, black, and white.

ence can be seen in the work of his nephew, who studied under him (Hunter-Anderson, 1983:84).

THE *PEBAEY*

The largest and most impressive structure in Bechiyal Village is the *pebaey,* the traditional center of political activity in the community. The elevated stone platform of the *pebaey* is hexagonal and contains an area of some 2,355 square feet, about the size of many residences in the United States. The structure is about 31 feet wide, 83 feet long, and 36 feet high measuring from the top of the paving of its adjoining *wunbey.* The maximum dimensions of the *wunbey* are approximately 66 feet east-west by 106 feet north-south. The plan of the *pebaey* presented here has the same scale and orientation as the residence, canoe shed, and *faluw* to assist the reader in comparing the buildings with each other.

The *pebaey* is placed in the southeast area of the *wunbey.* The sitting platform is about 32 feet wide to the north and almost 20 feet wide to the west. The dancing area to the north is 2 feet below the level of the *wunbey.* Circular stone valuables (*rai*) rest against the *wunbey,* demonstrating the wealth of the community. A total of thirty-five stone backrests are located on the *wunbey.* Well-fitted stones face the walls and paving of the *wunbey* and *dayif.*

The sides of the *pebaey* are open because the building is not normally used for sleeping. Its gable ends, which face north and south, are open woven to facilitate air movement. Colorful decorations on the gables represent stylized fish, stars, diamonds, and other abstract designs according to Yapese traditions. Colors traditionally used in the *pebaey* are red, yellow ochre, black, and white. In Bechiyal color is used only in the *pebaey* and on the outrigger canoe.

The Bechiyal *pebaey* was the result of a five-year building program employing up to fifteen villagers, who worked one or two days per week. Most of the time was spent in harvesting, cutting, curing, transporting, and storing construction materials. Time was traded during the building period according

A 5-foot-square sorting table occupies the center of the *pebaey*'s 7-foot-wide east aisle where the village elders congregate.

to Yapese traditions. Food and fish also were traded for time spent on construction (Kugfas, 1984).

Typical of all Yapese meeting houses and residences, the *pebaey* is a wood-framed structure with a high central ridge running continuously along its main axis. Its symmetrical roof planes extend from the ridge down to lintel beams at head height along its sides. The lowest sections of the roof flare outward to provide additional protection from the sun and rain. Gables enclose the ends of the *pebaey.* Here lower shed roofs are introduced for additional protection against the elements. In plan both ends of the building thrust outward at the centerline, forming hexagonal extensions. This configuration recalls the double ends of outrigger canoe hulls. Although the two ends of the *dayif* are symmetrical in plan, their column locations and framing differ significantly.

In plan the floor of the *pebaey* is divided into five longitudinal sections. The outer section is about 5 feet wide and continues around the ends of the building beneath the gables. Columns supporting the ridge beam occupy the 8-foot-wide center section. The seven main columns range from 2 to 3 feet in diameter and rise more than 30 feet to the ridge.

Additional columns flanking the main columns curve outward gracefully as they rise to support main roof purlins. Parallel rows of eight perimeter columns curve slightly inward to support the lower roof structure. All of the main columns extend 5 to 6 feet down into the stone foundation to resist horizontal wind forces. No diagonal bracing is used. The central columns lean progressively outward toward the gables along the building's longitudinal axis. This compensates dimensionally for outward projection of the roof ends.

A 4 × 6-inch flat wood plate surrounds the plan at the edge of the *dayif.* The plate is notched to interlock at its six corners. Eight pairs of 4 × 6-inch white-painted posts rise from the perimeter plate to support the outermost roof edge. The paired posts flank seven main openings along the *pebaey*'s long sides, providing a rhythmical composition of alternating wide and narrow post spacings on the elevations. The base of each perimeter post aligns precisely with floor dividers that flank interior columns.

Sections of palm logs divide the floor of the *pebaey* into rectangular matted areas. Small compartments in the floor near the column bases contain coral that may be used to produce lime associated with betel nut chewing. Five stone-lined fire pits are located at equal intervals along the west aisle. Fires at night provide warmth and illumination and deter mosquitoes. Young men sit in the west aisle of the *pebaey*. In the east aisle old men lounge and sometimes sleep after feasts. Traditionally, women of menstruating age were not permitted to enter the *pebaey*.

Near the center of the *pebaey* is a 2-foot-high, 5-foot-square stone table where fish and food are divided for members of the community. Two storage lofts are located some 6.5 feet above the floor along the building's centerline. Both lofts measure about 9 × 18 feet and are supported by posts around triple column clusters. Possessions belonging to the community are stored in the lofts. The decorations in the *pebaey* represent yellowfin tuna, octopi, swordfish, sharks, the sun and moon, stars, money, and abstract designs, such as black diamonds on a white background. The latter is a recent design referring to playing cards. Three-dimensional painted carvings of birds, monitor lizards, and other creatures also adorn the *pebaey*. The irregular wood disks on the loft beam tips are in the personal style of the *salop*, Tamag.

Mueller's (1917) plan of a *pebaey* in Gagil, which was recorded seventy-five years ago, corresponds closely with the plan of Bechiyal's *pebaey*. Both structures had seven main columns along their centerlines and two rows of eight columns each along the roof edges. The interiors of both buildings were divided into five sections longitudinally. In detail, however, the Bechiyal *pebaey* seems more carefully resolved. Gagil's twelve exterior posts at equal spacing along the main sides have no apparent relationship to the eight interior columns, and the location of several plan elements seems arbitrary.

The ratio of the plan width to length at Bechiyal is 1:2.71; at Gagil, 1:2.43. Per-

haps these differences in detail are indications of the stylistic preferences of the respective architects. Minor differences in dimensions may be due to the difference in the lengths of the respective architect's arms, for the basic unit of measure in Yapese architecture is two arms' length, a measurement similar to the original fathom.

Yapese houses, particularly *pebaey* and *faluw*, represent the highest level of architectural achievement in the island group. Mueller (1917:291–292) described these structures as follows: "To appreciate their true value one must remember that the Yap people, like all inhabitants of the tropics, make night their day. The houses are not planned for any external effects, although in bright sunshine such a structure half covered with greenery or jutting out in the open into the sea on huge squared stones is not lacking in effect. The essential thing, however, is the interior. Lying in deep shade during the day, these rooms 10 to 12 meters (33 to 39 feet) high show their full beauty at night. The lighting from the floor with the bright flames of the coconut shells, the distribution of the sources of light on several hearths along the middle line of the house, heighten the impression of enormous space reaching for heaven and extending into infinity, which is further accentuated by the painting of the posts with a coating of yellow earth deliberately and effectively applied."

Construction Materials, Fabrication, and Erection

Andrew Kugfas (1984) provided the following description of construction materials used in Bechiyal. The main columns and posts are mahogany (*Calophyllum*), breadfruit, mangrove, or occasionally driftwood. Bark always is stripped away from logs used for construction. Native mahogany, the hardest and most termite resistant wood on Yap, usually lasts sixty-five years or more. If buried in moist earth, mahogany, like any other wood, eventually will rot. The columns will last for many generations if they are protected from the rain and are placed in well-drained foundation pits lined with stones.

Floor log dividers are split coconut palm logs. In smaller houses areca palm or pandanus more frequently is used. Areca palm trees resemble small, straight palms. Floor slats are split areca wood strips laid in sand on the *dayif* of the *pebaey*. The floor slats are surprisingly soft to walk or sit on. The palm log dividers make comfortable seats, particularly when one leans back on one of the many columns of the *pebaey*. Columns and floor dividers serve as built-in seating in Yapese structures.

The ridge beam and main roof purlins are bamboo bundles that are bound around areca palm trunks. In smaller structures the trunks are omitted. Overlapping bamboo joints make possible 80-foot-long lightweight beams that adequately resist tension and bending. Roof rafters are nipa wood, a type of palm that grows in swamps with mangrove trees. Nipa lasts for many generations. Its fronds are used to thatch Yapese roofs, while the thatch of infilling walls is woven from pandanus that grows in the interior uplands.

Lashing cords are made from the mature husks of a special species of coconut. The husk is soaked in salt water for three days and then beaten to separate the fibers. After drying for two weeks, the fibers can be plaited or twisted on the leg into cord. Cord bindings are used exclusively in the nonrigid joinery of the *pebaey*. Pegs, spikes, bolts, and nails are not used. Column and post ends sometimes are notched to provide better supports for beams. Joints of woven cords are flexible enough to yield slightly in high winds. Intricate bindings encase the lintel beams throughout their lengths. Some of the more intricate bindings required as many as twenty men working simultaneously, each with an individual strand (Kugfas, 1984).

The construction materials used in Bechiyal vary slightly from those reported for Rumung and Gagil. Presumably, the predilection or experience of the architect also may account for differences in materials used.

The sequence of construction begins by building the *dayif*. Then the main columns, posts, and beams are erected. Next the roof purlins, rafters, and roof thatch are installed. Once the roof is in place, the stone facing of the *dayif* is placed. Floor dividers, matting, lofts, fire pits, coral bins, and dividing table are installed last. Sculptures, painting, and decorations complete the building. More complete details of Yapese construction processes may be found in the bibliographical references for Kobayashi (1978) and Mueller (1917).

A rectangular wood member traditionally was hewn out of a log by first cutting notches at close intervals on opposite sides of the log and then splitting and chipping away the remaining wood from the faces of the beam with an adz. Using an entire log to obtain a single beam seems to have been wasteful in view of Yap's limited forest resources. Muller reported that work songs were sung while beams were hauled or carried on cribs of bamboo. He also noted that stone money disks were hewn with adzes and polished with water and coral stones. A drill consisted of a bowstring that rotated a wood drill shaft. A hard stone tip was attached to the end of the shaft. This type of drill was used widely in Micronesia.

Color Sources

Several systems are used for producing the paints, dyes, and stains used in traditional Yapese structures. The most durable paints, such as those used on canoes, employ vehicles of sap extracted from breadfruit or other trees. The vehicle for stains, such as those used on the interior columns of the *pebaey*, is water.

Yellow ochre and red pigments are made from naturally colored stones found in certain upland interior sites on Yap, such as those in Tomil. The production of the pigment is a tedious procedure. The pigmented stones are scraped, ground, and pulverized into a powder, which is strained through coconut husks before being mixed with the appropriate vehicle. White pigment is produced by burning and slaking coral and collecting the resulting powder several days later. Black pigment is made by straining charcoal through coconut husks.

Turmeric is used widely in Micronesia as a cosmetic for coloring human bodies. In Yap it also has medicinal uses. The turmeric

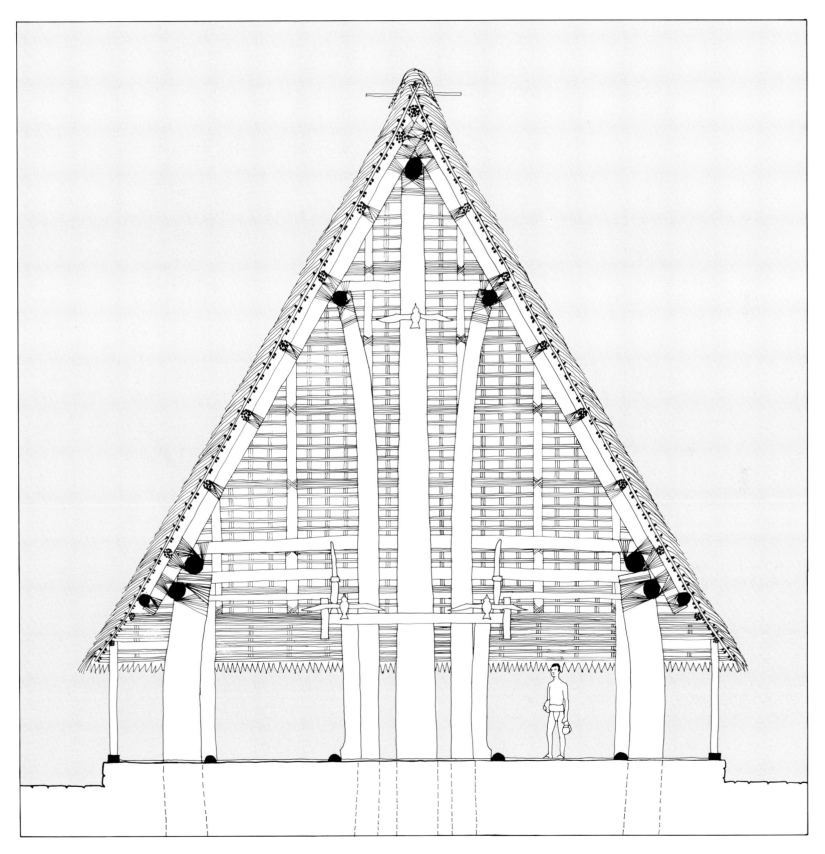

Bechiyal *pebaey,* longitudinal section.

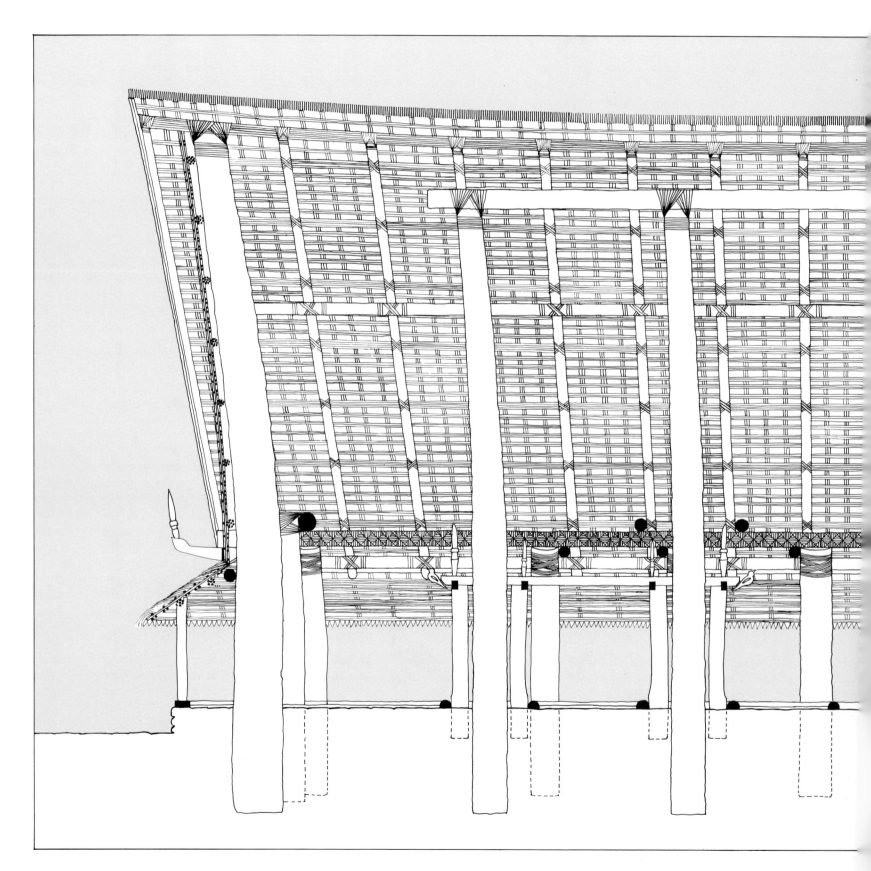

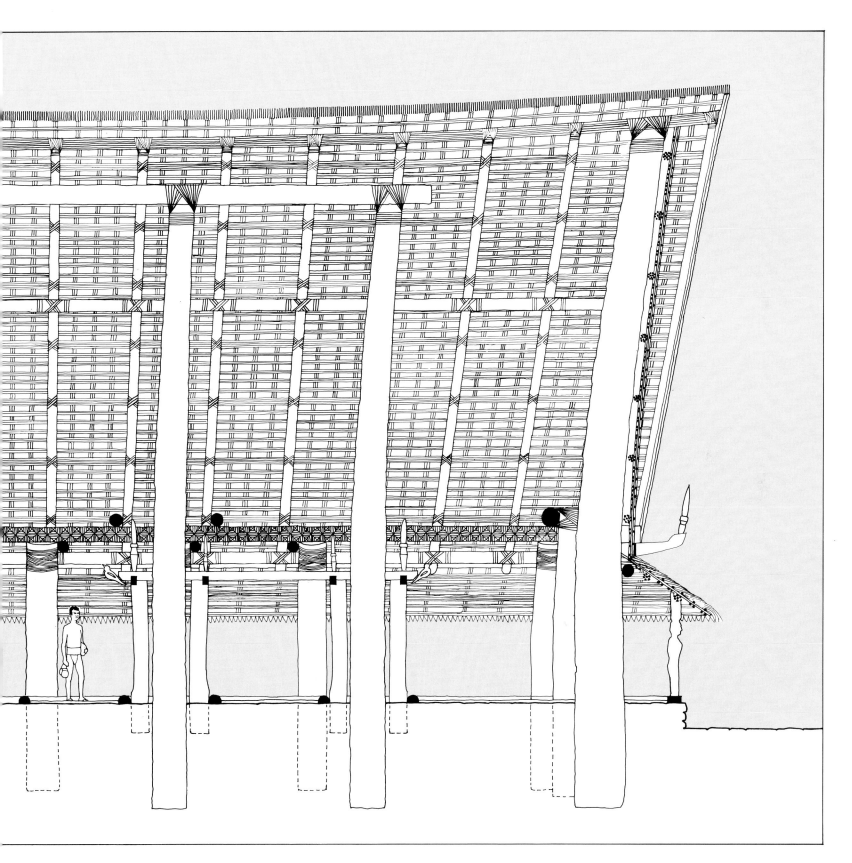

The *tabinaw* of Chief John Tamag is a traditional Yapese residence. Hexagonal walls enclose its central sleeping and storage area.

is ground, strained, and combined with sap, and the sediment is collected and hardened by drying. Depending on the grade of turmeric, the resulting color ranges from reddish to light ochre to pure yellow (Kugfas, 1984).

THE *TABINAW*

The *tabinaw* shown here is the residence of John Tamag, chief of Bechiyal. Of the thirty-four residential foundations in the village, only two presently have houses. The chief's *tabinaw* is located a short distance north of the *pebaey* in the direction of the lagoon. Like the *pebaey* the *tabinaw* has an associated *wunbey,* or seating platform, and the foundation of the *tabinaw* is hexagonal. The outermost dimensions of the structure are about 20 × 54 feet. The paved-stone platform contains an area of some 970 square feet, well less than half the size of the *pebaey.*

Because it is used for sleeping, the *tabinaw* has walls enclosing an inner hexagonal structure that measures roughly 15 × 31 feet. The area within the walls is perhaps 415 square feet, about the size of a typical efficiency apartment in the United States. In Yap a family consisting of husband, wife, and children younger than 8 or 9 years of age would sleep there. The north and south porches of the *tabinaw* contain some 200 square feet each. The floor of the north porch is covered by areca palm slats laid in sand on the *dayif.* The inner gable is embellished by the largest and most intricate cord bindings that I saw on Yap. The north porch is a place for receiving visitors and relaxing.

The south porch, which is paved with rough coral, is the most sacred part of the house, used only by the male head of the family. At the south end of the porch is an elevated coral slab about 5 feet in diameter. It serves as a dividing table for sorting and distributing fish, food, gifts, and other items among the members of the *tabinaw.* The center posts of the porches are about 30 inches in diameter, the largest wood members in the *tabinaw.* They are flanked by corner posts of about 18-inch diameters. Bamboo posts perhaps 4 inches in diameter support the lower roof edges at the perimeter of the elevated foundation.

The building's walls rest on 14-inch-high by 10-inch-wide rectangular wood sills. The sills are notched to fit at all six corners and extend short distances beyond the corners. Wood posts measuring 7 × 14 inches support the enclosing wall. Eight ventilating shutters serve as doors to the *tabinaw*. Each shutter is top hinged and can be propped open by a window pole stored on the sill. The portals, barely 2 feet wide and about 3 feet high, are located at equal centers around the perimeter to afford uniform ventilation. The two portals on the long sides are placed between three pairs of woven pandanus wall panels in a well-proportioned composition.

The interior of the *tabinaw* seemed very dark when I entered. For his afternoon nap the chief had closed the four west shutters and had opened the east flaps only a few inches. The temperature was pleasantly cool and the slight breeze was refreshing. A row of five posts divided the interior space into east and west halves like the *pebaey*, but on a much smaller scale. No color at all was used in the *tabinaw*. All wood surfaces were natural in finish. The space seemed to soar indefinitely upward in the dimly lit interior. The lower walls were supported by rows of seven columns on each side.

Palm log dividers and areca floor slats covered the east half of the interior. The west half was paved with small pieces of rough coral. Here the chief's modest possessions were stored. A single central fire pit about 2 feet square occupied the geometric center of the *tabinaw*. The central three columns, each 14 to 15 inches in diameter, were offset from the centerline. The posts curved slightly as they rose to support the ridge along the centerline of the roof.

The present *tabinaw* was completed in 1948. Its construction required up to twenty workers over a three-year period. The residence's design, like that of the other main structures in the village, was attributed to Tamag. At the time of my visit the east wall plate and several posts were being repaired.

In 1976 Yapese workers erected a traditional *tabinaw* at the Little Museum of Man in Nagoya, Japan. The workers were

not from Map Island, but the structure they erected was very similar to the *tabinaw* of Bechiyal. Kobayashi (1978) recorded the following information on the functional areas and sequence of erection of the house. It is divided into quadrants by longitudinal and transverse axes that intersect in the central fire pit. The eastern half contains the sleeping area; this half is open to any member of the family and is considered impure. The western half is restricted only to men and is considered pure. The southern half is the area of daily living. The northern half is taboo for women and children. Here aged men and high-ranking guests are received.

The northwest quadrant is the most sacred interior part of the house. Magic is performed in this area. The western half is constructed first, beginning at the north end and moving to the south. Next the northeast corner is built, and the southeast corner is added last. Yapese architectural traditions required the proper sequence of construction from the most sacred area first to the most impure area last in order to assure the structural soundness and longevity of the building.

The furnishings of the traditional *tabinaw* were modest. According to Mueller (1917) sleeping mats were woven from coarse co-

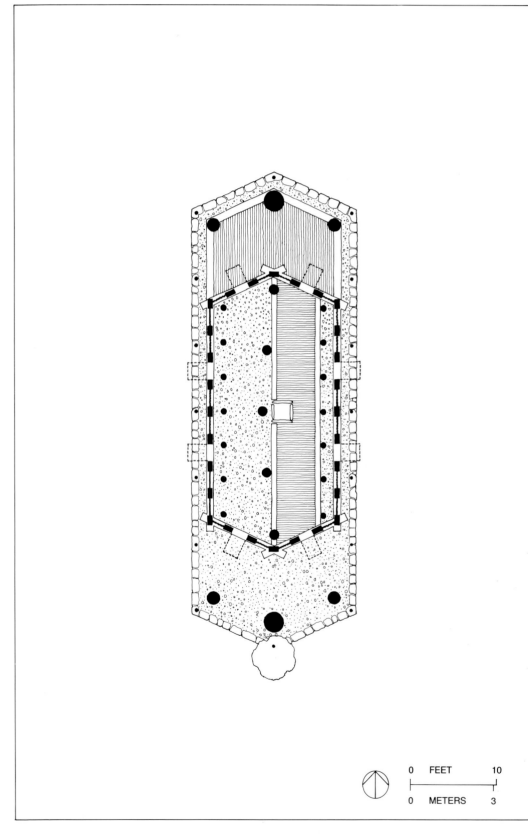

0 FEET 10

0 METERS 3

conut mats with pandanus mats over them. Rounded floor dividers served as headrests. Pillows were not used. Open woven netting served as bags for carrying coconuts or fruits. For protection against rats and ants, foodstuffs were stored in coconut frond baskets hanging from wooden hooks. Cupboards of wood or bamboo latticework stored valuables. Oblong wooden cases with curved sides contained ornaments, such as feathers used for decorative headdresses. A variety of wood bowls, some with feet or pedestals, served as food utensils.

Magic during Housebuilding

Pebaey, tabinaw, faluw, and other important structures on Yap traditionally required the services of a sorcerer, called *tamarang,* as well as an architect. The Yapese believed that every building was inhabited by one or more spirits that must be placated during the construction process. Like the Yapese architects, some sorcerers had better reputations and more experience than others. Demand for their services varied accordingly. According to Mueller (1917) both the architect and the sorcerer were required to practice sexual abstinence during the building process.

At the beginning of a project, Mueller observed, the sorcerer performed magic for which he needed very young coconuts that then remained on the site. The magic was repeated when the framing was completed. During the ceremony magic words were spoken and talismans were placed on beams, in corners, and on porches. Painted stones or bundles of herbs sometimes served as talismans, depending on the sorcerer. Similar magic was required for new *wunbey* and backrests.

When a roof of the *tabinaw* was completed, a small celebration was held. The host served a little food and the guests returned the favor with some valuables. The final completion of a *tabinaw* was celebrated by a large exchange of valuables. A friendly village donated valuables according to the relative rank and wealth of the two villages. Many months or years later the donor received commensurate gifts in return (Mueller, 1917).

The remarkable northwest corner of the Bechiyal *sipal* seems to have no supporting posts. The imaginative structure shelters the village canoe.

The remarkable northwest corner of the Bechiyal *sipal* seems to have no supporting posts. The imaginative structure shelters the village canoe.

THE *SIPAL*

About 160 feet northwest of Chief Tamag's *tabinaw* is the *sipal,* now the only canoe shed in Bechiyal. Formerly, the village would have had several. In plan the shed is in the shape of the letter T, corresponding to the shape of the double-ended canoe and outrigger that it shelters from the sun and rain. The *sipal* faces the lagoon 85 feet to the north at high tide. The structure measures about 44 feet along its ridge and is perhaps 29 feet wide in the area extending across the pontoon. The ridge peak is about 16 feet above the shed's sand floor.

The supporting system for the roof is

unique among wood structures of Yap. The posts below the roof's northwest corner are omitted to permit the canoe and outrigger to enter the shed without obstruction. The northern section of the roof is supported by two curving wood posts, which cantilever up from the east row of column supports and extend westerly to support the ridge beam. The plan and section shown here illustrate this unusual structural arrangement.

The northwest corner of the shed is entirely cantilevered from the rest of the roof structure. Mueller (1917) noted that temporary posts were placed under the cantilevered corner of the roof once the canoe had been moved in or out, but removable

posts are not used at Bechiyal. However, the cantilevered corner of the roof was cambered upward slightly, perhaps as a precaution against deflection over an extended period of time.

The *sipal* is the most utilitarian of Bechiyal's major structures and the least labor intensive. It was constructed during six months in 1983, using at most ten workers. Unlike the *pebaey, tabinaw, faluw,* and most of Bechiyal's other structures, the *sipal* has no stone foundation. The sandy shore suffices for storing and moving the outrigger canoe on logs used as rollers. The *sipal* is not used for human habitation and thus intricate bindings, sculptures, and ornamenta-

Bechiyal *sipal,* plan and transverse section.

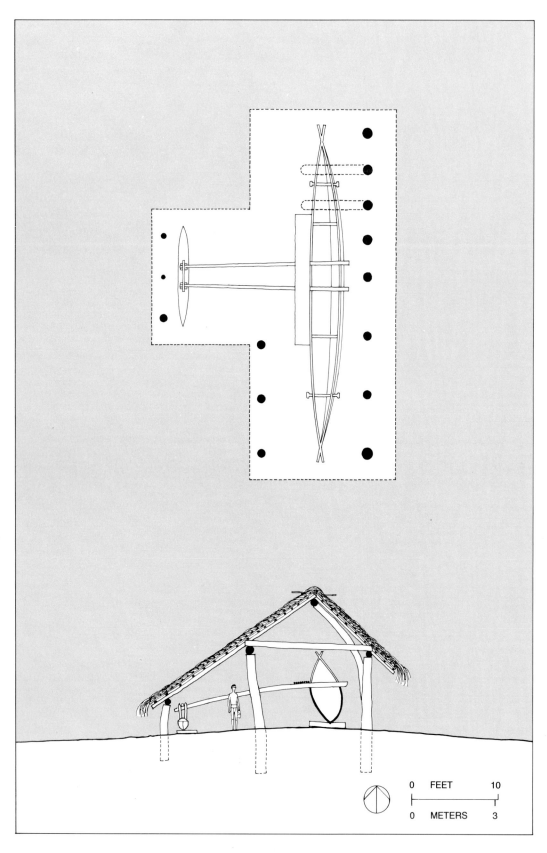

0 FEET 10

0 METERS 3

tion are not required according to Yapese architectural traditions.

The east side of the shed is supported by a row of eight wood posts, 10 to 14 inches in diameter. Three posts, 5 to 10 inches in diameter, support the roof above the pontoon. The center of the roof to the south is supported by three posts, each about 12 inches in diameter. The roof is asymmetrical. The ridge is located above the canoe's hull, and the roof extends westerly to a point only 3 feet above the ground.

If the *sipal* is said to be a humble and utilitarian structure, the opposite must be said of the canoe that it shelters. The double-ended outrigger canoe is one of the most remarkable achievements of ancient Micronesia, a graceful craft capable of voyages throughout the islands and beyond. Yapese outrigger canoes, called *popo,* sailed frequently to Truk and the Palau Islands and even as far as Okinawa, 1,350 miles to the northwest across the Philippine Sea (Kugfas, 1984). The lateen sails of the *popo* traditionally were woven from pandanus. A minimum crew of five is required to man the Bechiyal canoe, but twenty or more persons can be accommodated when the occasion requires.

The overall length of the canoe's hull is about 34.5 feet; the hull's beam, 4.4 feet. The maximum width is some 19.4 feet, measured from the outside of the outrigger to the outside of the canoe hull. Additional space for crew and cargo is provided by a platform along the hull on the outrigger side and another platform that cantilevers out from the canoe's hull on the opposite side. The cantilevered platform is detached from the hull before storing the canoe in the *sipal.* It does not appear in the plan and section shown here.

The main hull of the canoe is carved skillfully from the trunk of a large breadfruit tree. The shape of the hull is asymmetrical for the purpose of increasing the speed and seaworthiness of the vessel underway. Gunwales are joined to the upper edges of the hull by cords laced through augered holes along the upper edges of the hull and the lower edges of the gunwales. Sap extracted from breadfruit trees is used to caulk the seams. The pontoon, which is carved from a solid log, measures roughly 11.3 feet in length by 1.3 feet in width and is hexagonal in cross section.

The colors of the canoe's hull are primarily red and black. White coloration is used sparingly for decorative emphasis on the sides of the hull and in combination with black on both bowsprits of the double-ended canoe. No color is used on the pontoon. My guess would be that the personal style of the canoe's architect appeared in the shaping of the hull and bowsprits and in the painting and decoration of the hull.

THE *FALUW*

The *faluw* of Bechiyal Village is the young men's clubhouse. Like other Yapese *faluw,* it is built on an elevated stone platform that extends beyond the beach and onto the tidal flat. Water surrounds the platform on three sides at high tide. The normal tidal range is at most 5 feet. At low tide beach sand surrounds the platform. The *faluw* is oriented parallel to the beach rather than perpendicular to it like all other Bechiyal structures. Except in a few villages on Map and Rumung, all Yapese *faluw* are built perpendicular to the beach. Some *faluw* are attached at one narrow end to the beach, while others are surrounded entirely by water and are connected to land by a wooden bridge.

The foundation of the *faluw* is made of large blocks of coral faced with schist. The paving on the seaward side is coral; schist paving is used elsewhere. The platform measures perhaps 46 × 95 feet and has four backrests along its west end, the most comfortable backrests and seats that I found on Yap. The platform is subject to subsiding into the sandy beach if it is not constantly maintained. Rain water causes stones to sink rapidly into sandy beaches on Yap. This is less of a problem inland, where clay soils predominate.

One or more *faluw* are associated traditionally with a single *pebaey.* The remains of a second *faluw* at Bechiyal lie 130 feet to the west of the existing *faluw.* The young men's clubhouse serves as a general work and recreation area. Those who are unmarried can

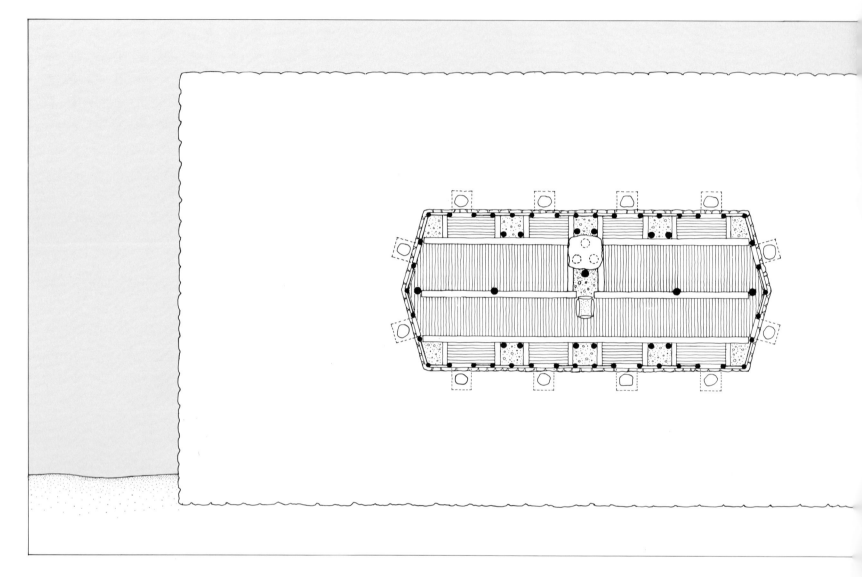

sleep here. Sometimes young men arranged for young women to serve as entertainers in the *faluw,* a practice no longer followed. Primarily the fisherman of Bechiyal, young men also were the village's first line of defense against enemies arriving from the sea.

Reconstruction of the Bechiyal *faluw* was completed in 1978. The project required a maximum of twenty workers over a three-year period. The hexagonal stone foundation is raised about 3 feet above the platform level. The structure measures at most some 18 × 43 feet and contains about 730 square feet, less than one-third the area of the *pebaey.* Although its foundation is smaller than Chief Tamag's house, the *faluw* contains al-most twice the interior area of the *tabinaw.* The enclosing walls of the *faluw* are located at the edge of the foundation. Consequently, it has no porches or verandas.

Twelve portals, each about 2.3 feet wide, provide access into the *faluw.* A stepping stone is located beneath each portal to facilitate access. Top-hinged, outswinging shutters at the portals may be propped open by short poles that are stored on the sills. The shutters provide ventilation and protection against the sun and rain. The proximity of the *faluw* to the lagoon assures constant breezes.

Three rows of columns divide the interior floor plan into four sections longitudinally. The inner sections are about 5.5 feet wide; the outer sections, 3.5 feet. Five columns ranging from 8 to 12 inches in diameter support the ridge beam. The center ridge column is offset from the building's centerline to accommodate the stone-lined fire pit in the center of the structure. Traditionally, there would be several fire pits in a *faluw,* but Chief Tamag anticipated tourists' staying in the Bechiyal *faluw* and thus installed only one fire pit. Customarily, young men would sleep in a row between the fire pits.

Two rows of paired columns support the lower roof along the long walls of the *faluw.* Five crossbeams just above head height are secured to the lower sections of the roof to

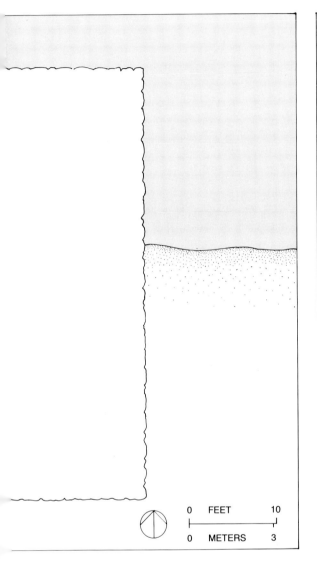

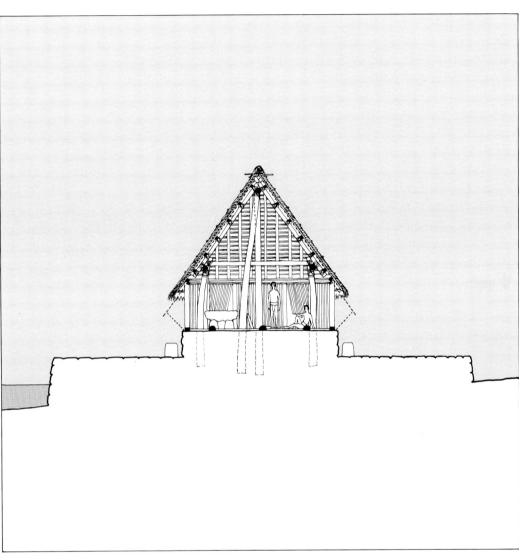

0   FEET   10

0   METERS   3

resist outward thrust. The crossbeams also serve for storage of sails, masts, ropes, rigging, nets, and fishing gear. Sometimes entire canoes would be dismantled and stored in a *faluw*.

Half sections of palm logs line the four sections of the floor. The logs are notched to fit around the bases of the center columns. Most of the floor area is covered with slats of nipa laid in sand on the stone foundation like the floors of the *pebaey* and *tabinaw*. Five floor bins along both main walls contain coral for producing lime used in betel nut chewing. North of the fire pit is a 2-foot-high dividing table, a coral slab supported by three upright coral slabs.

Perimeter posts at equal spacings frame the exterior walls and support the lower edges of the roof. The walls consist of panels of small bamboo poles woven together. Poles, and sometimes worn-out fishing nets, protect the roof thatch against the wind and rain in the exposed coastal location of the *faluw*.

OTHER YAPESE STRUCTURES

Each village on Yap had a varying number of secondary structures in addition to its traditional *pebaey, tabinaw, faluw,* and *sipal.* The illustrations of secondary structures are based on the fine drawings of Jan Kubary (1895) and observations by Wilhelm Mueller (1917). The areas around both primary and

secondary Yapese houses are cleanly swept with brooms made of the ribs of coconut fronds.

The *fang* was any small wood frame house built on stilts often several feet above the ground. It traditionally served as a place for young men to sleep or lounge or as a temporary residence for newlywed couples until they could build a traditional house. Mueller noted that some young men apparently preferred to sleep in a *fang* rather than in the *faluw.* The former was less expensive and easier to build than a *tabinaw*, the traditional residence. Building a *fang* was a method for young men to learn and practice house-building skills. Compared to the *tabinaw,*

The interior loft of the *faluw* serves as a storage place for sails, masts, ropes, rigging, nets, fishing gear, and, sometimes, canoes.

the *fang* was much smaller in size, had a clear-spanned interior space rather than a row of columns along its center line, was rectangular rather than hexagonal in plan, and had no stone foundation (*dayif*) or platform (*wunbey*). Access from the ground was provided by a ladder made of a notched tree trunk.

The *ta'ang* was a cookhouse built on a low, rectangular stone platform. Its construction was a diminutive version of a larger wood structure, except that paired wall posts, rather than a row of central columns, supported the roof. Several *ta'ang* were required for each family, depending on the ages and sexes of the family's members. Cooking was done on a tripod made of three stones. Near the cookhouse, typically, stood an upright stick with branches that served as a rack for hanging baskets, fish, utensils, and food. Mueller noted that larger families sometimes built structures like *ta'ang* for their elderly or newlywed members, either on stone bases or on stilts like *fang* 15 to 20 inches above the ground. He also observed that cookhouses with elevated floors could easily be converted to sleeping quarters when the family's size required.

The *toorba* is a copra drying house. Copra is dried coconut meat, an important economic resource for trade with foreigners beginning in the late nineteenth century. The *toorba* is built on a stone foundation and has an asymmetrical roof that slopes down to the rear. Sections of its walls are left open to facilitate the copra drying process. Sheds similar to *toorba* are walled in with panels of vertical bamboos and are used for storing such items as nets, firewood, and nuts.

Kubary also illustrated a type of canoe shed that was built on a stone pier in the lagoon. The upper structure resembled the *sipal* of Bechiyal, but the outrigger canoe's hull rested on a stone platform above the high-tide level and the pontoon was supported above the water level by short wood posts. The outermost rows of columns apparently were subjected to wetting and drying as the tide rose and fell.

One of the photographs presented here shows the east end of the men's house at

Balebat Village in Rull District. Unlike the Bechiyal *faluw,* the men's house is placed perpendicular to the sea, the preferred orientation for buildings on Yap. Like the major structures of Bechiyal and other traditional villages, the Balebat edifice has been reconstructed recently. It has a porch, or veranda, at its west end, similar to the porch of the *tabinaw* at Bechiyal, while the east end is built to the edge of the stone foundation like a traditional *faluw.*

VARIATIONS IN ARCHITECTURE

Although rectilinear village plans, detached houses, community buildings, ceremonial areas, and stone-paved pathways are found in all Yapese settlements, marked architectural variations between villages occur according to their relative ranks on Yap. Thus, the cultural organization of the island group is directly expressed in its architecture and community planning.

Within the Gagil hegemony of northern Yap, only Rumung Island is ranked lower than Map Island. Immediately southeast of Bechiyal on Map lies the higher-ranked village of Toruw; in the highlands to the south, the low-ranking village of Nlul. In a study of the physical differences between Toruw and Nlul, Hunter-Anderson (1984) recorded clear contrasts. Geographically, Toruw lies along the northeast coast of Map with direct access to the abundant resources of the lagoon and fertile coastal farming land. Nlul occupies relatively infertile upland hillsides with limited fishing rights in the lagoon north of Bechiyal. It lacks a *faluw* since young men traditionally applied themselves to fishing. The higher-ranking village traditionally had several *faluw* and numerous stone fish traps.

The prehistoric population of Toruw probably exceeded four hundred, while perhaps only eighty persons lived in Nlul. The land areas of the two villages are in direct proportion to their former populations. The higher-ranked village had extensive access to building materials within and beyond its borders subject to trade agreements, but building materials in Nlul primarily were limited to those within its borders. The average size of house foundations in Nlul is about two-thirds the area of those in Toruw; sitting platforms, perhaps three-fourths; and cookhouses, a little over half the area of those in Toruw. The blocks of stone in the structures of Nlul are smaller than those of their neighbors, who also used coral from the plentiful lagoon and some very large slabs of schist brought from Rumung.

Toruw had many stone backrests, numerous stone-paved paths, and many circular stone valuables (*rai*) typically lining both sides of dance areas (*malal*). Relatively few backrests and only one stone path are found in Nlul. The *rai* of impoverished Nlul are few and seem to be associated with payments for services. The numerous *rai* of prosperous Toruw suggest exchanges between families, friendly villages, and competitive rivals.

Perhaps the most striking difference between the higher- and lower-ranked villages on Yap relates to the distribution of graves. Although forty-five graves were estimated for Nlul, only five were recorded in residential Toruw, with three more near inland gardens. On Yap the "dead are regarded as contaminating to higher-ranked persons. Serfs had the obligation of handling the corpses of their overlords and of burying them in traditional cemeteries geographically far removed from the dwelling sites of the overlord estate or within the residential areas of serf villages. The exceptions were high-ranking warriors killed in battle defending their village and distinguished, well-respected chiefs whose memory would be maintained through the building of prominent graves located within the residential part of their own village" (Hunter-Anderson, 1984:100). Traditional Yapese customs with respect to burial practices account for the abundance of graves in Nlul, including three-tiered earth terraces faced with stone, and the scarcity of graves in Toruw.

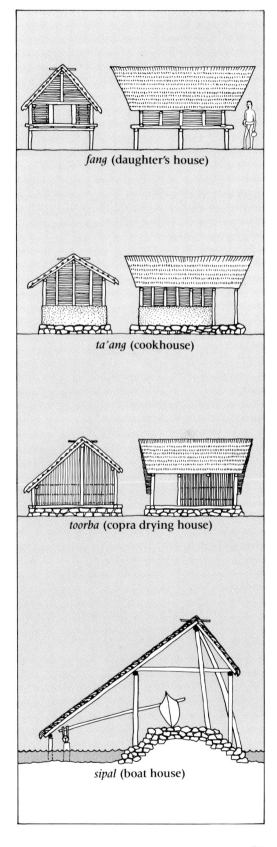

fang (daughter's house)

ta'ang (cookhouse)

toorba (copra drying house)

sipal (boat house)

SUMMARY

Prehistoric Yapese architecture survives today in the form of extensive stone structures forming elevated house foundations with large sitting platforms, raised and paved pathways with stone-lined gutters, grave facings, sea walls, docks, piers, and fish traps built in the waters of the lagoon. Traditional architecture on Yap possesses several special characteristics that are not found elsewhere in Micronesia.

While gable-roofed houses raised above grade on stone foundations are found in many prehistoric sites, the consistent use of elevated, solid stone foundations for major buildings distinguishes Yapese architecture from that of its neighbors. Important prehistoric structures in Palau and the Marianas were placed on individual stone piers on columns. Their floors were wooden platforms built above grade. The floors of ancient Kosraean buildings were placed at grade level. The foundations of traditional Pohnpeian structures differ widely from the hexagonally shaped stone platforms (*dayif*) of Yap.

The use of central rows of columns to support roof ridge beams is another unique characteristic of traditional Yapese architecture. Column-free interior spaces are the rule elsewhere in prehistoric Micronesia. The hexagonal configuration of floor plans and foundations also identifies Yapese buildings. The preferred orientation of Yapese structures is perpendicular to the coastline, with such exceptions as some of the *faluw* on Rumung and Map. This is another distinguishing trait of traditional Yapese architecture. Prehistoric structures in the Mariana Islands often were placed end to end in rows parallel to the nearby coastlines or watercourses. The feast houses and residences of Nan Madol and Leluh were oriented with respect to the walls of their enclosing compounds rather than coastlines.

The burial practices of Yap differ widely from those found elsewhere in Micronesia, with the exception of Palau. Three-tiered earth graves faced with stone usually were located in upland cemeteries or serf villages remote from higher-ranking coastal settlements. The Yapese custom contrasts sharply with the Chamorro practice of interment beneath or very near *latte* house platforms, where higher-ranked persons presumably lived.

The remains of deceased Kosraeans apparently were committed to special areas in the lagoon. Pyramidal stone tombs in Leluh seem to have been used as intermediate repositories for deceased royalty and perhaps certain members of the nobility. The nobility of Pohnpei apparently were finally laid to rest in large stone tombs of mortuary compounds, such as Nandauwas in Nan Madol. Palauan burial practices, however, seem to resemble more nearly those of Yap, its relatively nearby neighbor in the western Carolines.

On Yap no major administrative or ceremonial center is found that would compare to Leluh on Kosrae or Nan Madol on Pohnpei. Yapese villages, like those of Palau and the Marianas, generally tended to contain within themselves the institutions necessary for the basic functioning of the community. This suggests that no king or paramount controlled the society of prehistoric Yap. Social rankings and rival alliances provided the basis for the order that is expressed in traditional Yapese planning and architecture.

Poles protect the roof thatch against the wind and rain in the exposed coastal location of the men's house at Balebat, Rull District.

3. POHNPEI

No site in Oceania surpasses the dramatic beauty of ancient Nan Madol, perched on the very edge of the vast Pacific Ocean. Situated on the east coast of Pohnpei (also Ponape), the elite administrative and ceremonial center grew, flourished, and declined during the centuries preceding Western contact. Here in a shallow lagoon the ancient Pohnpeians constructed a magnificent complex of ninety-two artificial islets interconnected by a network of waterways. Today the islets are mostly covered by dense jungle growth, and the waterways are largely choked with mangrove swamps. Even in their present state, the megalithic ruins of Nan Madol are present-day reminders of the splendid achievements of prehistoric people in Micronesia.

The traditional name of the island is Pohnpei, meaning "upon a stone altar." Its people are referred to as Pohnpeians. Until the recent re-adoption of the traditional name, the island was known as Ponape; its inhabitants, Ponapeans.

Pohnpei is a mountainous high island, one of the most beautiful in Micronesia. Dense forests grow down to the edge of the surrounding lagoons in most places. Numerous smaller islands lie within the barrier reef. Seemingly endless coves, fringing reefs, inlets, and outcroppings, such as the spectacular Sokehs Rock, lend variety to the coastline. Of comparatively recent geological age, Pohnpei's mountainous interior is dominated by numerous peaks. The highest rises 2,595 feet above sea level.

Sheer cliffs occur in several locations. Often the cliffs are of prismatic basalt, the material used in constructing Nan Madol and other ancient structures around the island. Dozens of streams and rivers flow from the interior. More than 180 inches of rain annually, a tropical climate, and fertile soils account for the island's luxuriant growth. Typhoons occur here less frequently than in western Micronesia, but several struck Pohnpei in the early twentieth century.

Exceeded in size only by Guam in the Marianas and Babeldaob in Palau, 129-square-mile Pohnpei is the third largest island in Micronesia. Kosrae, 340 miles to the south-east, and Truk, some 400 miles to the west, are Pohnpei's closest major island neighbors. Guam, Yap, and Palau lie a thousand miles and more to the north and west. The mid-1981 census reported 23,920 residents on Pohnpei, most of whom live along the coasts or in the administrative center of Kolonia.

The staples of Pohnpeian subsistence agriculture are bananas, breadfruit, and yams, but more than forty different crops are cultivated on the island. Traditionally, men tended the more important agricultural crops while women exploited the fringing reefs with handnets (Alkire, 1977). Like the Kosraeans, the Pohnpeians have one of the most complex sociopolitical organizations in Micronesia. For information on social stratification and the complex rank and title system, see the bibliographic reference to Riesenberg, 1968.

Today the island is divided into five districts, which were autonomous polities before the advent of successive Spanish, German, Japanese, and American administrations. Each district is presided over by dual leaders called *nahnmwarki* and *nahnken,* who are the equivalent of royalty in Pohnpeian society. Traditionally, the ranked title holders who assisted them were the island's nobility. The titles of commoners were not inherited, as was largely the case with the nobility. During the German administration of 1899 to 1914, land reform was instituted with the distribution of property titles to male heads of households. Formerly, only the high chiefs owned land, granting use rights to their subjects in return for tribute payments and obeisance. A principal component of traditional chiefly power was thereby destroyed by the Germans.

Feasting ceremonies (*kamatihp*), the raising of giant yams to be eaten at them, and competition for titles suggest the flavor of Pohnpeian life and what it means to live in a chiefdom society. Clan and subclan memberships, which are based on matrilineal inheritance, are extremely important aspects of Pohnpeian social organization. High chiefs generally inherit their positions based on rank inherited through the mother's side of the family.

PREHISTORY AND LEGEND

In the following discussion of Nan Madol, the numbers shown in parentheses after islet names refer to the 1910 listing by the German ethnologist Paul Hambruch (1936). The complete list appears later in this section. The numbers are intended to assist the reader in locating the islets on the accompanying map of Nan Madol.

At what time the first settlers arrived on Pohnpei is unknown. Eventually stone platforms, house foundations, walls, pavings and tombs, earth terraces and mounds, and other architectural features began to appear at various locations along the coasts, in valleys, and on hillside sites of the island's interior. During the first or second century A.D., people apparently were inhabiting the coastal area that became the site of Nan Madol. Here Stephen Athens (1983:53) has recorded radiocarbon dates of this time range from archaeological deposits found below the artificial fill and low-tide level of Dapahu Islet (93). Geologic subsidence coupled with sea level rise on Pohnpei accounts for the present-day inundation of early coastal habitation areas.

William Ayres and Alan Haun (1978) of the University of Oregon have documented several stages of construction for the Usendau (104) and Pahnkadira (33) islet bases, the former going back to the eighth or ninth century A.D. About 1000 or 1100, pottery ceased to be used at Nan Madol. The early use of pottery followed by its discontinuance is a common pattern in Oceania.

Apparently not until sometime around 1200 to 1300 did elaborate megalithic architecture begin at Nan Madol. By this time Pohnpei is believed to have been conquered and unified by a paramount chief called the *saudeleur,* meaning lord of Deleur, a small political unit that evidently encompassed Temwen Island and neighboring areas. Eventually, the hegemony of the *saudeleur* seems to have extended throughout the entire island of Pohnpei.

Under the reign of the *saudeleur,* Nan Madol flourished and expanded to its present size. This was the time of greatest archi-

Pohnpei.

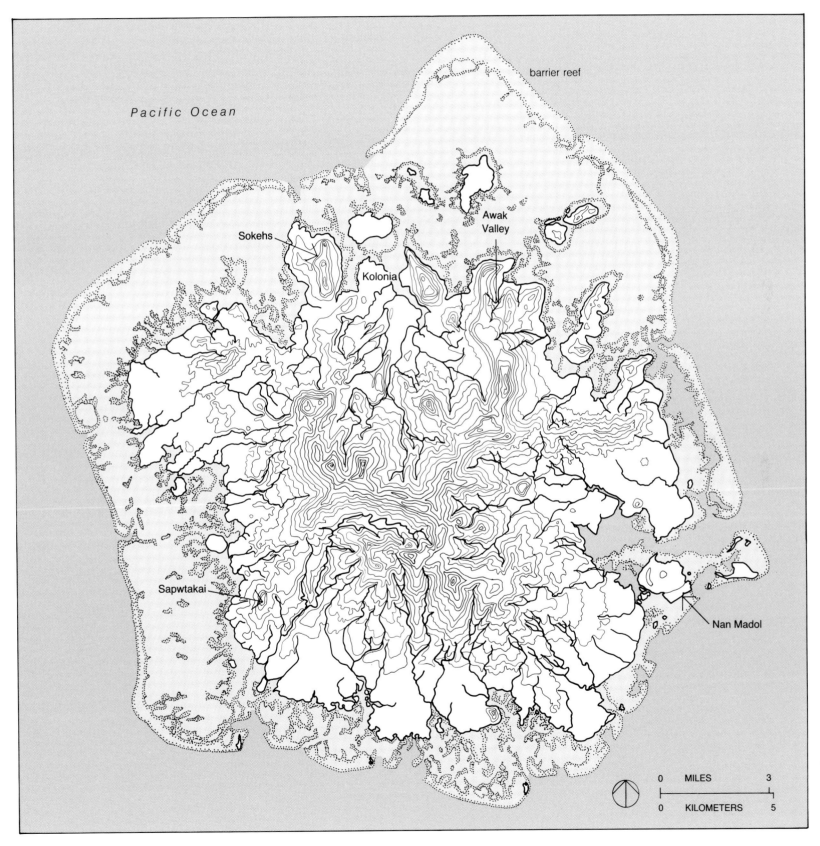

Pacific Ocean

barrier reef

Sokehs

Awak
Valley

Kolonia

Sapwtakai

Nan Madol

MILES
0   3

KILOMETERS
0   5

tectural achievement, when walls of stacked prismatic basalt 18 to 25 feet high were constructed around Nandauwas (113) and the number of artificial islets increased substantially. Some had coral fill up to 7 feet above sea level at high tide, while one of Pahnwi's (9) platforms was some 20 feet high. Several of the islets measure well more than 100 yards on a side and contain areas roughly equivalent to three football fields. Immense seawalls and breakwaters were erected to protect the chiefly center from the relentless pounding of ocean waves in the exposed coastal site.

The downfall of the *saudeleur* is estimated to have occurred during the early 1600s.

Pohnpeian oral traditions link the paramount's demise to the Thunder God, whose temple is located on a large, three-tiered platform on Pahnkadira Islet (33), where the *saudeleur* lived. The Thunder God's son, the legendary Isokelekel, is said to have established a new political order presided over by a high chief called the *nahnmwarki*. Perhaps as a safeguard against the reemergence of a paramount on Pohnpei, Isokelekel divided the island into three autonomous chiefdoms.

Isokelekel himself became the first *nahnmwarki* of Madolenihmw, the chiefdom that included Nan Madol, where the next six *nahnmwarki* resided. It is estimated that

during the early 1700s the *nahnmwarki* removed his residence from Nan Madol, but people seemed to have continued living there a little while longer. By the 1820s, when intensive Western contact began with Pohnpei, people had ceased to live at Nan Madol though it continued to be used through the mid1800s for periodic religious observances.

EUROPEAN CONTACT

In 1528 Álvaro de Saavedra Cerón, commander of the Spanish galleon *Florida*, probably reached Pohnpei or one of its neighboring atolls. Saavedra named the island "Barbudos," a reference to the beards of the natives. Sixty-seven years later Pedro Ferdi-

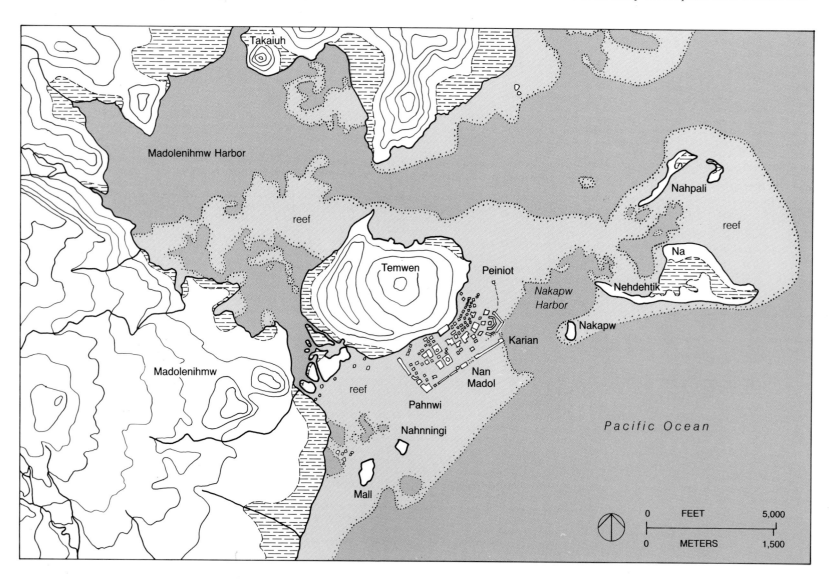

nand de Quiros nearly foundered on an island that was almost certainly Pohnpei. He named his discovery "Quirosa" but did not land on the island (Hezel, 1983). In time mariners began to refer to the island as "Ascension," before Ponape and now Pohnpei became the accepted name.

Not until 1828 was Pohnpei rediscovered by the Russian explorer Capt. Fyedor Petrovich Lütke, who named it "Senyavin" in honor of his ship. Shortly thereafter British and American trading vessels began to frequent the island's ports, and a colony of often unruly beachcombers began to grow. As whaling activities increased dramatically in the 1840s, so did the number of deserters from visiting ships.

The population of Pohnpei at the time of initial European contact is estimated to have been in the range of 20,000 to 35,000 people (Reisenberg, 1968). The population declined precipitously, however, with the introduction of diseases by visiting whalers, traders, and explorers. The most dramatic and unfortunate event was the smallpox epidemic of 1854, when the contagion killed over 2,000 islanders, more than one-third of the then surviving population. Venereal diseases also contributed to the population decline.

Early in the 1850s American missionaries arrived on Pohnpei. They attempted to curb prostitution and alcohol trading by the beachcombers and *sakau* drinking and spirit worship by the natives. Today Pohnpeians continue to prepare *sakau*, a narcotic, on pounding stones for special occasions. After several decades of strife, Christianity became accepted, but only within the framework of traditional Pohnpeian sociopolitical institutions. By the 1880s money began to replace barter as the basis of the island's trade.

OBSERVATION AND RESEARCH

The first Western observation of Nan Madol, completely abandoned, was by James F. O'Connell between 1828 and 1833. In 1852 Luther H. Gulick, an American missionary, noted that the ruins covered one half of a square mile, and he correctly suggested that they were built by ancestors of the present-

day Pohnpeians. Gulick documented the spectacular nature of the ruins and recorded accounts of the ritual activities practiced by the natives in the ruins on ceremonial occasions.

The German ethnologist Jan S. Kubary prepared the first outline map of Nan Madol in 1873. Further observations on the site and its contents were made by the Englishman F. W. Christian in 1896. In 1910 Paul Hambruch conducted a detailed survey of Nan Madol, using only a hand-held compass and tape measure in the extraordinarily brief span of ten days.

Recent instrument surveys by Stephen Athens have altered the overall configuration of Hambruch's map very little. However, the recent work shows the details of surface features on each islet, which Hambruch largely ignored. Besides mapping, Hambruch (1936) also conducted excavations, collected oral accounts, and recorded the existence of thirty other important sites elsewhere on Pohnpei.

Germany purchased Pohnpei from Spain in 1899 but was forced to sell its South Sea island possessions to Japan at the outbreak of the First World War. Limited scholarly research was conducted on Pohnpei during the Japanese administration. In 1945 the United States assumed control of the island and began its administration under the mandate of a United Nations trusteeship. Recently, Pohnpei joined Yap, Truk, Kosrae, and other islands of the Carolines in forming the Federated States of Micronesia, an autonomous political entity in free association with the United States.

In 1963 the Smithsonian Institution conducted the first modern archaeological investigations at Nan Madol. Since that time scientific research has increased significantly, including the work of Athens, Ayres, Bath, Davidson, Haun, Mauricio, Saxe, Streck, and others. Presently, substantial support is needed for clearing the site of fast-growing tropical trees, underbrush, and vines that destroy the ancient stoneworks. The magnificent monuments also are in urgent need of restoration and preservation if they are to continue to exist as the record of a distinguished past and thus an inspiration for future generations.

NAN MADOL

Nan Madol was a special place located away from the main island of Pohnpei, perhaps to symbolize and reinforce the unique character of the people who lived there and their ritual activities. Built by well-organized indigenous Micronesians, the complex belongs to relatively recent prehistory. The site extends along the southeast shore of hilly Temwen Island for a distance of approximately 4,600 feet and reaches into the lagoon about 2,450 feet. The area occupied by the islets, their waterways, and the breakwaters is roughly 200 acres. The remains are accessible by a one-hour boat ride from Kolonia or by a somewhat longer journey by vehicle along the coastal road followed by a one-hour hike across Temwen.

Greater Nan Madol extends beyond the immediate vicinity of the islets proper. For a discussion of the neighboring islets, structures, and other architectural features closely associated with the elite center, the reader may wish to refer to the bibliographic reference for Saxe, Allenson, and Loughridge, 1980b. One such neighboring islet is Nahnningi, located in the lagoon some 2,000 feet south of Nan Madol. A short distance south of Nahnningi lies Mall. Both of these islets appear to have been constructed by the builders of Nan Madol. They are surrounded by stacked prismatic basalt walls several feet high and their surfaces are raised well above the high-tide level on coral fill. Another important islet contemporary with Nan Madol is Nakapw, a basically natural island with some stonework. It is located across the bay east of the ancient center.

Nahnningi also is known as Joy Island. My party stayed here during our visit in 1984. The rectangular islet contains numerous coconut palms through which the prevailing northeasterly ocean breezes blow constantly. The reef protecting the lagoon from the open Pacific lies a short distance east of the islet. We could have walked across the shallow lagoon to Nan Madol at low tide when the water was only knee to waist deep, but we preferred to go by boat at high tide. The boat facilitated transportation of our photographic equipment, compass, tape, note and reference books, food, water, and related paraphernalia.

The temperature on shady Nahnningi was about 4 degrees cooler in the daytime than at Nan Madol, where we recorded a temperature of 91 degrees in the shade at 4:00 P.M. In the evenings the temperatures on breeze-swept Nahnningi dropped to about 68 degrees. At night we slept under blankets. We paused for lunch one day on Usennamw (91), where the temperature of the dark gray basaltic stones was 103 degrees in the shade and 116 degrees in the sun.

Nan Madol consists of ninety-two artificial islets, many surrounded by retaining walls of immense basalt boulders and stacks of naturally formed prismatic basalt. Some islet walls extend only to the surface of the interior coral rubble fill, while others rise 6 to 30 feet above the surfaces to form enclosures for mortuaries and residences. For stability, the higher walls on some islets rise in parallel rows linked with crosspieces. This is a system of horizontally laid stones in alternating parallel and perpendicular courses, known to brick masons as headers and stretchers. Stone pavings and platforms—foundations for residences and meeting houses, walls, tombs, tunnels, and other features—are found on the islets.

Not all of Nan Madol's islets are surrounded by basalt retaining walls. The coral fill of Pahnkatau (94) terminates at the water's edge with no protective basalt facing at all. The perimeter stones of this low-lying islet may have been robbed to construct other islets. Pahnkatau contains three tombs consisting of coral mound walls with large basalt cobbles on top. Other low-lying islets with partly eroded perimeter walls are Sapwengei (69), Sapwolos (70), Sapwenpwe (71), and Sapwuhtik (76).

Loose coral taken from the nearby reefs was used to fill and pave islet cores, and considerable remodeling by successive occupants has occurred on many of the islets. Most islets are orthogonal in plan and have flat platforms that originally supported pole-

and-thatch structures. The spaces between the islets are flooded at high tide. Thus, the ancient center is interlaced by a network of waterways reminiscent of Venice.

Most of Nan Madol's islets were used for burials or residences. The more spectacular burial places possess a central vault or tomb constructed with four vertical walls of stacked prismatic basalt. These structures usually are surrounded by an enclosing wall. Other burial places are indicated by only a simple rectangular or square basalt cobble paving on the islet surface.

House platforms are rectangular stone foundations elevated several feet above grade. They often have fire pits recessed into the centers of their platforms and range in size from about 60 square feet for commoners' houses to some 800 square feet for dwellings of the nobility (O'Connell, 1972). The residence of the *saudeleur* was even larger, containing an area of about 1,470 square feet.

The Pohnpeians call meeting houses *nahs*. Among the largest traditional structures on the island, *nahs* will be described in greater detail later in this section. Another type of structure found in Nan Madol is an enclosing wall. Enclosures seem to have been erected for special purposes, such as providing privacy for dwellings of high-status people or setting apart sacred areas for tombs or religious activities.

Nan Madol is divided into two main areas separated by a central waterway. To the southwest lies Madol Pah, the lower town. It was the administrative sector, where royal dwellings and ceremonial areas were located. To the northeast lies Madol Powe, the upper town. This was the mortuary sector, where the priests dwelled and major tombs were located. Recently, more burials have been found along the lagoon breakwater islets, suggesting that mortuary activities may have been more important at Nan Madol than previously realized. The maximum population of the ancient center may have been between 500 and 1,000 people, although it is very difficult to arrive at a precise estimate due to the lack of reliable information.

Two lines of rectangular platforms with canoe channels left between them form the southeast and southwest seawalls, about 3,500 and 1,500 feet long, respectively. The northern edge of Nan Madol apparently was left open to the elements. A number of the structures in the complex in fact seem to have been left unfinished. The seawalls were built stoutly of huge basalt boulders packed with smaller stones on which prismatic basalt was stacked in a cribwork of header and stretcher coursing.

Provisional Map for Nan Madol

The map of Nan Madol presented here is based primarily on Paul Hambruch's original map; the 1983 topographic map of Pohnpei prepared by the U.S. Geodetic Survey; recent detailed surveys of twenty-nine islets directed by Stephen Athens with Joyce Bath and Charles Streck; surveys of Pahnkadira (33), Usendau (104), and Pahnwi (9) by William Ayres and Alan Haun; and aerial photographs provided by the Bishop Museum, Joyce Bath, and Newton Morgan. The map is termed provisional because of the lack of precise current information on the remaining sixty-one islets and other features of the elite center.

Hambruch's original map, dated August 1910 and published in an obscure German journal in 1911, was unknown for a long time until it was rediscovered a few years ago. The map named each islet, showed a scale, and presented an identification on the legend. A later version of the map accompanied Hambruch's widely circulated 1936 volume, published after the author's death. The later map contained a number of unfortunate errors, quite possibly due to inattentive draftsmanship. The difference between the two maps can be ascertained immediately by noting the alignment of the segmented breakwater connecting Peiniot (118) with the outer seawall of Nandauwas (113). The segments do not form a straight line as erroneously shown in the 1936 version, and many other details disagree with the more accurate map of 1910.

Hambruch listed two breakwaters as the remains of unfinished islets. One lies north of Karian (122); the other, east of Lemenkou (129). Stephen Athens has suggested, and I would agree, that these features seem to have been constructed originally to serve as breakwaters rather than islets. Their huge stones are placed at regular intervals in rows that permit canoes to pass through easily. Unlike in islet retaining walls, no intermediate stones lie between the monoliths. The breakwaters continue today to dissipate the force of ocean waves and facilitate the cleansing action of sea water flowing through the canals with each tidal change.

Hambruch listed a total of 130 features for Nan Madol, including channels, canoe passes, reef pools, building foundations, and other architectural features. Of these features 93 were islets, some with more than one number denoting features associated with individual islets. Subtracting the 2 breakwaters originally recorded as islets, 91 islets remain. During a recent survey, Stephen Athens discovered that Likinpei (88) actually consists of two neighboring islets, now designated 88A and 88B. Thus, the total number of islets shown on the provisional map is 92.

Apparently, all of the islets originally were surrounded by water except for Peinkitel (55), Peitu (57), and Puilelt (58). Built partly on the southeast shore of Temwen Island, the large mortuary enclosure of Peinkitel contains an impressive tomb within a secondary enclosure entirely on the shore. The tomb is believed to contain the remains of Isokelekel. When the German governor Berg began exploring the tomb in 1905, the natives requested him to refrain for fear of incurring the wrath of their legendary hero. The governor persisted but died a short while later of sunstroke. The Pohnpeians were certain his death had been revenge for the destruction of Isokelekel's grave (Hambruch, 1936).

Most of Nan Madol's waterways, particularly those closer to Temwen Island, today are choked with mangrove swamps and thus are largely impenetrable. Mangrove trees, coconut palms, breadfruits, and, particularly, *Thespesia populnea*, along with dense tropical undergrowth, cover most of the islets,

An aerial view of Nandauwas (113) shows the
outer seawall facing the Pacific Ocean. Karian
(122) appears in the upper right.

largely obscuring the original appearance of the site. Recently, efforts have been undertaken to clear the islets of the destructive jungle growth, but the task is formidable. The provisional map presented here shows water in all of the canals and waterways with the view of reconstructing the original appearance of the ancient center.

The thick black lines shown on the map denote basalt-faced walls exceeding 7 feet in height. Parallel lines define lower walls. Single lines around islet perimeters indicate the absence of basalt retaining walls, and dashed lines show stone alignments that are submerged. Small squares and rectangles indicate such features as pavings, house platforms, or excavations. Most of Nan Madol's architectural features are rectangular or linear; triangles, polygons, circles, and other geometric configurations do not appear. Exceptions are natural features, such as the reef pools on Peikap (39) and Dorong (50) and west of Lemenkou (129).

Most of the islets are oriented with respect to a generally northeast to southwest axis. House platforms usually are arranged orthogonally with respect to their islet foundations or enclosing walls, perhaps suggesting the orientation of pole-and-thatch houses with gables facing the northeast to capture prevailing breezes.

Pottery remains have been found on islet surfaces and fill closer to Temwen Island, where the earliest islets were built. During the *saudeleur* expansion period, probably between about 1200 to 1500 or 1600, magnificent megalithic architecture was constructed at Nan Madol and the islets farther from the shore were built. Here no pottery remains are found, indicating that pottery making had been abandoned by that time. More precise information on the sequence of constructing Nan Madol's islets presently is lacking.

The Islets

The following list of islets is based on the numbering system and names originally published by Hambruch on the ancient center. The spellings of many of these names have been revised to correspond with mod-

The provisional map of Nan Madol shows the 92 artificial islets of the elite center surrounded by canals and lagoons. To the left lie the 34 islets of Madol Pah, the lower town; to the right, the 58 islets of Madol Powe, the upper town.

The 34 islets of Madol Pah, the lower town:

5	Ponkaim (above the corner)
7	Panmueit (below the passage)
8	Mueit (passage)
9–10	Pahnwi (under the Barringtonia Trees) *
12	Kapennot (new Not)
14	Pikalap (large sand)
16	Lemensei
17	Peinmet
18	Likinsau
19	Sapuei

20	Sapenlan (place of the sky)
21	Batenlan (stone of the sky)
22	Pilenlan (water of the sky)
23	Pantibob (under the Terminalia Tree)
24	Betebete
25	Peienapue
26	Nikonok
27	Reilap
28	Loleeue
29	Peiian
30	Reitik
31	Uasau

32	Kalapuel
33	Pahnkadira (place of the announcement)
38	Peienmueik
39	Peikap (new grave enclosure)
43	Idehd (place of the sacred eel) *
44	Reitaub
45	Taketik (small island)
46	Paniso
47	Penieir
48	Mant
49	Palakapw *
50	Dorong *

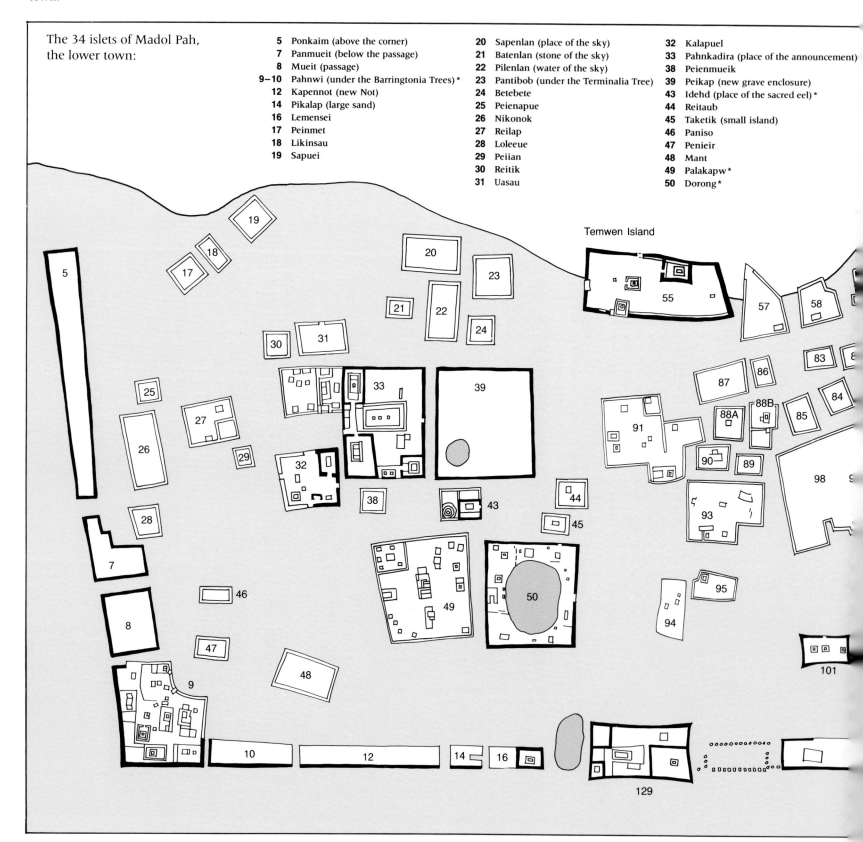

Temwen Island

66

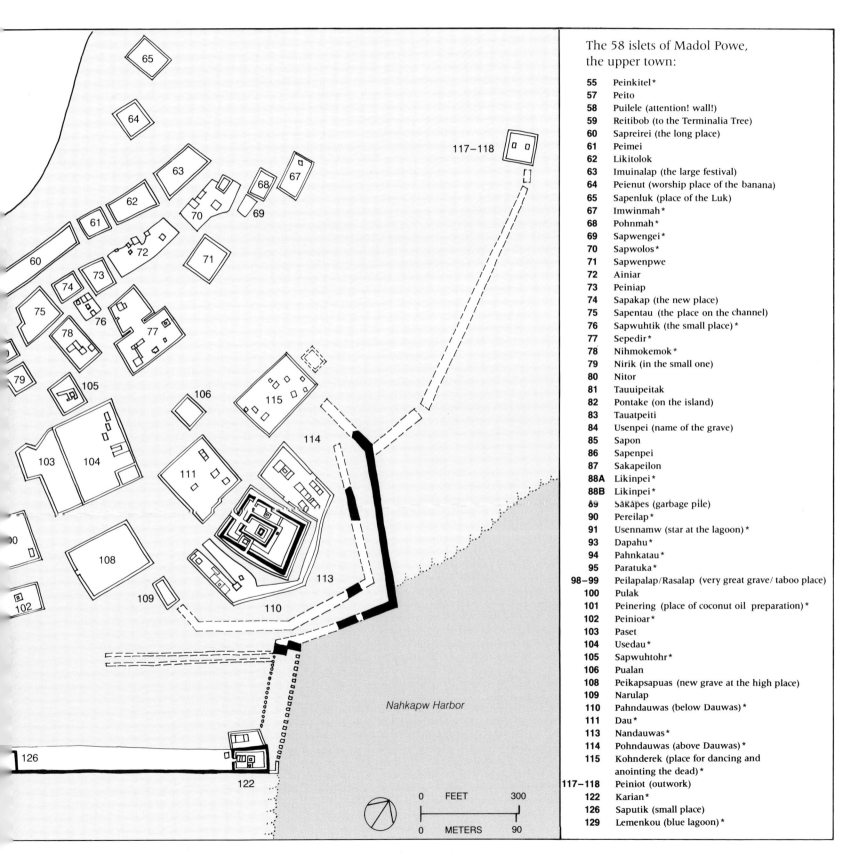

The 58 islets of Madol Powe,
the upper town:

55	Peinkitel*
57	Peito
58	Puilele (attention! wall!)
59	Reitibob (to the Terminalia Tree)
60	Sapreirei (the long place)
61	Peimei
62	Likitolok
63	Imuinalap (the large festival)
64	Peienut (worship place of the banana)
65	Sapenluk (place of the Luk)
67	Imwinmah*
68	Pohnmah*
69	Sapwengei*
70	Sapwolos*
71	Sapwenpwe
72	Ainiar
73	Peiniap
74	Sapakap (the new place)
75	Sapentau (the place on the channel)
76	Sapwuhtik (the small place)*
77	Sepedir*
78	Nihmokemok*
79	Nirik (in the small one)
80	Nitor
81	Tauuipeitak
82	Pontake (on the island)
83	Tauatpeiti
84	Usenpei (name of the grave)
85	Sapon
86	Sapenpei
87	Sakapeilon
88A	Likinpei*
88B	Likinpei*
89	Sakapes (garbage pile)
90	Pereilap*
91	Usennamw (star at the lagoon)*
93	Dapahu*
94	Pahnkatau*
95	Paratuka*
98–99	Peilapalap/Rasalap (very great grave/ taboo place)
100	Pulak
101	Peinering (place of coconut oil preparation)*
102	Peinioar*
103	Paset
104	Usedau*
105	Sapwuhtohr*
106	Pualan
108	Peikapsapuas (new grave at the high place)
109	Narulap
110	Pahndauwas (below Dauwas)*
111	Dau*
113	Nandauwas*
114	Pohndauwas (above Dauwas)*
115	Kohnderek (place for dancing and anointing the dead)*
117–118	Peiniot (outwork)
122	Karian*
126	Saputik (small place)
129	Lemenkou (blue lagoon)*

Nahkapw Harbor

0 FEET 300

0 METERS 90

ern orthography and, in a few cases, with information developed since 1910, when Hambruch worked at the site. The meaning of the names according to Hambruch (1936) is shown within parentheses. Features other than islets are omitted. Asterisks indicate islets that have been surveyed accurately in recent years.

Nandauwas

The crowning architectural achievement of Nan Madol is Nandauwas (113), the royal mortuary compound of the *saudeleur* and, later, of the *nahnmwarki*. Certainly no more magnificent example of prehistoric architecture exists in all of Micronesia. The gracefully upswept walls of the extraordinary monument exceed 25 feet in height at their corners and entryways. The design is powerfully conceived, sensitively sited, and skillfully executed.

Although I had seen photographs and drawings of the remarkable structure previously, I was unaware of its appropriate sense of place in the islet environment. My party approached by canoe from the open lagoon and then moved along the central canal that leads through Madol Powe. Passing jungle-covered islets on both sides of the canal, we caught our first glimpses of Nandauwas' southwest corner through the trees. A few moments later the canoe turned to the left, slowed, and stopped before the main entry landing of the west front. For several minutes I sat quietly in the boat, gazing at the magnificent west façade, the stately podium, the noble entryway, and the ascending steps that led to the interior courts, enclosures, and tombs.

Nandauwas and its immediate neighbors are the only islets in Nan Madol that are oriented with respect to a due east-west axis. East, the direction of the rising sun, was the cardinal point of the compass for prehistoric Micronesians. Pohndauwas (114) and Pahndauwas (110) flank Nandauwas to the north and south, respectively. Perched near the edge of the lagoon facing the open Pacific Ocean, the royal mortuary is protected by two massive seawalls that project into Na-

kapw Harbor to the east. In places the outer seawall is 15 feet high and 35 feet thick. The sound of powerful waves breaking on the stout seawalls is ever present at Nandauwas.

The reconstructed aerial view of Nandauwas presented here is based on an accurate instrument survey directed by Stephen Athens and conducted by Joyce Bath, photographs taken in 1984, and my notes and sketches. The podium or base of the islet measures some 208 × 258 feet along the centerlines. Its area exceeds 53,600 square feet, well more than the equivalent of a football field in size.

The podium of Nandauwas is a unique feature for Nan Madol. The high walls of the mortuary enclosure are set back 10 to 24 feet from the podium's edge, providing a level walkway all the way around the perimeter. Along the west side the islet podium is 4 to 5 feet higher than the surrounding canal. Huge basalt boulders form the lower courses of the walls near the islet's corners. Most of the retaining wall consists of prismatic basalt stacked in six alternating courses of headers and stretchers. The stones range in size up to 2.5 feet in diameter and 17 feet in length. One amorphous basalt cornerstone is estimated to weigh more than 50 tons.

Along the south edge of the podium, and at points on the east and north, the podium sags down almost to the water level at high tide. This may be the result of damage by jungle growth, geological subsidence, and possibly structural settling due to the immense superimposed weight over the centuries since Nandauwas was constructed.

Comparatively well preserved, the exterior façades of the north and west main enclosure walls are exceptional examples of Nan Madol's megalithic masonry. They clearly illustrate the three subtle curves that together produce the illusion of gracefully upswept corners seemingly poised to soar into the air. In plan, the walls curve outward to thicken at the corners and portals. In elevation, the walls curve upward 4 feet higher at their ends than in their centers, rising to a maximum height of 25 feet above the canal. In vertical plane, each wall slopes inward

about 1 foot for the lower two-thirds of its height and then corbels outward so that the top course lies directly above the base.

The builders of Nandauwas maintained the coursing of their stones while increasing the wall height by using larger stones near corners and by introducing additional headers and stretchers in each header course. This arrangement is illustrated in the accompanying photographs and drawing. Other examples of upswept corners in Nan Madol are found on Dorong (50), Peinering (101), Kohnderek (115), Karian (122), and Lemenkou (129). However, the walls of these islets are less dramatic in appearance and lower in height than those of Nandauwas.

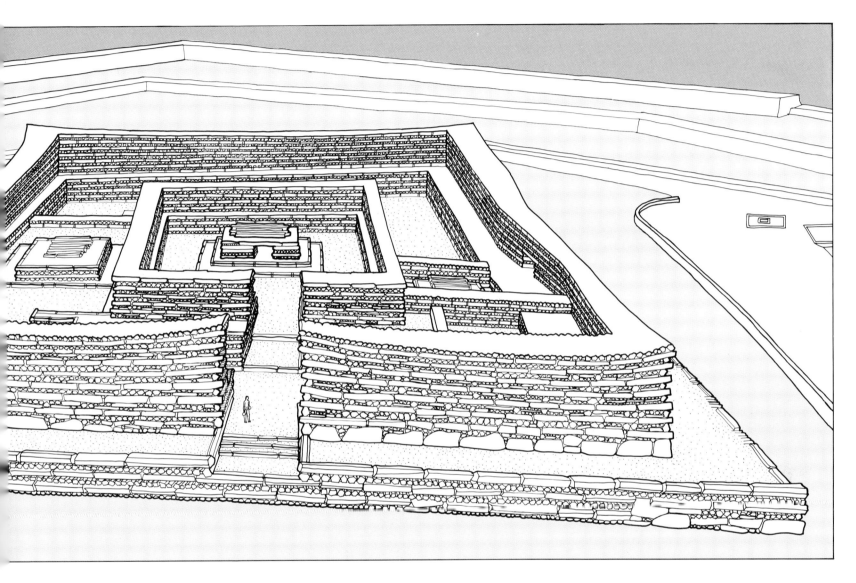

The landing in front of the main entry is set down two courses, apparently to facilitate access from canoes. Two tunnels also give access through the main enclosure walls. The 4-foot-high by 8-foot-wide tunnel through the south wall appears to the right in the perspective. A second tunnel, 4 feet high by 4 feet wide, leads through the north wall. The tunnel in the south wall 28 feet from the outer west corner apparently is not an original feature.

Several steps lead up from the canoe landing to the outer courtyard. The entry exceeds 14 feet in width and 22 feet in height. The south wall of the portal is 18 feet thick at its base where the hexagonal prismatic basalt stones exceed 2 feet in diameter. The surface of the outer courtyard is about 1.5 feet higher than the podium outside.

On both sides of the courtyard are raised ledges or galleries about 10 feet wide and elevated approximately 5 feet above the surface paving. The galleries continue all the way around both sides of the entire outer courtyard. Hambruch was told that the galleries served as the sites for exposing corpses before burial. The top four courses of the 13-foot-high interior enclosure wall project noticeably, forming a decorative cornice.

The entry into the inner courtyard directly aligns with the entry through the outer enclosure. However, the portal of the tomb closure. However, the portal of the tomb lies north of the entry alignment, suggesting that tomb portal may be only a temporary feature. Perhaps the wall of the tomb traditionally was resealed after each new interment.

The inner courtyard is elevated about 1.5 feet above the outer courtyard. The approximately 21-foot-square central tomb is almost 10 feet high. Its west face has an unusual double stretcher coursing of carefully matched and placed prismatic basalt. Two stone tiers lift the tomb above the level of the inner courtyard. The roof of the crypt is spanned by eight prismatic basalt stones, each measuring up to 18 feet in length and weighing one ton or more.

The 260-foot-long north wall of Nandauwas (113) sweeps gracefully upward at its ends. Naturally formed prismatic basalt was laid in skillfully fitted stacks to form the wall.

The north wall of the central tomb is about 1 foot lower than the south wall, probably due to subsidence. The portal of the crypt is some 4 feet high and 4.7 feet wide. The interior of the crypt measures roughly 10 × 13 feet in plan and about 7 feet in height. Here voluminous shell artifacts were found by Christian in 1896 and Hambruch in 1910, including adzes, circular beads, elegant bracelets, needles, breast pendants, necklaces, pearl-shell shanks of fishhooks, and other valuable objects. Even a gold crucifix and silver-handled dirk were found by visiting ships' captains between 1834 and 1840, suggesting possible Spanish contact before the 1820s.

Between the inner and outer walls of Nandauwas are three additional crypts built of prismatic basalt. Smaller than the central tomb, they still are impressive. Those to the north and south are set off by low enclosing walls. The small crypt to the east is recessed into the gallery paving of the inner enclosure wall. The surface of the east court, which is about 1.5 feet lower than the islet's podium, becomes water logged as high tide approaches. Here, near the outer enclosing wall, was discovered recently an approximately 2.5-foot-square culvert or channel running perpendicular to the east wall. The culvert's use is unknown.

The east wall of the outer enclosure is somewhat higher than the west wall, apparently an intentional feature. The east wall is protected by the two staunch seawalls of Nandauwas facing the open Pacific. The stoutest and best reinforced walls of Nan Madol face the open lagoon, such as those of Pahnwi (9) and Karian (122).

Karian

The skillfully built mortuary compound of Karian (122) lies some 570 feet east of Nandauwas (113). Karian is situated on the edge of the reef abutting the deep waters of Nahkapw Harbor and the open Pacific. The islet, which forms the eastern terminus of Nan Madol's southeast seawall, has the feel-

ing of a bastion set boldly on the edge of the sea. The sound of waves crashing on two sides of Karian is a constant reminder of the islet's exposed coastal location.

The outer walls of the islet enclose a rectangular area of some 11,200 square feet, only about one quarter the size of Nandauwas. The northeast and southeast walls, 97 and 128 feet long, respectively, rise more than 17 feet above sea level. They are constructed of huge basalt boulders in keeping with their functions as bulwarks against the sea. Unfortunately, they are much in ruins today. Among the most stoutly built of Nan Madol's walls, they range in thickness from 11 to 15 feet.

The aerial perspective from the southeast presented here is based on an accurate survey directed by Stephen Athens and conducted by Joyce Bath, photographs taken in 1984, and my notes and sketches. The islet base rises some 6.5 feet above sea level. Areas of coral fill retained by basalt walls extend to the northwest and southwest, protecting Karian's inshore walls.

In the foreground of the perspective is the approximately 77-foot-long southwest wall, shown also in the accompanying photograph. Most of the exterior facings of this wall and the northwest wall are in an excellent state of preservation and are among the finest examples of megalithic architecture in

Nan Madol. The southwest wall is about 11 feet high near the center and curves gracefully upward to its 13-foot-high corners. The tops of the inshore walls align with those of the seaward walls.

Like the somewhat higher enclosure of Nandauwas, Karian's walls are composed of stacked prismatic basalt in alternating courses of headers and stretchers above amorphous basalt boulders. Here, however, the boulders account for a larger proportion of the total wall surface, underscoring Karian's role as a seawall as well as a mortuary enclosure. The top of the north corner affords an excellent view of Nandauwas across the breakwater.

The second entryway in Nandauwas (113) leads to the inner courtyard and central tomb, where the remains of the deceased *saudeleur* and, later, the *nahnmwarki* were interred.

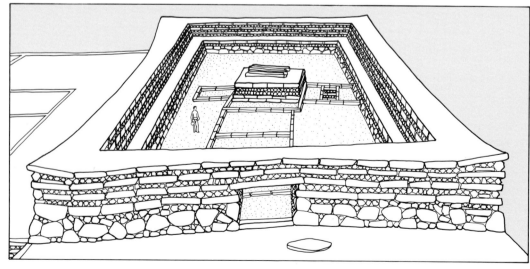

The mortuary islet of Karian (122) anchors the east corner of Nan Madol. An unusual archway gives entry to the courtyard.

The most remarkable architectural element of Karian is its distinctive entry portal located near the center of the southwest façade. The lintel of the portal is composed of five carefully selected and placed prismatic basalt stones, each about 12 feet long. The lintel supports four courses of stacked prismatic basalt. Karian's entryway is the largest and most beautiful of its type at Nan Madol, mutely attesting to the excellent technical skills of its builders.

The entry portal measures about 9 feet in width by 5 feet in height on the exterior of the enclosure, but increases to some 10 feet in width and diminishes to 4 feet in height on the interior. Perhaps the diminishing height of the portal is a reminder to bow when entering the sacred mortuary compound. The thickness of the walls enclosing Karian varies from 6 to 12 feet.

Just outside the portal is a 7-foot-long *sakau* pounding stone. Six more grooved pounding stones were found outside the walls; three others in the courtyard. The presence of ten pounding stones for *sakau* preparation at Karian indicates the importance of the ceremonial beverage in the ancient rituals of Nan Madol.

The interior courtyard of Karian originally was surrounded on all four sides by a gallery engaging the base of the enclosing walls. The gallery varied from 3 to 6 feet in width but maintained a constant height of about 5 feet above the courtyard paving. Due to the present ruinous condition of Karian's interiors, the entire gallery is no longer clearly distinguishable. Unlike the similar galleries of Nandauwas, the lower two courses of Karian's gallery are amorphous basalt boulders rather than stacked prismatic basalt. This feature may be another reflection of the concern of Karian's builders for constructing massive walls capable of resisting the relentless pounding of the sea.

The proportion of the courtyard's width to the enclosing wall height is at most 5 : 1 in its shorter dimension and about 11 : 1 in its maximum extremity. The sense of spatial enclosure is less compelling here than at Nandauwas. Near the center of the courtyard is a roughly 16.5 × 25-foot tomb about 5 feet high. The construction of the tomb is unusual in that its lower two courses and its top course are entirely stacked prismatic basalt stretchers; the intermediate two courses are only headers. This is an exception to the alternating header and stretcher coursing more frequently found elsewhere in Karian and other high wall structures of Nan Madol.

The walls of the central tomb have no entry portal. Within the tomb is an 11-foot-square crypt about 5 feet high. Originally, the crypt seems to have been roofed by eight prismatic basalt stones, each perhaps 12 feet long. Several of the roof stones were missing at the time of my visit. A second crypt, measuring about 4 × 9 feet in plan and 5 feet in depth, lies between the central tomb and the southeast wall. The smaller crypt had no roof but was lined with four courses of stacked prismatic basalt. Several stone-paved areas outlined by prismatic basalt are located in the courtyard and in the areas of coral fill northwest and southwest of Karian.

Peinering

The most beautifully proportioned islet that I found in Nan Madol was Peinering (101). According to Stephen Athens' accurate survey, the plan measures about 94 × 152 feet, a ratio of 1 : 1.608. This is very nearly the proportion of 1 : 1.618, familiar to students of Western architecture as the golden section (Dixon, 1981). The appearance of this proportion in the plan of Peinering seems to have been unique among the islets of Nan Madol. I repeatedly sought examples of perfect squares or golden rectangles at Nan Madol, but I found no evidence of their conscious employment either here or elsewhere in Micronesia. Isolated examples occurred in various monuments, but I was unable to identify an underlying rule of constantly recurring proportions in the prehistoric architecture of Micronesia.

A second reason for enjoying Peinering was that it was relatively well preserved and totally cleared of trees and tropical under-

growth at the time of my visit. In plan the four sides of the islet curve outward slightly at their corners, a configuration similar to Karian (122), Nandauwas (113), and other important monuments at Nan Madol.

Peinering's 8-foot-high walls also curve upward at their corners and entry portal and are slightly concave in their vertical planes. The top courses of the walls consisted of prismatic basalt headers that tilted markedly upward and projected beyond the exterior faces of the walls to form a cornice. This feature also was employed at Nandauwas and elsewhere in Nan Madol. The ancient builders of Peinering seem to have been consciously aware of the architectural problems of defining the top and bottom of a wall and of turning the corner of a wall with clear resolution.

Peinering's entryway was the most sensitively proportioned example of stacked prismatic basalt masonry that I saw in Nan Madol. It measures about 6 feet in width, 4 feet in height, and 6 feet in wall thickness. The sides of the entryway are exactly parallel, and its paving is precisely square in plan. The wall stones are carefully chosen and fitted together with exceptional skill. What Peinering lacks in size and impressiveness it more than offsets with architectural proportions, scale, and craftsmanship.

The islet's base is raised on coral fill to a level 4 feet above the waters of the surrounding lagoon. The enclosing walls of stacked prismatic basalt are some 6 to 7 feet thick at their bases. Near the center of Peinering are two approximately 20-foot-square mortuary features with holes dug in their centers by investigators during the Japanese administration. The features originally were basalt pavings elevated slightly above the surface of the islet, a type of structure found very frequently at Nan Madol. They typically contain multiple secondary interments.

Near Peinering's east wall along the islet's longitudinal centerline lies an approximately 13-foot-square house foundation with a 3-foot-square central fire pit about 2 feet deep. The vertical surfaces of the foundation are faced with rubble basalt; its paving, with coral fill. A pole-and-thatch house

originally may have been erected on the foundation, possibly oriented with its gable end toward the northeast. The structure may have housed a priest who was responsible for the preparation of coconut oil. In Nan Madol coconut oil traditionally was used to anoint the bodies of the dead and for other ceremonial purposes.

Other Islets of Madol Powe

Most of the fifty-eight islets of Madol Powe, the upper town, apparently served as dwellings for priests. Some were tomb enclosures, including Nandauwas (113), Karian (122), and Peinkitel (55). Other islets seem to have accommodated special functions related to ceremonial rituals, such as Peinering (101).

Usennamw (91), a large islet of irregular shape, contains several house platforms and an impressive *nahs* foundation. Hambruch (1936) reported that Usennamw served as the kitchen of the *saudeleur* and, later, of the *nahnmwarki*. Here the leaders were reported to have appeared at times to distribute food to their followers. Pottery was found primarily on the northern islet protrusion, an area that is completely flooded at high tide. Apparently, this is an earlier portion of the islet that was not resurfaced with additional coral fill during the *saudeleur* reign. Usennamw's fill elsewhere is elevated higher above the water level than most of the islets in the elite center. The impressive *nahs* of Usennamw will be described later in this section.

Containing several dwelling house platforms, Usendau (104) served as the residence of successive *nahnmwarki* and also of Hambruch in 1910. Relatively small Kohnderek (115) contained nine house platforms and is said to have been used for mourning the deceased with a kind of dance. The small islet of Sapwuhtohr (105) has abundant pottery remains and a large *nahs* foundation.

Peinioar (102) contained a single mortuary feature, while Pahnkatau (94) had three. Dapahu (93) is said to have been used for canoe making and for distributing food to participants in a ceremony honoring the deceased *saudeleur* at Nandauwas. Dau (111)

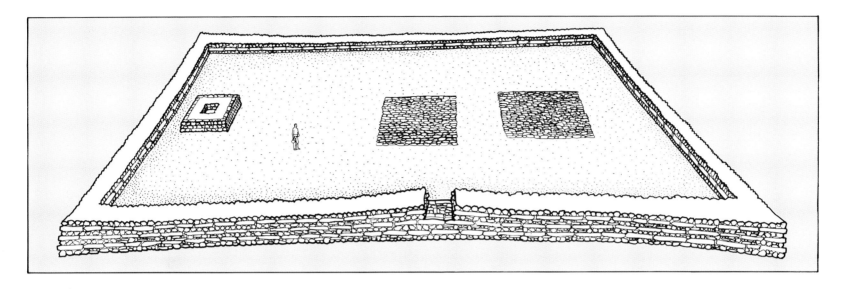

was reported to have been the place where the guards of Nan Madol resided.

Surrounded by high walls of stacked prismatic basalt, Lemenkou (129) has secondary wall enclosures in three corners. One enclosure has a raised house platform with a central fire pit. Three basalt-lined burial features recently were found in the western part of Lemenkou near the 20-foot-deep reef pool. A large number of *sakau* pounding stones also were found on the islet.

Pahnkadira

The residence of the *saudeleur* was the large, high-walled islet of Pahnkadira (33), shown here in a reconstructed aerial view from the southwest. Pahnkadira probably was once the most complex and impressive compound in Madol Pah, the lower town. Known as "place of the announcement," the islet consists of the approximately 105,500-square-foot main enclosure together with an attached attendants' area of some 33,500 square feet. Well more than twice the size of Nandauwas (113), Pahnkadira contains an area equivalent to almost three football fields.

A third functional unit associated with the royal residence seems to have been the islet of Kalapuel (32), where visitors apparently were quartered when they called on the *saudeleur*. The basis of the reconstruction presented here is an accurate survey of Pahnka-

dira by William Ayres and Alan Haun, the account of Hambruch (1936), and photographs and notes recorded during my visit.

The royal residential compound is surrounded by stacked prismatic basalt walls up to 16.4 feet high. Four entries give access from the canal into the main enclosure: the approximately 13-foot-wide main entry from the southwest, two 8-foot-wide entries from the southeast, and a roughly 8-foot-wide entry from the northeast. Near the center of the compound is a three-tiered platform with three fire pits outlined by basalt. The top platform measures about 62 × 120 feet.

Hambruch was told that the platform was the site of the pole-and-thatch temple of Nan Zapue, the Thunder God. Here Hambruch found the remains of corner posts suggesting a structure some 33 × 79 feet in size. Near the west corner of the temple platform is an approximately 33-foot-long bench of prismatic basalt. A row of pounding stones lies along the southwest side of the temple base, where two conch shell trumpets were excavated.

In the west corner of Pahnkadira is the secondary enclosure of the residence of the *saudeleur*. Its 8-foot-thick interior walls enclose a courtyard measuring about 63 × 107 feet, an area of roughly 6,740 square feet. The residential platform is about 32 feet wide and 42 feet long.

The royal family resided in the southeastern area of Pahnkadira. The approximately 94 × 135-foot south enclosure, which contains a single house platform, comprises an area of some 12,650 square feet, almost twice the size of the paramount's enclosure.

The almost square east enclosure measures 64 × 67 feet and contains about 4,300 square feet in area. Less than two-thirds the area of the enclosure of the *saudeleur*, it also contains a single dwelling platform. Between the east enclosure and the temple platform is a paved area beside a 26 × 33-foot excavation dug through the islet fill down to the original reef. The excavation is said to have been a bathing pool. The servants of the royal family are reported to have dwelled in the northern area of Pahnkadira.

The walls around the attendants' annex are substantially lower than those of the main enclosure. Here the first court attendant of the *saudeleur* is said to have lived. No portal interconnects the attendants' area with the main enclosures, and access was afforded only by two approximately 6.6-foot-wide entries through the southeast wall. Within the annex are several house platforms with central fire pits. One measures about 25.6 × 29.5 feet and has a roughly 5 × 6 foot fire pit. Like the main enclosure, the attendants' area is predominantly coral paved with basalt outlining house platforms.

Although Pahnkadira had been com-

75

pletely cleared and surveyed in 1981, the jungle had reclaimed it by the time of my visit three years later. Underbrush and dense jungle grass up to four feet high rendered observations at the site very difficult. The spatial relations of the enclosures were easily perceived by walking on the tops of the interior walls, but finding house foundations, the bath, and the temple's base was arduous.

Kalapuel (32) lies just across the canal from the main entry to Pahnkadira. It appears in the foreground to the right in the aerial perspective. The last *saudeleur* is said to have made Kalapuel available as a dwelling place for Isokelekel and his 333 warriors when they asked for hospitality. In the absence of an accurate survey of the islet, the detailed map published by Hambruch (1936) is the basis of the reconstruction presented here.

In plan Kalapuel is a slightly irregular square measuring at most 200 feet on each side and containing about 36,000 square feet, an area slightly larger than the attendants' annex of Pahnkadira. The northwestern walls are perhaps 12 to 13 feet high above water level; the southeastern walls, about 6 feet. The islet base is elevated some 3 feet above the lagoon. Four entries give access into the islet, one on each side. The north corner of Kalapuel has a roughly 69 × 95-foot residential courtyard separated by possibly 8-foot-high walls from the rest of the islet. It once contained a single dwelling in an enclosure similar in size to the *saudeleur's*. Hambruch recorded four other house platforms and several low walls elsewhere on Kalapuel.

Other Islets of Madol Pah

Most of the other islets of Madol Pah seem to have served as dwellings for the nobility, but some served special ceremonial purposes. The islet of Idehd (43), "place of the sacred eel," appears to the upper right in the aerial perspective of Pahnkadira (33). A comparatively small islet, Idehd measures only about 102 × 141 feet and contains at most 14,400 square feet, little more than one-tenth the size of Pahnkadira. The care-

fully built, stacked prismatic basalt walls of Idehd are perhaps 6 feet high except at the east corner enclosure, where they rise to some 8 feet. Here, near the base of a wall, I found the longest prismatic basalt stone that I saw in Nan Madol: it measured 19 feet 7 inches in length.

A single entry, some 13 feet wide, gives access into the islet from the northwest. The entry leads into an approximately 67 × 80-foot courtyard where the sacred eel reportedly was kept in a well about 2 feet square. Periodically, turtles were brought to Idehd, where they were killed and cooked and their entrails were fed to the eel. The turtles were kept in an artificial basin on Paset (103) in Madol Powe.

A mound of rubble some 10 feet high is located in the outer courtyard of Idehd. Hambruch (1936) reported that inside the courtyards, under the sacred eel's protection, the people of Nan Madol were said to have kept weapons, including spears and stones. The wood of the weapons had perished, but beautifully polished stones the size of ostrich eggs remained when Hambruch visited the islet in 1910. Too large to be managed with a sling, the stones were thought to have been thrown by hand.

In 1963 the Smithsonian Institution sponsored scientific investigations on Idehd. During the ancient ritual of cooking a turtle for the sacred eel, the highest priest is said to have performed a ceremony of atonement for himself, other priests, the *saudeleur*, and, finally, all the people. Over the years, cooking residue accumulated to form Idehd's rubble mound. Radiocarbon dates from the mound were A.D. 1260 near the base, 1295 toward the middle, and 1380 in the upper level. Stephen Athens and David Welch recently confirmed the Smithsonian dates and established the fact that megalithic construction with basalt columns was under way in Nan Madol by at least 1200 to 1300.

The islet of Peikap (39), "new grave enclosure," appears in the upper center of the aerial perspective of Pahnkadira. It is located some 33 feet northwest of Idehd (43). A narrow canal separates Peikap from Pahnkadira to the southwest. Hambruch recorded di-

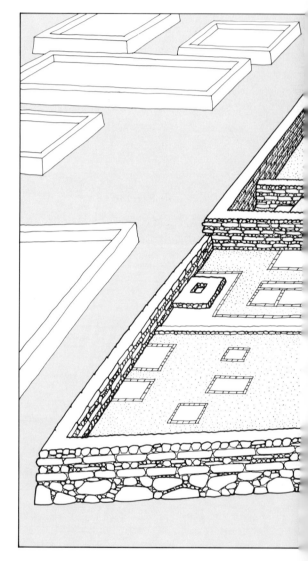

mensions of about 362 × 367 feet for the islet, suggesting an area almost as large as Pahnkadira. The high walls of Peikap are built of stacked prismatic basalt on amorphous basalt boulders packed with smaller stones. Some of the boulders are shaped like turtle shells. Near the islet's south corner is a natural reef pool much smaller than Dorong's (50).

The west corner of Dorong appears in the upper-right-hand corner of the aerial perspective. The roughly 315 × 335-foot islet, enclosed by high walls of stacked prismatic basalt, was an important ritual site. Hambruch recorded an approximately 6.6-foot-wide entry facing the canal to the northwest

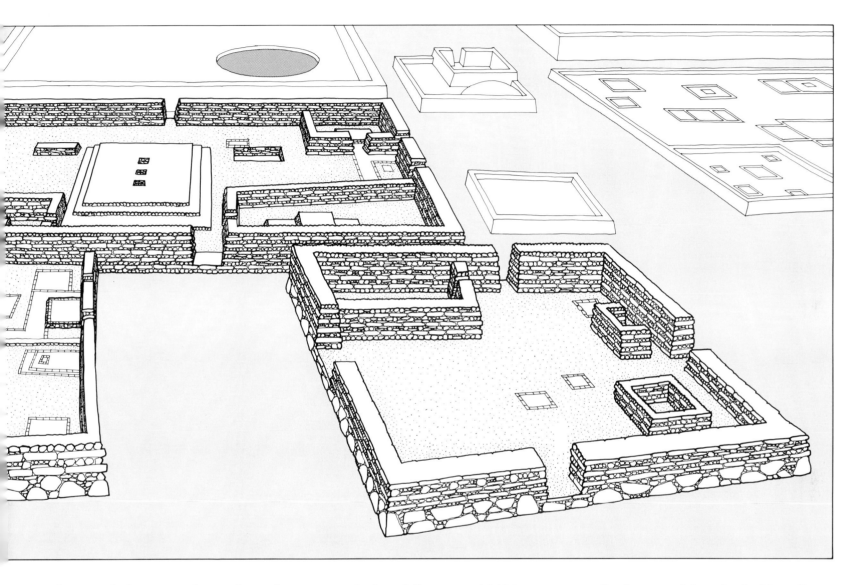

Pahnkadira (33), the royal residential compound, is shown near the center of this aerial view from the southwest. In the lower left and right, respectively, appear the royal attendants' compound and Kalapuel Islet (32).

and a portal about 16.5 feet wide in the northeast wall. Constructed symmetrically around a large, natural reef pool, Dorong is said to have been used to raise and keep clams. At appropriate times the clams reportedly were collected ceremoniously for the nobility. Numerous clam shells lying on the islet surface confirm the oral account. Hambruch reported that Dorong also provided coconuts, breadfruit, pandanus, and fruits destined for sacrifice.

The wall-enclosed basalt pavement on Dorong is a mortuary feature. Near it a huge, two-ton *sakau* pounding stone was found. Eleven small tunnel-like channels run through the islet's fill. They are con-

structed of carefully cut coral laid between basaltic prisms. One of the tunnels, which is much larger than the others, is said to have been used to keep the sacred eel. A small *sakau* stone is located next to it. The other ten channels apparently allowed fresh sea water into the reef pool to assist in cultivating clams. Platforms and a *nahs* foundation also are located on Dorong.

The north half of Palakapw (49) appears to the right in the aerial perspective. The islet lies across the canal southwest of Dorong. Palakapw measures at most 318 × 328 feet, about the size of Dorong. The enclosure of Palakapw has a double wall of basalt with a core of coral fill. Not all the

walls of Nan Madol used a double wall system. Palakapw has fourteen or fifteen house platforms where members of the nobility once resided. Some of the platforms here were larger than those on Usennamw (91).

Pahnwi (9) is located at the south corner of Madol Pah. The coral-paved islet is a complex ensemble of platforms, basalt-faced tombs, house platforms, enclosures, and other architectural features. At the time of my visit the islet was being investigated by a University of Oregon team under the direction of William Ayres, with the sponsorship of the National Geographic Society.

Pahnwi's walls facing the lagoon are among the largest in Nan Madol. The terraces

Immense basalt boulders packed with smaller prisms of basalt form the canal walls of many of Nan Madol's islets.

within the islet step up to the 20-foot-high platform in the south corner, the highest platform in Nan Madol. The 36-foot-high south corner, the highest wall in Nan Madol, is an impressive feat of engineering. Here three immense basalt boulders are piled one on top of the other and crowned by very large stacked prismatic basalt. Unfortunately, a huge tree presently threatens to destroy the magnificent corner.

MEGALITHIC CONSTRUCTION

The basalt boulders and prisms used in constructing the walls of Nan Madol came from quarries on the main island. Prismatic basalt columns are natural stone formations

resulting from volcanic activity. Scientists have identified a number of prismatic basalt outcrops, and oral accounts also indicate several quarry locations.

Each basalt flow tends to have distinctive proportions of trace elements, making it possible to match individual stones with particular quarries. David Mattey, an English geochemist, has matched one stone in Nandauwas (113) with a mainland quarry on the opposite side of Pohnpei from Nan Madol. The study of quarry sources for the structures of Nan Madol is being pursued by Stephen Athens.

In their natural state prismatic basalt columns usually are attached to larger crys-

talline formations. Oral traditions said that the prisms were dislodged by building large fires at their bases and suddenly cooling the stones with sea water to cause them to fracture. The stones then were placed on rafts and floated within the fringing coral reefs to the building site. Apparently not all the stones reached their intended destinations, for basalt stones can be seen on the bottom of the coastal lagoon between Nan Madol and Sokehs. The stones lie on coral and sand, clearly the result of the activities of humans rather than nature.

Moving and placing the basalt stones was a highly labor intensive process. Oral accounts reported the use of levers, inclined

planes of coconut palm trunks, and strong ropes of hibiscus fiber. These methods for moving megaliths were within the technical abilities of the ancient Pohnpeians. Similar systems were reported for erecting huge stone structures in Kosrea and for moving heavy logs in Yap and Palau. The nearby reef was the source of coral for islet fill and wall cores at Nan Madol. Many of the coral slabs are light enough to be passed from hand to hand, a much easier task than erecting megalithic walls of basalt.

HOUSE DESCRIPTIONS

Although the wood components of ancient Pohnpeian houses perished long ago, several early observers left descriptions of the residences they found on the island. James F. O'Connell lived on Pohnpei from perhaps 1828 until November of 1833, a relatively long period of residence before a regular Western contact began. He noted that "the dwelling houses vary in size and in shape according to the taste and rank of the proprietor" (1972:125).

O'Connell also observed that "dwelling houses seldom exceed forty feet by twenty, and *Nigurts* [probably a reference to commoners] are sometimes contented with ten by six and less. But the war canoe houses, which serve also the purpose of council rooms and halls for feasting and other ceremonies, are often a hundred feet in length, and forty to fifty wide" (1972:127). The latter probably refers to a *nahs*.

Concerning carpentry tools, O'Connell described *Tridacna* shell adzes as "made of a hard white stone, found on the beach, broken to the shape of a hatchet, and rubbed to a very good edge on rough rocks. A native will be sometimes two or three months preparing his hatchet, working at intervals upon it, before he fastens it to the handle. . . . For smaller works sea shells are used, and coral forms their rasps. They have also dogfish skin for polishing" (1972:128–129).

Another early description of Pohnpeian houses was made by a Dr. Campbell, a surgeon serving aboard the British cutter *Lambton* when it visited Pohnpei in 1836. He observed that the houses "are neat and com-

Photographs of houses in Uh (*left*) and Kiti (*right*) municipalities, Pohnpei. Both photographs were taken by Paul Hambruch (1929) and numbered G105.

The *nahs* of Usennamw (91) measures about 49 feet × 70 feet in plan. Its original height may have been some 40 feet.

fortable; the walls being constructed entirely of small bamboo, and are raised two or three feet from the ground on a solid platform of stone, built without cement; the interior might answer the description of a birdcage; the various beams and uprights being fastened (like the canoes) with party colored twine made from the bark of the cocoa nut. The floor, composed of bamboo, is as soft as carpet; though they do not cook anything in their houses, a square place is left in the centre of the floor, where generally they have a fire, round which may often be seen the old and infirm. . . . They sleep on mats, . . . and have a blanket inside of bark interwoven with a soft fibrous filament" (Campbell, 1836, in Athens, 1981:4).

Andrew Cheyne stayed on Pohnpei for five months in 1842 and 1843 and visited the island on other occasions. Concerning Pohnpeian houses, he wrote, "They all form an oblong square. . . . A foundation of stone work is raised to a height of from three to six feet above the ground, for the frame of the house to rest upon. In the center of this, a space of about four feet square, and two in depth, is left for a fire-place; and the remainder of the floor is covered with a species of wicker-work, made of small cane, or reeds, neatly seized together. The sides are about four feet high, and are also covered in with this wicker-work, having several small open spaces left for windows, and for which they have shutters made of the same materials. The whole frame of the house is made of squared timber, and the uprights are all morticed into the wall-plates. The rafters are formed of small straight rickers, about two feet apart, which reach from the ridge-pole to the wall-plates on each side, and are seized to both with small senit. The thatch is made of pandamus leaves, sewed to a reed, which forms a long narrow mat, about six feet in length, by one in breadth" (Cheyne, 1852:111).

The Nahs of Usennamw

The reconstructed drawing of the *nahs* (meeting house) of Usennamw (91) presented here is based on the accurate survey by Stephen Athens, photographs G105 and

G175 published by Paul Hambruch (1929), and my personal observations of wood structures in Pohnpei. The wood structures of Pohnpeian *nahs* existing at the time of Western contact perished long ago. It is important that the reconstruction suggested here be regarded only as an approximation, pending the development of more definitive information.

Many foundations of ancient *nahs* have been found in Nan Madol and elsewhere in Pohnpei, and modern versions of traditional meeting houses continue to be built and used on the island today. Although the structures' foundations vary in dimensions and construction, the *nahs* of Usennamw will suffice to illustrate the typical building type. The form is said to have been initiated with the *nahnmwarki* title system. In plan the structure is a U-shaped rectangle measuring about 49 × 70 feet. At one end is an open space level with the adjacent grade.

The main level of the structure is raised some 4 feet above grade. The walls of the elevated platform consist of rubble basalt retaining coral fill. Reed mats probably covered the floor of the platform originally. On the centerline of the *nahs* opposite the area on grade is a second platform raised an additional 4 feet above the level of the main platform. The higher platform measures perhaps 16 feet square and contains a roughly 6-foot-square fire pit at its center. The coral surface of the fire pit is recessed into the platform and is lined with rubble basalt. The coral floor of the upper platform probably also was covered with reed mats.

My speculation is that the foundation of the *nahs'* wood superstructure rested on four rows of hewn wood base plates extending the length of the building. The plates received wood posts as shown in Hambruch's photographs. The wood posts would have been located not more than 12 feet apart. The center row of posts probably was omitted to double the width of the center span. My guess would be that the roof ridge quite possibly was supported by horizontal beams bearing elevated posts in a king post truss arrangement. Joints bound with ropes of woven fiber seem likely.

Longitudinal roof beams would have been placed on top of the posts to receive rafters sloping at an angle of about 45 degrees with the horizon. This is the roof slope shown in Hambruch's photographs and is somewhat lower than the traditional roofs of major structures on Kosrae, Yap, and Palau. The roof probably was constructed of wood purlins and rafters covered with thatch, the system traditionally used in Micronesia. The vertical areas between perimeter wall posts may have been filled in with mats of woven fiber or reeds except at portals for access and ventilation. The reconstruction suggests rafters at most 39 feet long and posts not more than 18 feet high. Timbers of this size are assumed to have been reasonably available in prehistoric Pohnpei.

A basalt stone that projects from the northwest face of the Usennamw *nahs'* foundation probably served as a step to assist persons climbing up to the main platform. Two pounding stones are located on grade near the center of the structure. In this area servants traditionally prepared *sakau* and food for those assembled on the platforms. According to present-day practices in Pohnpei, only the highest-ranking people would occupy the upper platform of the *nahs*. Because seating is assigned according to a rigid system of social ranking, persons of the lowest rank would sit farthest from the upper platform.

PEINLOLUNG

On the coastal road between Nan Madol and the administrative center of Kolonia is Peinlolung (exact location not certain). In Pohnpeian the name means "platform of burial." The photograph of the site presented here shows a modern house built on top of an ancient platform with rectangular walls of stacked prismatic basalt. Peinlolung is an example of the present-day practice of placing modern structures on top of ancient monuments in Pohnpei.

STONE PLATFORMS IN KITI

Kiti, one of the five municipalities of present-day Pohnpei, is located on the southwest coast of the island. One of the important prehistoric sites in Kiti is Sapwtakai, an ancient administrative center built on a mountain peak. In a recent survey of Sapwtakai and its environs, Joyce Bath (1984) identified dozens of stone burial sites, platforms, and enclosures. The examples shown here illustrate broad variations in size, type of construction, configuration, and details.

Alauso (Po-D32-7) is a comparatively small but beautifully constructed two-tiered platform with a central fire pit. The site lies less than one quarter of a mile south of Sapwtakai on a 460-foot-high mountain ridge with a beautiful view of the seacoast to the southeast. The 1-foot-high lower platform measures about 14.8 × 23 feet overall, an area of some 340 square feet. Alauso's roughly 10 × 13-foot upper platform is 2 feet high and contains a stone-paved 3 × 4-foot pit. All of the structure's facing stones are amorphous basalt. The overall height slightly exceeds 3 feet.

About 800 feet south of Sapwtakai is the Kiti Rock Complex, which includes a 22 × 24.6-foot two-tiered platform (Po-D35-15, Feature 1). The platform's area is about 540 square feet. One of the unusual features of the structure is its very low steps; each riser is only 9 inches high. Other unusual features are the four upright basalt prisms near the outer corners of the approximately 12.7 × 16-foot upper platform. Each of the uprights is about 18 inches high. A platform with upright corner prisms was reported at Wene (Po-D11-5; Ayres and Haun, 1980), but it does not resemble the Kiti Rock platform. Also unusual is the disproportionately large central fire pit, measuring some 8.2 × 9.2 feet.

Diadi (Po-D30-16) is a rectangular enclosure with a platform as high as its enclosing wall. The site is an upland marsh half a mile south of Sapwtakai. The 2-to-3.5-foot-high outer wall measures about 29.5 × 36 feet in plan, an area of approximately 1,060 square feet. A single 3-foot-wide entry leads to an unpaved aisle around the inner platform. Near the center of the platform is a 3-foot-square central pit surrounded on three sides by an approximately 1 foot deep by 1 foot wide recess into the platform's surface,

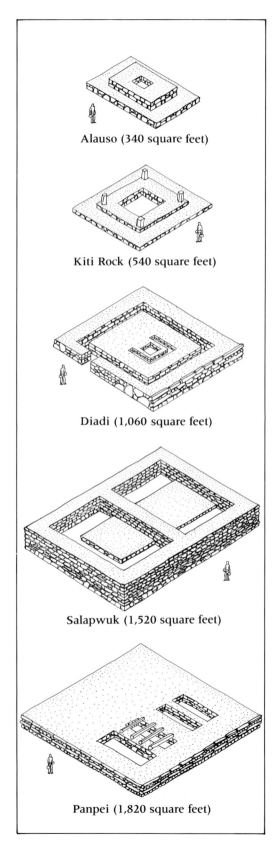

Alauso (340 square feet)

Kiti Rock (540 square feet)

Diadi (1,060 square feet)

Salapwuk (1,520 square feet)

Panpei (1,820 square feet)

a highly unusual feature for prehistoric Pohnpeian architecture. Also unusual is the mixture of types of masonry in Diadi's platform walls. Headers and stretchers of prismatic basalt are used at some corners, flat surfaces of stones placed on edge face some parts of the walls, and stacked, randomly coursed stones appear in other parts of the walls.

Slightly less than one mile northeast of Sapwtakai is Salapwuk (Po-D24-7), a rectangular enclosure with a bisecting interior wall and two low platforms. The site is a swampy upland meadow covered with wild grasses, canes, and ferns. Salapwuk's overall dimensions are about 33 × 46 feet, an area of some 1,520 square feet. The 4.6- to 7.5-foot-high exterior walls vary from 3 to 5 feet in thickness. The inner platforms are only 1 foot high. The walls are constructed of randomly stacked, roughly dressed vesicular basalt boulders. Vesicular basalt contains many small spherical cavities, a feature sometimes found in volcanic rocks. The dual courtyards of Salapwuk are highly unusual features for prehistoric Pohnpeian architecture.

The Panpei Complex is located about one quarter of a mile southwest of Sapwtakai. The site includes an 1,820-square-foot burial platform with four crypts (Po-D35-3). The approximately 42.7-foot-square structure is slightly more than 3 feet high. The crypts vary in length from 12.5 to 14.8 feet, in width from 3 to 5 feet, and in depth from 20 to 24 inches. The two larger crypts originally may have been roofed by prismatic basalt, perhaps 7 feet long. Four of these prisms remained in place in 1983. The walls of the burial platform are constructed of prismatic basalt headers and stretchers similar to many of the walls of Nan Madol.

SAPWTAKAI

Believed to have been a regional political center, Sapwtakai (Po-D35-1) is located on a mountain peak some 720 feet above sea level. Radiocarbon dating indicates that the earliest occupation of the site occurred between A.D. 1300 and 1400, about the time of major expansion at Nan Madol. The site apparently was abandoned about 1800.

The plan presented here is based on the excellent survey prepared by Joyce Bath (1984). Walls almost entirely enclose the mountain peak, except along the southeast perimeter of the site, where a lineal earth mound falls off steeply toward a deep gorge to the east. Toward the north and northwest a second wall is located about 50 feet beyond the main wall. These freestanding walls ranged in height from 4.7 to 6.5 feet. They seem to have been erected primarily for defensive purposes.

The walls to the south are on the average only about 2.4 feet high. Apparently, they served mainly as retaining walls for terraces rather than as defenses. The maximum dimensions of the site are some 245 feet in width by about 760 feet in length, measured to the outermost walls. The site area within the main walls is slightly less than three acres.

The arrangement of stout defenses to the northwest suggests the existence of unfriendly neighbors in that direction. The defense of the northern perimeter appears to have been a major problem throughout the entire period of occupation at Sapwtakai. Access from the densely populated areas to the south and east seems to have been under control by other means, as the mountain-top site lacked defenses toward the southeast.

At the northwest corner of the site is a platform 6 feet higher than the main walls. The structure is faced and paved with well-fitted basalt. At the northeast corner of the main wall is a U-shaped platform about 20 inches high. In plan the structure measures at most 20 × 32 feet. Apparently built in two phases, the platform very probably was not a *nahs*.

Centered near the north end of the walled enclosure is a large stone arrangement with walls now 20 to 24 inches high. The original wall alignments appear to have been disturbed, and evidence collected on the site indicated two periods of occupation. Local tradition reported that Sapwtakai was conquered by rival clansmen, who occupied the site and wrought great destruction.

The central area of Sapwtakai seems to have been the main residential area. Four stone-paved platforms lie immediately west of the main wall, here some 6.5 feet high. Within the enclosure are three truncated platforms with central fire pits. Probably once residences used over long time periods, they range from 260 to 860 square feet in area and up to 7 feet in height.

Two large paved areas, together containing an area of about 5,300 square feet, lie in the east-central area of Sapwtakai. One of the pavings projects beyond the east wall, here perhaps 6 feet high. A retaining wall extends from the paved terrace down to grade. The three circular features shown on the terrace are stone-lined breadfruit storage pits with raised stone rims. Associated with the pits was a large breadfruit mortar rock.

Immediately south of the two large residential terraces is a small paved area about 2 feet lower in elevation. Here a 4-to-5-foot-wide and 7-inch-high stone-paved walkway leads some 36 feet south to the feature shown as two concentric stone circles. The circles represent a stone-lined depression that was more likely a water reservoir than a fire pit or a breadfruit storage pit. To the northwest of the reservoir is a semicircular rock oven.

East of the walkway is a low platform with a central pit. Here a number of large, round river stones were discovered. Weighing 5.5 to 44 pounds each, the stones are believed to be either magic stones or sling stones, although they are too heavy to be managed by a sling. Hambruch (1936) recorded similar stones in Nan Madol, as previously noted.

The southernmost feature of Sapwtakai's central residential area is a two-tier stone platform with two terraces descending in 18-inch steps to the east. The lower platform contains some 1,100 square feet and is about 19 inches high. The upper tier is perhaps 300 square feet in area and 18 inches high. Constructed of well-fitted columnar basalt, the platform and terraces together occupy an area of almost 2,300 square feet. The platform's central pit yielded shell and fish and turtle bones, confirming that the structure was a house platform.

In the center of Sapwtakai's southern zone is an approximately 2,500-square-foot tomb containing two crypts. The height of the tomb's base varies from perhaps 3 feet in the north to about 6 feet in the south due to the terrain's slope. Although some stacked-basalt header and stretcher construction is in evidence, most of the walls are in advanced stages of deterioration.

A roughly 11.4 × 16.4-foot paving some 20 inches high covers the central crypt. The relatively well preserved crypt measures about 3 feet wide by 9.6 feet long and 4.8 feet deep. The second, unopened, crypt lies along the south edge of the structure. Along the eastern side of the tomb's main platform is an approximately 3-foot-wide curbing elevated some 7 to 20 inches above the platform level.

In the southwest corner of the main enclosure lies Sapwtakai's second two-tier stone platform. The roughly 325-square-foot upper tier contains a central pit and rests on an approximately 2,170-square-foot platform. The terrace is level with grade at its north corner, perhaps 3 feet above grade at its east and west corners, and some 8 feet high to the south due to the terrain's slope. The upper tier is about 2 feet higher than the platform.

Sapwtakai's central house platforms may have served purposes similar to those of Pahnkadira (33) in Nan Madol. Here perhaps was located the residence of the highest-ranked person in the ancient political center, his family, attendants, and quarters for the accommodation of important visitors. Turtle bones recovered from one of the fire pits may recall the ritual preparation of turtles for sacrifice on the islet of Idehd (43). Thus, north and central Sapwtakai may be the functional counterpart of the Madol Pah, or the lower town of Nan Madol.

The tomb and the area south of it may have had mortuary functions similar to the tombs of Madol Powe, such as Nandauwas. Subject to further investigation, the southern area is tentatively interpreted as the sacred area of Sapwtakai. Alternately, Sapwtakai may have been entirely secular except for the known tomb, with its mortuary or sacred areas being located in nearby areas downslope.

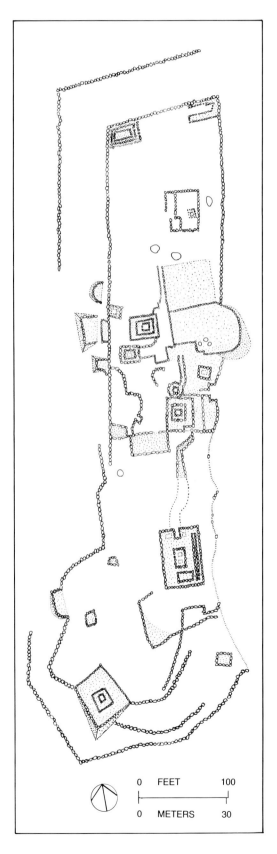

Photograph of the house at Peinlolung,
Pohnpei.

SUMMARY

Although dozens of ancient sites exist on Pohnpei, none exceeds the elite center of Nan Madol in architectural magnificence. Indeed no greater record of prehistoric achievement exists in all of Micronesia than the ninety-two islets of ancient Nan Madol. Set apart from the main island of Pohnpei, the ceremonial center was the scene of human activity as early as the first or second century A.D. By the eighth or ninth century islet construction had begun, but the distinctive megalithic architecture of Nan Madol probably was not begun until perhaps the latter twelfth or early thirteenth century. About that time, apparently, a paramount conquered and unified Pohnpei, beginning the reign of the *saudeleur*. By the end of the *saudeleur* reign in the seventeenth century, Nan Madol had reached essentially its present form.

The elite center was a special place of residence for the nobility and of mortuary activities presided over by priests. Its population almost certainly did not exceed one thousand and may have been less than half that. Madol Powe, the mortuary sector, contains 58 islets in the northeastern area of Nan Madol. Most of the islets once were occupied by the dwellings of priests. Some islets served special purposes, such as food preparation on Usennamw (91), canoe making on Dapahu (93), and coconut oil preparation on Peinering (101). High walls surrounding tombs are located on the mortuary islets of Peinkitel (55), Nandauwas (113), Karian (122), and Lemenkou (129).

The crowning achievement of Nan Madol is the royal mortuary islet of Nandauwas (113). Here walls 18 to 25 feet high surround a central tomb enclosure within the main courtyard. Karian (122) anchors the east corner of Nan Madol on the edge of the reef facing the open Pacific. Karian's most distinctive feature is its handsome main entry portal below a massive lintel supporting the upper wall.

Peinkitel (55) is built partly on the shore of Temwen Island, one of the few islets in Nan Madol not bounded on all four sides by the waters of the lagoon. Here, within a secondary enclosure, lies a large tomb that is said to contain the remains of the legendary Isokelekel. The hero is supposed to have conquered the *saudeleur* and instituted the *nahnmwarki* title system that persists on Pohnpei to this day.

Madol Pah, the administrative sector, contains 34 islets in the southwestern area of Nan Madol. This was the area of dwellings for the nobility. The high walled islet of Pahnkadira (33) contained the residences of the *saudeleur* and his family and the three-tiered stone base of the Thunder God's temple. The annex of Pahnkadira was the dwelling place of the first court attendant of the *saudeleur*. Kalapuel (32) was said to have quartered Isokelekel and his warriors when they first came to Nan Madol.

Turtle entrails were prepared for feeding to the sacred eel on the islet of Idehd (43). Clams were cultivated for the nobility in the large reef pool of Dorong (50), where another sacred eel is said to have been kept. The 36-foot-high south corner of Pahnwi (9) is the highest wall in Nan Madol. Pahnwi also contains the highest platform in the elite center and a large tomb within a secondary enclosure.

A network of waterways reminiscent of Venice interconnected the islets of Nan Madol, while immense seawalls and breakwaters protected the island center from the unrelenting waves of the Pacific Ocean. Most of the islets were rectangular in plan, and all were constructed artificially with cores of coral rubble fill. The majority of the islets were surrounded by retaining walls of basalt boulders and stacked prismatic basalt.

Walls extending above islet bases usually consisted of prismatic basalt stacked in alternating courses of headers and stretchers and filled with coral rubble. Often immense, the megalithic prisms weighed up to 5 tons or more and sometimes exceeded 19 feet in length. Other immense boulders weighed up to 50 tons. The megaliths were taken from quarries on the mainland, floated to the remote lagoon site on rafts, and lifted into place with ropes, levers, and inclined planes.

In order to appreciate more fully the scope of prehistoric architectural activity on Pohnpei, the mainland sites of Sapwtakai and its environs have been examined. Stone platforms at Alauso, the Kiti Rock Complex, Diadi, Salapwuk, and the Panpei Complex reveal similarities as well as rich contrasts with the ancient architecture of Nan Madol.

Parallels with Nan Madol may exist in the functional organization of Sapwtakai. Nan Madol construction methods and materials appear in Sapwtakai's tomb structure, which utilizes headers and stretches of prismatic basalt. Also found at Nan Madol were rounded basalt boulders, such as those of the northern and western walls of Sapwtakai.

Similarities also appear between the structures of Nan Madol and those of Leluh on Kosrae. Both centers were situated in isolated sites on the east coast of their main islands. Both had artificial islets and walls of basaltic construction. But many differences also occur between the two centers, such as house foundations, types of tombs and ritual structures, configurations of wall portals, types of walls, locations of functional sectors in the overall plan, and other details. Major construction on Leluh began perhaps two centuries later than on Nan Madol. Neither center is known to have had ocean-going canoes at the time of Western contact, and large migrations or political linkages between Nan Madol and Leluh seem most unlikely.

The *saudeleurs* in some sense united all of Pohnpei. Their architectural monuments may have validated their august positions, as well as solidified the social system of ancient Pohnpei. The prehistoric architecture of Nan Madol is the living symbol of the social institutions that long ago brought the magnificent monuments into being.

4. KOSRAE

Perhaps the Micronesian landmark best known to Western mariners during the nineteenth century was the impressive stone city of Leluh on the island of Kosrae. Here in the six centuries preceding European contact a complex hierarchical society had developed. Its people erected an island city consisting of more than one hundred compounds, some surrounded by stone walls up to 21 feet high. The urban complex of Leluh was the administrative and ceremonial center of Kosrae, a 42.8-square-mile island some 340 miles southeast of Pohnpei.

One of the most beautiful islands in Micronesia, Kosrae rises majestically from the midst of a seemingly endless sea. Mount Fin-kol, the island's highest peak, towers 2,077 feet above the mountainous interior. Of volcanic origin, the mountains and escarpments are basalt. Outcropping boulders and prismatic basalt cliffs provided stones for building the impressive walls of Leluh. Most of the island is covered with luxuriant tropical forests fed by 185 inches of rain annually in coastal areas, while more than 300 inches of rain falls annually in the interiors. Many perennial streams and rivers flow down to the sea and in seven places breach the living coral reef that surrounds the island.

Mangrove swamps and sandy beaches line the shore within the reef. Fresh water rivers flow into Kosrae's three major harbors: Leluh Harbor on the east coast; Utwe Harbor, also known as Port Lottin, on the south coast; and Okaht Harbor on the northwest coast. Within the reef the lagoon is relatively narrow by Micronesian standards. At low tide it is shallow enough for wading in many places. At high tide the lagoon provides a protected waterway suitable for the navigation of rafts that carried large basaltic stones to Leluh and other architectural sites around the island.

Yenyen Islet lies in the shallow lagoon 360 feet north of Leluh. In the background are Mount Finkol to the left and Mount Motonte to the right.

Kosrae.

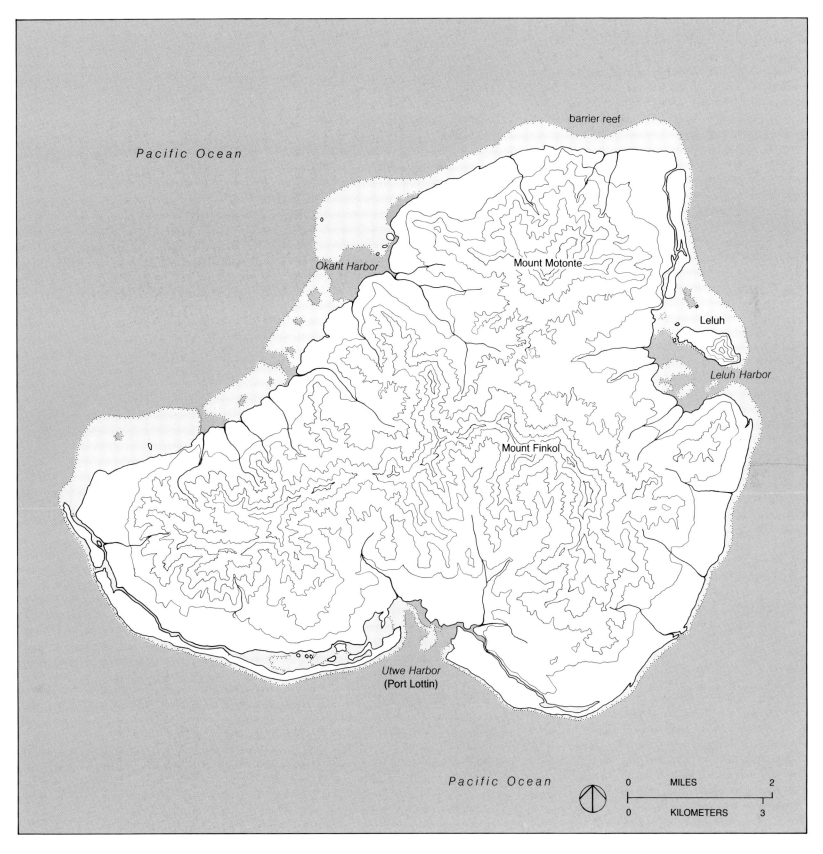

barrier reef

Pacific Ocean

Okaht Harbor

Mount Motonte

Leluh

Leluh Harbor

Mount Finkol

Utwe Harbor
(Port Lottin)

Pacific Ocean

| 0 | MILES | 2 |
| 0 | KILOMETERS | 3 |

The island city of Leluh lies on a shallow reef
some 1,600 feet from the east coast of Kosrae.

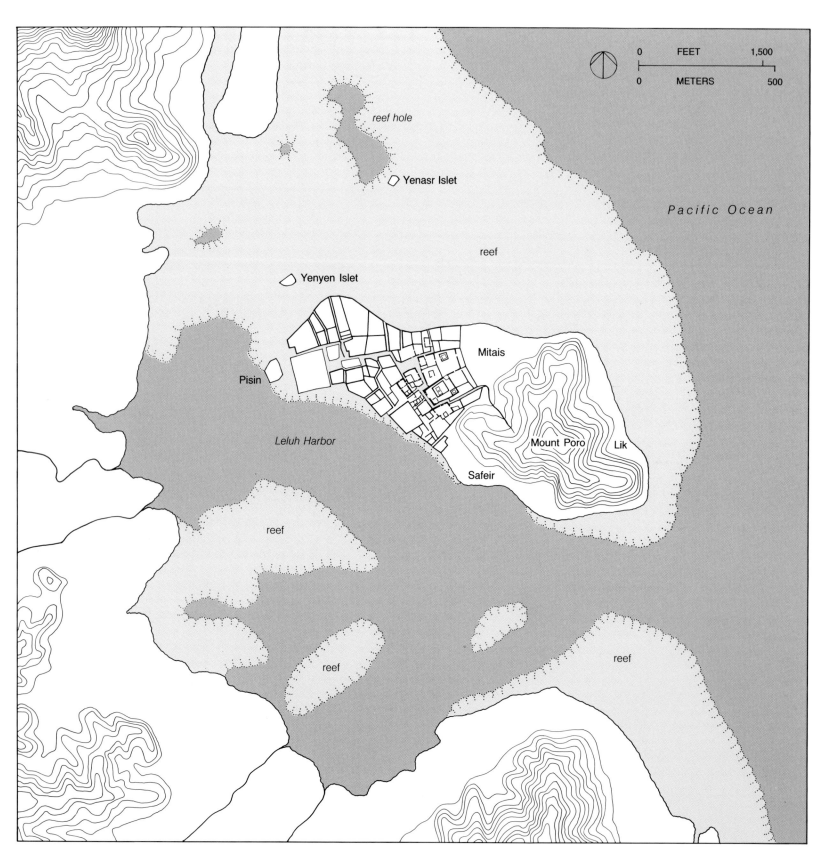

Pacific Ocean

reef hole

Yenasr Islet

reef

Yenyen Islet

Mitais

Pisin

Mount Poro   Lik

Leluh Harbor

Safeir

reef

reef

reef

reef

0   FEET   1,500
0   METERS   500

Typhoons occur less frequently on Kosrae than in the areas of Micronesia farther to the north and west. The favorable temperature, the rainfall, and the fertile soils combine to produce abundant natural foods. At the time of Western contact these included bananas, coconuts, taro, breadfruit, sugarcane, and citrus fruit. The reef abounds with several species of fish, mollusks, starfish, lobsters, crayfish, turtles, and crabs, including large mangrove crabs. The availability of abundant natural foods assured logistical support for the workers who built Leluh.

Hibiscus trees provided firewood and framing material for houses. Other common trees were banyan, mangrove, palms, pandanus, and probably bamboo. Fruit pigeons roosted in trees, but no pigs or dogs were found on prehistoric Kosrae. Early observers also noted several species of butterflies and birds, bats, lizards, wild chickens, ornamental flowers including orchids, fibers suitable for ropemaking, and rats. In fact, rats were numerous in the islands of prehistoric Micronesia.

The maximum population of the island before European contact probably was in the range of five to six thousand people. Of these perhaps fifteen hundred lived in Leluh. Although the largest settlement and the most extensive stone ruins are found on Leluh island, the remains of much lesser prehistoric architectural sites have been found elsewhere on Kosrae, including former house compounds surrounded by low stone walls, small house platforms, pavings, and enclosures (Cordy, 1983a).

LELUH AND ITS ENVIRONS

The island city of Leluh lies within the reef on the east coast of Kosrae, more than 1,600 feet from the closest point on the mainland shore. To the south is Leluh Harbor. A narrow pass through the coral reef connects the harbor to the open Pacific Ocean. European sailing vessels found that this harbor was easy to enter during the day because of prevailing winds from the east.

Leluh before 1250, the original island; 1250–1400, early expansion; 1400–1600, the building of the great walls; 1600–1650, consolidation of central Leluh (after Cordy, 1981).

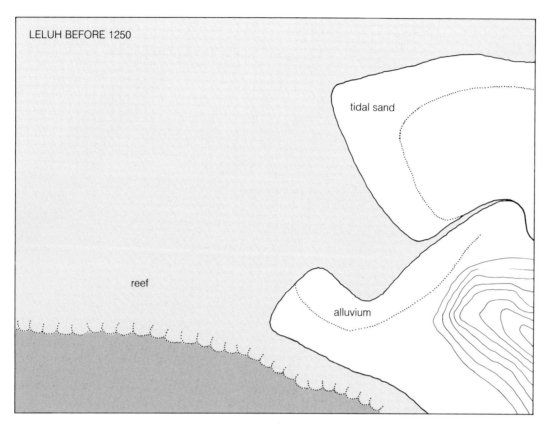

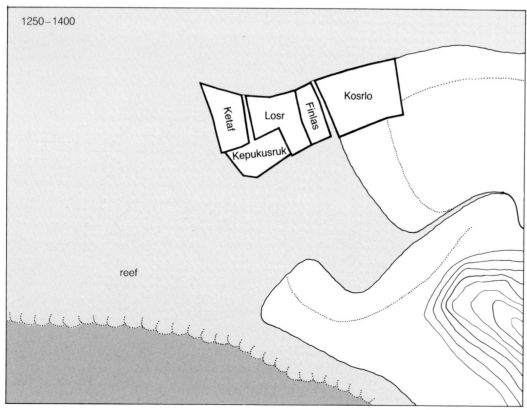

However, winds from the west blow only at night, rendering departure through the coral reef pass difficult and dangerous (Duperrey, 1828). The earliest European navigators to visit Kosrae anchored in Okaht Harbor, but the whaling ships that came later preferred to anchor in Leluh Harbor.

Yenyen Islet lies on the shallow reef 360 feet from Leluh's northwest shore. Yenasr Islet is located farther to the north next to a deep hole in the reef. The sand spit presently along the reef east of Leluh was created by a typhoon in 1905. Since the spit was not present at the time of the prehistoric city, it is omitted from the map shown here. Also omitted are other present-day features, such as the 1,800-foot runway for small aircraft north of Yenyen, the vehicular causeway that presently connects Leluh to the mainland, and recent fill that extends beyond the sea wall of the ancient island city.

At the time of European contact, Leluh was very nearly at the high point of its architectural development. Early visitors found a feudal state that was presided over by the king (*toḳosra*) of Kosrae (Cordy, 1981). The complex society had three levels below the king. All of the island's high chiefs (*lem fulat*) resided on Leluh with the king and led lives of leisure. The low chiefs, or land section managers (*mwetsuksuk*), supervised production on the main island and assured a constant flow of tribute to the high chiefs and the king. Land section managers also lived in the villages on Kosrae, although some also may have maintained residences in Leluh.

At least two-thirds of Leluh's inhabitants probably were commoners (*mwetsrisrik*). Most of them lived on the main island, where they gathered food, farmed, and fished. The king and high chiefs alone owned land, while the commoners had only land use rights and thus were peasants. The commoners typically lived in one of Kosrae's approximately fifty small villages dispersed around the island.

Famine resulting from the typhoon of 1800 may have reduced Kosrae's population by about 50 percent. By 1824 perhaps only five to eight hundred people lived in Leluh.

The island was politically unified and geographically isolated although it was very infrequently in contact with Pohnpei.

OBSERVATIONS AND RESEARCH

Information on the prehistoric architecture of Kosrae comes primarily from the remains themselves and from the accounts of early European visitors who were present when Leluh was at its pinnacle of development. Today relatively little of the original city remains. During the past century, modern Leluh has been built on top of most of the prehistoric city, leaving only a few of the compounds in nearly original condition.

Seawalls have been extended beyond the areas of original fill. Silt fills the canal in many places and nipa palms choke the former waterway in others. Leluh's commercial center and maritime port occupy the site of prehistoric Posral and several adjoining compounds. Recent preservation efforts fortunately have begun to protect the remains of the ancient island city.

In view of the present condition of remains, the accounts of early observers are essential for understanding more clearly the prehistoric architecture of Leluh. The ten-day visit of the French corvette *La Coquille* in 1824 and a three-week visit by the Russian corvette *Senyavin* in 1827–1828 resulted in the earliest informative accounts.

During the mid-nineteenth century, whaling ships frequented Kosrae's ports, and American missionaries introduced new ideas to the island. Eventually, a Western-style monetary system replaced the feudal economic system, Christianity was accepted as the new religion, and democracy replaced feudalism. The power of the king and high chiefs waned, and prehistoric Leluh declined as the new city emerged.

Claimed by Spain in the sixteenth century, Kosrae was sold in 1899 to Germany. In 1910 the South Sea Expedition produced detailed maps of Leluh, gathered artifacts from the site, and recorded Kosraean legends and recollections of elderly residents who still remembered specific features of the ancient city (Sarfert, 1919). Considering the brevity of the expedition's stay on Kos-

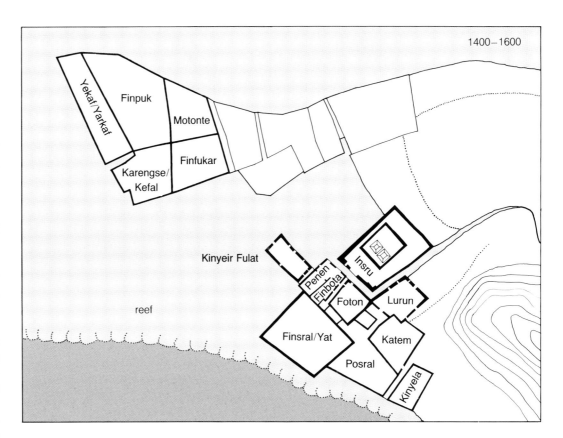

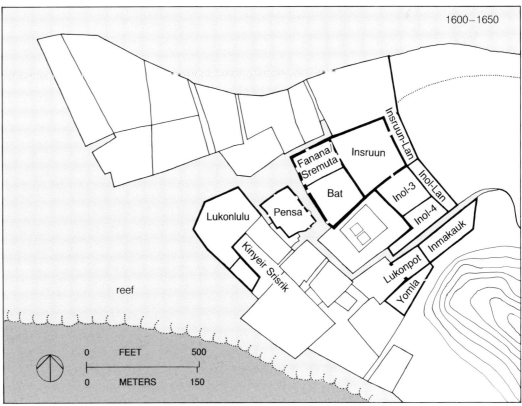

91

rae, the German records were remarkably accurate. During the Japanese administration (1914–1945), several tombs were excavated and a few artifacts were collected at Leluh.

Following World War II, the United States assumed trusteeship over the island under a United Nations mandate. Kosrae recently joined the Federated States of Micronesia, a self-governing political entity in a compact of free association with the United States. In the past few years archaeological investigations have intensified on Kosrae, greatly expanding our knowledge of prehistoric architecture on Leluh.

THE EVOLUTION OF LELUH

Most of the island city was built on artificial fill over a shallow reef in the lagoon west of Leluh Island. Apparently, construction activity occurred over the period of perhaps A.D. 1250 to 1850. Radiocarbon dating indicates that Leluh's first compounds were built on artificial fill between 1250 and 1400, but that the original island was inhabited earlier. The building of artificial islets at Nan Madol on Pohnpei appears to have occurred during the earlier period of Leluh's construction.

Before 1250: The Original Island

The highest point of Leluh Island is 363-foot-high Mount Poro. The eastern edge of the island is protected by the coral reef, and from the slopes of the wooded mountain a fresh water stream flows down to the west. Prior to the expansion of Leluh, sand fringed the western shore and alluvial deposits occurred along the stream. A fresh water swamp suitable for taro cultivation was fed by the stream. As Leluh expanded in succeeding centuries, alluvium was used as fill material on some of the nearby artificial islets. Basalt outcroppings on the original island of Leluh probably provided some of the stones that were used to build the ancient city, but most of the megaliths appear to have come from quarries on the main island of Kosrae.

1250–1400: Early Expansion

The Kosraeans gave names to each of the compounds and areas of Leluh. Finlas, Losr, and Ketaf seem to have been built and occupied first in the sequence of westward expansion. The mixed coral and basalt foundation wall style of these compounds suggests that they were conceived and executed as a single unit. Kosrlo, built directly on the tidal sand closest to the original island, also probably was occupied early in the expansion sequence. Alluvial deposits from the stream may have begun to accumulate southwest of Losr and Ketaf. Here Kepukusruk was added and the last compound of the initial expansion was completed. Apparently no compounds were enclosed by stone walls at this time. About 1400 Kosrae's several societies became united under the leadership of Leluh, thus enabling the rapid expansion of the island city (Cordy, 1981).

1400–1600: Building of the Great Walls

The largest and most impressive walls of Leluh were constructed between 1400 and 1600. The walls were built of stacked prismatic basalt up to 21 feet high. The highest walls enclosed Posral, the royal residential compound. Where the walls faced the open lagoon or habor, sturdy foundations of immense basaltic stones were carefully placed and fitted. The construction of these walls required skillful planning and substantial logistical support. These factors clearly suggest that the complex society of prehistoric Kosrae was functioning by not later than the fifteenth century.

The southern expansion area of this period contains the largest walls. The compounds of Kinyela, Posral, Finsral/Yat, Penem, Finbota, Foton, and Katem were built partly on the original shore of Leluh and partly out over the shallow reef.

The magnificent walls of the Lurun and Kinyeir Fulat dwelling compounds share common architectural characteristics and probably were built at about the same time. The stacked prismatic walls of these compounds attained heights of 17 to 19 feet,

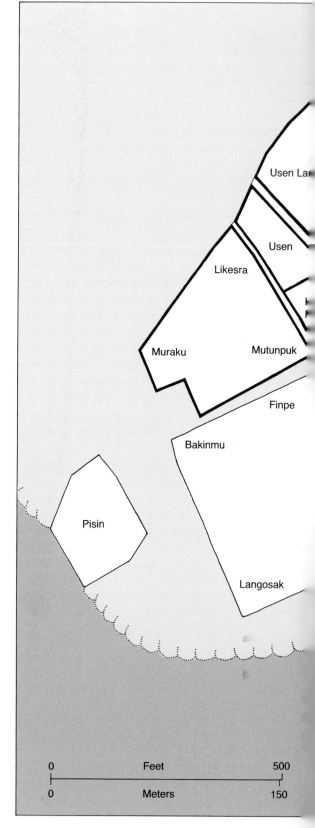

1650–1800, the completion of Leluh (after Cordy, 1981). The map shows Leluh as it probably appeared when the first recorded European visitors arrived in 1824.

Metais

Katem
Kosra 2

Yepangin

Finkulkul

Ineoluk

Naunik

Finmong

Kenwen

Yatkaf

Bot

Yurlap

Mutunkin

Untan

Mutunsoik

Kalung

reef

Safeir

Leluh Harbor

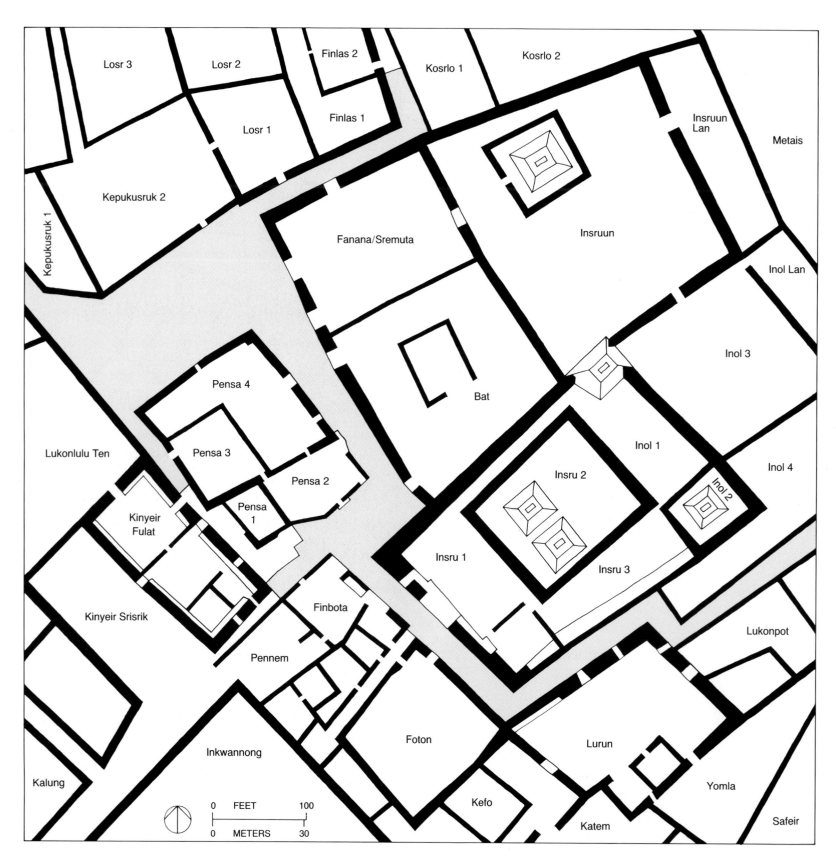

Central Leluh.

94

the highest now standing in Leluh. Fortunately, these walls continue to exist today in very nearly their original configurations. Nowhere are to be found better examples of the architectural achievements of ancient Kosrae. The western corner of Lurun abuts the eastern corner of Foton, which had been built earlier. At this time Kinyeir Fulat projected into the lagoon with seawalls on three sides. This seems to confirm the Kosraean legend related to Hambruch in 1910 that Kinyeir Fulat originally faced the sea (Sarfert, 1919).

The sacred and royal tomb compound group of Insru and Inol was constructed on artificial fill north of the canal that serves to drain the Leluh stream. Some of the high walls of these compounds have unique truncated coral caps. Insru and Inol remain today in relatively good condition, although continuing preservation efforts are required and accurate restoration would be desirable.

A second major construction area during this period was the western extension of Leluh's northern peninsula, adding Motonte, Finfukar, Karengse/Kefal, Finpuk, and Yekaf/Yarkaf. Here the compound walls were of dominantly coral construction up to 6 feet in height. Motonte is the name of Kosrae's second highest mountain as well as a compound in Leluh. Perhaps the names of some of the compounds refer to geographical areas on the main island, possibly districts owned by chiefs residing in compounds with corresponding names. Other examples are the references of the Yat compound to Tafeyat on the main island, Pennem to Innem, Kinyela to Yela, and Kepukusruk to Pukusruk.

By the end of the sixteenth century a shallow bay had been created near the center of western Leluh, and the high walls of Kinyeir Fulat projected into the bay. The three basic elements of the city plan now were present: compounds enclosed by walls, a canal through the center, and streets interconnecting the compounds and boat landings.

1600–1650:
Consolidation of Central Leluh

The infilling of Leluh's central core probably occurred between 1600 and 1650. Fan-

ana/Sremuta, Bat, Insruun, eastern Inol, and the adjoining compounds formed a single architectural unit with walls 14 to 16 feet high. Apparently, Insruun initially was a residential compound. Its royal tomb and funeral feast house seem to be later additions.

The compound walls of Inmakauk and Lukonpot extended the canal farther to the east. To this group Yomla was added. Pensa was constructed north of Kinyeir Fulat, and a short street interconnecting two canal landings was created between these compounds. Kinyeir Srisrik and Lukonlulu extended the center of Leluh to the west. Sarfert (1919) recorded that Lukonlulu meant "the edge of the lagoon."

This period marked the end of the building of high walled compounds at Leluh and seems to have been a time of consolidation rather than of major expansion. The new additions appear to have been supporting units for the major compounds constructed during the preceding two centuries. New dwelling compounds were added but no new sacred or mortuary compounds were built. During this time wall construction changed to round basalt with large to medium size stones. However, stacked prismatic basalt construction continued to be used at the outside corners of compounds and at entrance portals.

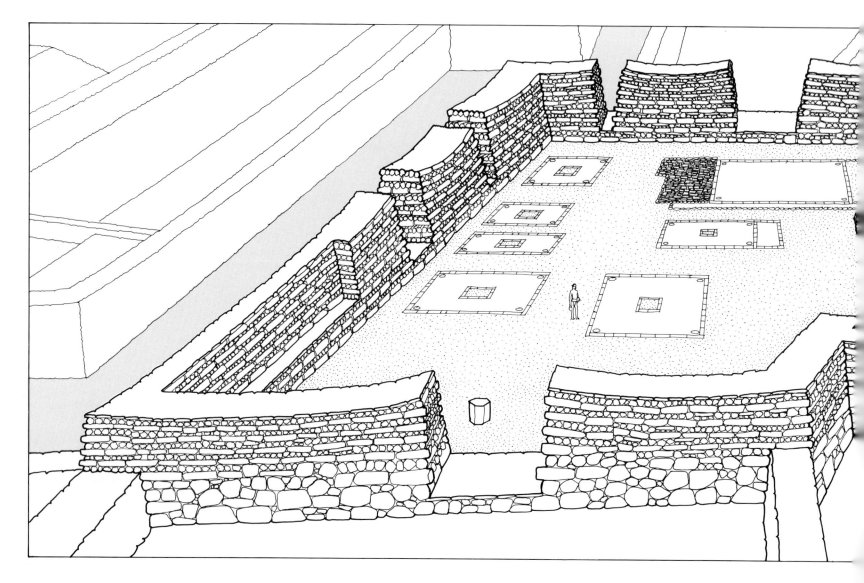

Aerial view of Lurun from the southwest. A street beginning in the foreground leads a short distance to Posral, the king's compound. The canal borders Lurun to the upper left.

1650–1800: The Completion of Leluh

The final phase of construction at Leluh extended the island city to its western terminus on Pisin Islet. The seven compounds of the Bot-Kenwen group seem to have been added between 1650 and 1700. The Mutunkin compound, which forms the southwestern corner of Leluh, probably was added next. Mutunkin's large basalt foundation would have protected later additions from storms and erosion. The Mutunpuk, Katem/Kosra, and Usen·block may have been constructed about 1770. The canal islets of Naunik and Yepangin, probably built about the

same time, were the last compounds to be built at Leluh. At this time walls up to 4 feet high were built of mixed coral on foundations of mixed coral and basalt or round basalt (Cordy, 1981).

Other additions during this period probably included Insruun's royal tomb and funeral feast house and the islets of Pisin, Yenyen, and Yenasr. Radio carbon dating indicates that Pisin was built within ninety years of 1660 (Marck, 1975). The foundation styles of all three islets are similar, and they probably were built about the same time. Yenasr's reef hole, however, probably was used much earlier as a final repository for remains brought from the royal tombs.

By 1800 Leluh had reached the pinnacle of its development. Its compounds extended half a mile west from the original island and measured almost a third of a mile from north to south. The population of Kosrae may have reached as many as six thousand people, of whom possibly fifteen hundred lived in Leluh. The island city and nearby Pisin, Yenyen, and Yenasr islets contained more than one hundred walled compounds, including seventeen sacred compounds, three royal tomb compounds, and an unknown number of unwalled areas where commoners lived.

A seawall surrounded the city and protected the artificial fill. Early observers reported that the seawall rose 5 or 6 feet above

sea level. In some areas the seawall was built up as high as 6 feet above the artificial fill, while in other places it probably was lower or flush with the level of fill.

A canal more than 3,000 feet long ran through the center of Leluh. Navigable throughout at high tide, the canal system gave maritime access to many of the compounds and numerous boat landings. Tribute of food and goods from the land sections on Kosrae were brought by boat to Leluh daily.

Walled streets, often 15 to 20 feet wide, interconnected the compounds and boat landings. Most of the streets were paved, usually with the flat coral stones on a foun-

dation of mixed basalt and coral. Today, however, the streets more frequently are unpaved and often are muddy at high tide and after rain showers.

Within the city lived members of Kosrae's four social strata: the king, high chiefs, low chiefs or land section managers, and commoners. The king resided in Posral surrounded by walls 18 and 21 feet high, the highest in Leluh. The royal compound was subdivided by lower internal walls. The largest compound in Leluh, Posral encompassed an area of perhaps 71,000 square feet, the size of one and one-half football fields. Near the royal residence were several important sacred compounds, the largest concentra-

tion in Leluh. This suggests a close relationship between the king's secular and sacred positions in Kosraean society.

High chiefs, of whom there were probably about twenty by 1800, lived mostly in central Leluh. Low chiefs, possibly fifty in number, may have lived in the remaining areas of Leluh. They also maintained residences in the land sections they managed on Kosrae. Commoners who served the king and chiefs resided in the unwalled areas of Lik, Mitais, and Safeir. The large majority of Kosrae's commoners resided on the main island.

Aerial view of Kinyeir Fulat from the southeast. In the foreground lies the Kinyeir-Penem street; to the right, Pensa's compounds and the canal.

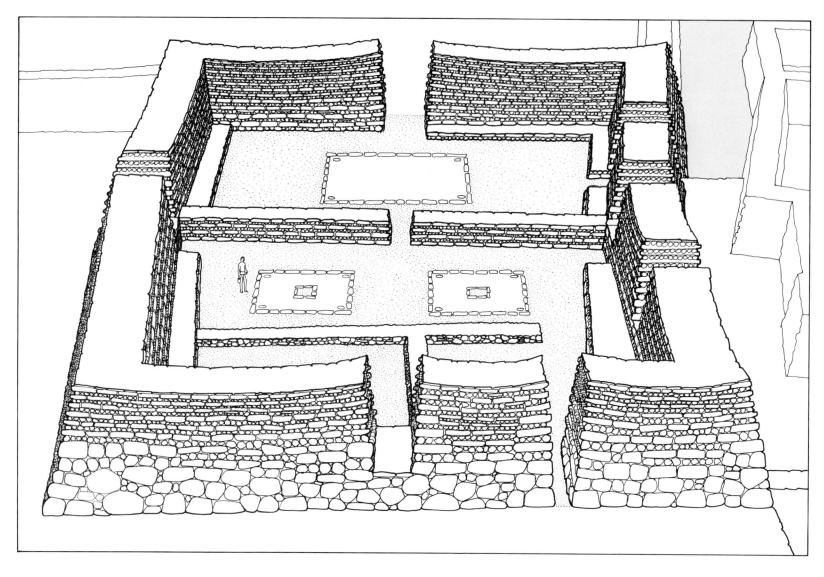

1800–1850: The Decline of Leluh

About 1800 a severe typhoon apparently struck Kosrae with winds of possibly two hundred miles per hour. Mutunkin's seawall was destroyed, and its shore was eroded perhaps 30 to 60 feet. The typhoon seems to have damaged irreparably the Insruun tomb and to have swept away entirely several islets and other geographical features in the vicinity of Leluh. Pisin and at least part of the Mutunkin block may have been abandoned after this storm.

Between 1800 and 1850 the Inol wall tomb probably was built to replace the Insruun tomb destroyed by the typhoon of 1800. The

Kefal tomb in the Yarkaf compound probably also was added during this time.

LIVING IN LELUH: AN EARLY ACCOUNT

Early French (1824) and Russian (1827–28) visitors left several valuable records of life in the ancient city. The Europeans approached Leluh in boats or by wading across the shallow lagoon. Behind the city's encircling seawall they saw the stone walls of Leluh's compounds, which ranged in height from a few feet to more than 20 feet. Above the walls rose a limited number of banana, coconut, and breadfruit trees and the graceful, saddle-shaped roofs of hundreds of resi-

dences and feast houses. Some of the upward-curving thatched roofs attained heights of 35 to 40 feet. The immense stone walls that lined the streets of Leluh amazed early visitors (Ritter and Ritter, 1982).

In 1827 Capt. Fyedor Petrovich Lütke visited the residential compound of a high chief, Sipé. Lütke recorded his observations and prepared a plan of the compound. His verbal account refers to the letters shown on the plan, such as the letter *L* placed at the ends and corners of the compound's walls. The following is a translation of his account.

The residence of the principal urosse [chief] is composed of several houses.

The detailed description of the habitation of the urosse Sipé will give a good idea of all the others.

L,L,L are walls constructed of huge rocks, which surround all the residences of the urosse. It is rather strange that although Yat [an area in south central Leluh], where, as we have already said, live most of the urosse, is the property of Sipé, the house of each urosse is surrounded by a similar wall. Coming from the street, very muddy, to mention in passing, first one finds a house (A) which contains what we would call salons, drawing rooms, dining rooms, etc., and which I call, to distinguish it from the others, the eating house.

It is there that the master passes the largest part of the day, ordinarily seated to the left of the entry in A. There, breadfruit is cooked, séka [saka, a ceremonial beverage] is prepared and served; it is there that he receives visitors, placing distinguished persons next to him, and the others in a circle toward B,B,B; the less important, and those who are occupied in some task which prevents them from taking part in the general conversation, sit at the other end (C,C,C). There from morning to night, flows a concourse of people who, during our stay, were ordinarily so numerous that most of them were obliged to remain outside the house. A wall made of partitions of split bamboo (K,K,K) separates the interior apartments of the urosse, where no one has entry except him and the people who are immediately attached to his house, among whose numbers we were counted. Entering by the door [M], one finds on each side a similar partition behind which are two separate houses. C is the residence, during the day, of the first wife of Sipé; the second wife lives in D. We always saw in B a large number of children, who were not even Sipé's but who belonged, in some way, to his family. There also slept his son, a nursing child, born of his favorite wife, under the surveillance of an old maid. I do not know what house E was for. After having passed across the corridor, one arrives at a little court, where there are three houses—two (F,G) about the same size as the others and the third, H, a lot smaller. Sipé ate and passed the night in G; Mrs. Sipé slept in H with her daughter of four years; it was also there that the friends of Mrs. Sipé gathered and played different games. F was the house which was designated for us, which we willingly inhabited and where we even transported our baidarke [small, portable boat]. In I[J] was one of those stones on which they pounded séka but which we never saw

used. In O was an enclosure for the sow which Captain Duperrey had left to them. All the space in K,K was covered with very clean bamboo laths except the areas N,N where several coconut trees, banana trees and breadfruit trees, forming a little domestic garden, agreeably varied the interesting family tableau. The entire compound was seventy paces long, thirty wide.

The description of the houses took us only a little time; the inventory of that which they contain did not cost us much time either, for they are almost entirely empty. Among a people who lead such a simple and monotonous life, the household articles can soon be counted.

In the middle of each house hangs from the ceiling a type of large, thin tray with low sides, serving to shelter food, etc. from the rats. In two or three other places are suspended other small trays, or simply poles with hooks on which one could hang small articles of all sorts, such as coconut shells which they use to drink out of and which are sometimes decorated with a very clean cloth, the tols [wide belts of fabric woven from banana fibers, Kosraean clothing worn around the hips], small fishing equipment, etc. That is also where they placed the small trifles they received from us. A trough made from breadfruit wood, three feet long and two and half feet wide, made in the form of a dingy, in which they brought the water for preparing séka, is an indispensable article in each house; when it is not being used for this purpose, it serves them as a chair. Some tubs for various uses and some small looms for weaving tols complete the furniture of the houses. (Ritter and Ritter, 1982:117–120)

The sow that Capt. Louis Isidore Duperrey had left three and a half years earlier was believed to be pregnant. This belief proved to be erroneous; there still was only one pig on Kosrae when the Russian expedition arrived. In gratitude for the Kosraeans' hospitality during his visit, Captain Lütke left them a sow that was indeed pregnant. Unfortunately, today many of the surviving compounds in Leluh are used as pigpens. Stones taken from the compound walls and floors have been used to build low walls across the compounds' entries to contain the pigs. The rooting and trampling of pigs further accelerate the deterioration of the architectural monuments.

CENTRAL LELUH

"Our arrival in Lele created intense joy. Men, women, and children rushed in great crowds in our footsteps. This astonishment was centered primarily on the color of our skin, which they touched with their hands and faces, at the same time emitting new cries of admiration. It was thus that they escorted us to the urosse-tone, or principal chief, in front of whom they knelt, at the same time keeping such a silence that we were strongly impressed by the respect that they had for his person" (Duperrey, 1828, in Ritter and Ritter, 1982:14).

The best preserved and most impressive remains of the island city today are found in the central core. Here are ancient streets, high stone walls, compounds serving several purposes, the central canal, boat landings, house foundations, stone benches or terraces, pounding stones, and other architectural features.

Dwelling compounds in Central Leluh were enclosed by high stone walls, often of basalt. Posral's walls originally attained a height of 21 feet. The walls of Lurun and Kinyeir Fulat were in the range of 17 to 19 feet high; those of Bat and Fanana/Sremuta, 15 to 17 feet. The compounds were entered from streets, boat landings, or adjoining compounds. Chiefs' dwelling compounds contained several houses. Lütke noted eight houses in Sipé's compound and Hambruch recorded seven for Lurun (Hambruch, 1919).

Feast houses were located at or near main entrances of compounds. They typically contained four to five times the areas of private houses and ranged in size from 900 to 2,000 square feet, but usually contained from 1,400 to 1,600 square feet. The funeral feast houses of Insru and Insruun, however, contained 5,000 square feet each. Their floors usually were paved with rectangular basalt, sometimes outlined by prismatic basalt. Coral paving was less frequently used for feast house floors, although Kinyeir Fulat's feast house was paved with coral.

The frame structure of a typical feast house probably was built of mangrove and hibiscus, and the floor likely was of bamboo. Candles consisting of copra (dried coconut meat) on stakes provided illumination. A hollow log on the floor may have served for pounding taro and as a drum for dancing. Often near the center of the feast house was a fire pit perhaps 5 feet square. From the rafters a storage tray probably was suspended by a rope to protect the contents from rats. Shelves also provided storage for such items as woven belts, adzes, clubs, shell trumpets, shell valuables, trade goods, drum sticks, baskets, bananas, and *saka.* Canoes sometimes were stored just above head height in the feast house (Cordy, 1981).

Outside the feast house, food was prepared by servants who pounded taro and other foods with hand-sized stones on large flat stones, peeled vegetables with shell peelers, removed bones from fish, and extracted meat from mollusks. Food was cooked in earth ovens lined with stones. *Saka,* a ceremonial beverage similar to *sakau* on Pohnpei, was prepared on pounding stones. Food and *saka* were consumed in the feast house.

Residences in a typical dwelling compound were located away from the feast house in areas remote from the main entrance. Bamboo fences, sometimes on low stone walls, formed private yards around the residences. Gates gave access to yards. The sizes of houses at Leluh ranged from 50 to 650 square feet, but most were about 150 to 300 square feet in area. Their floors frequently were paved with rectangular coral stones.

The furnishings of the residences were more modest than those of the feast house. Here the family slept, women ate their meals, and limited *saka* preparation may have occurred. Earth ovens and pounding stones are rarely found near private dwellings.

Courtyards were kept very clean and often were covered with bamboo and mats. Small gardens for the cultivation of coconuts, bananas, breadfruit, or taro were frequently found in yards. The family's dead seem to have been buried in small cemetery areas within the compounds.

The functions and characteristics of Leluh's seventeen sacred compounds are not clearly understood, but they probably contained spirit houses and priest houses. Spirit houses were small in size but their original appearances are unknown. Priest houses apparently were periodically refurbished to serve as temporary residences during special occasions, such as major annual feasts or the coronation or funeral of a king. A mound and an altar were found in one sacred compound, and three others have sunken ground levels. Sacred compounds do not show evidence of prolonged occupation.

Leluh's three tomb compounds—Insru, Inol, and Insruun—were enclosed by walls and contained coral stone tombs in the shape of truncated pyramids with small central crypts lined with stacked prismatic basalt.

Lurun

The high chief's dwelling compound of Lurun measures approximately 125 × 155 feet and contains some 19,400 square feet. The reconstructed drawing presented here shows a perspective view from the southwest. The walls, 17 to 19 feet high, were constructed of large prismatic basalt stones stacked on foundations of huge block basalt. They are among the largest constructed at Leluh and today are relatively well preserved. The reconstructions shown here are based on my observations of the site in 1984, information provided by Ross Cordy (1981 and 1986), and the report of the South Sea Expedition (Sarfert, 1919).

Seven entries give access to Lurun. In the foreground of the perspective is the entry from a short street leading to the king's residence in Posral. Near the entry is the king's sitting block, a multilateral basalt prism taller than it is wide. Along the canal to the left are three service entries. At these portals the wall exceeds 18 feet in thickness at the base. Lurun's main entry is shown toward the upper center of the perspective and in the accompanying photograph. The main portal opens into Lukonpot to the northeast. To the right are two smaller entries giving access from the southeast.

Lurun's main entry displays several distinctive architectural characteristics. The stacked basaltic prisms extend deeply back into the wall at the corners of the portal. The wall tapers inward slightly on both sides as it rises. The width of the opening is greater at the top than at the bottom, and the sizes of stones diminish toward the top of the wall. The upward sloping prismatic basalt stones flanking the entry give the appearance that the wall is swooping upward. They seem to celebrate the event of entering or leaving the compound. The portal's threshold, which is raised about 2.5 feet for the full thickness of the wall, clearly separates the interior space of the compound from the space outside.

Lurun once seems to have had seven houses located on the flat coral pavement that originally covered about two-thirds of the compound's floor (Hambruch, 1919). A large feast house lay directly in front of the main entry. The foundation of the approximately 1,420-square-foot structure was outlined in prismatic basalt. It had four corner posts, an earthen floor, and no fire pit. Nearby were several *saka* pounding stones. The area northwest of the feast house was paved with rectangular basalt.

Near the center of Lurun were three dwellings, each containing four corner posts, a central fire pit, and a coral-paved foundation outlined with prismatic basalt. These ranged in size from about 650 to 310 square feet. The remaining three residences, which were located along the canal wall, ranged in area from roughly 340 to 220 square feet. A low terrace or bench was recessed into the west end of the canal wall some 3.5 feet above the compound's floor. Several sections of pathways outlined with basalt also were found in the paved area of Lurun.

The southeastern third of the compound's floor was unpaved. A 5-foot-high coral wall near the center of the unpaved area enclosed a small cemetery (Hambruch, 1919). The remaining unpaved areas may have been used for small gardens or earth ovens.

Kinyeir Fulat

Kinyeir Fulat was a high chief's dwelling compound enclosed by walls up to 19 feet high. The source of the wall's huge basalt stones probably was a quarry near Utwe (John, 1984). The reconstructed drawing presented here is a perspective view from

the southeast. Fortunately, Kinyeir Fulat is one of the best preserved compounds remaining in Leluh and one of the easiest to interpret in terms of its original function and appearance.

At its time of completion Kinyeir Fulat projected into the shallow bay then west of Leluh. Water surrounded it on three sides. Primarily a residential compound, it may have served as a fortress in times of strife and also may have been used for ceremonies in its earlier days. Slightly smaller in area than Lurun, Kinyeir Fulat contains some 15,330 square feet within its 82 × 187-foot walls.

The Kinyeir-Penem street, which appears in the foreground of the reconstructed perspective, widens from 10 to 16 feet as it approaches the canal landing shown in the lower right. Originally, Leluh's south shore was about 300 feet to the left. At the lower left, the street is half as wide as the walls are high. Like most of the paved streets in ancient Leluh, the Kinyeir-Penem street is paved with flat coral on a foundation of mixed basalt and coral. The flat paving stones are not set in grout and many rock slightly under foot pressure. This produces a hollow ringing sound as pedestrians traverse the present-day remains of Leluh.

Four of Kinyeir Fulat's seven entrances are walled up to the height of 5 to 6.5 feet. The remaining northernmost two portals were the main entries. The seventh entry into Kinyeir Fulat is illustrated in the accompanying photograph, which shows a view into Kinyeir Fulat from the Kinyeir-Penem street. The portal is only about eighteen inches wide at its base. To the right in the perspective drawing is a short street, some 13 to 16 feet wide with canal landings at both ends. Part of Pensa's four dwelling compounds appear to the upper right.

The floor of Kinyeir Fulat was paved with flat coral and was divided into four courtyards by low interior walls. A feast house containing approximately 1,120 square feet probably was located in the north courtyard, near two main entrances (Cordy, 1981). Near the feast house were found eight *saka* pounding stones, two food pounding stones, and the remains of earth ovens and shell food. In

Aerial view of Insru and Inol from the southwest. In the center of the mortuary and sacred compounds are Leluh's unique royal tombs shaped like twin truncated pyramids.

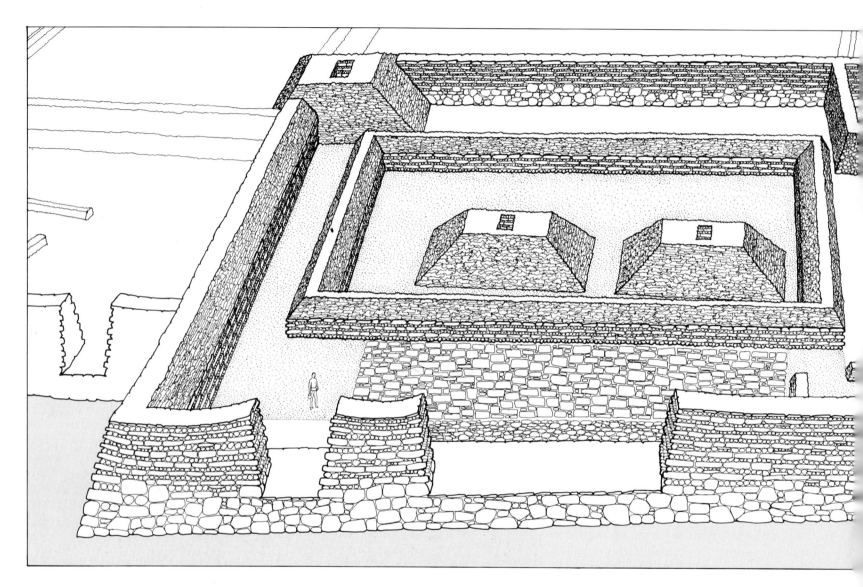

1910 Hambruch (1919) recorded a 5 foot high by 3 foot wide wall separating the north and central courtyards.

Probably two dwellings, each perhaps 430 square feet in area, occupied the central courtyard. A roughly 12 inch high by 32 inch wide coral wall defined two small courtyards in the southeast and southwest corners of the compound. Bamboo fences extending above head height may have been located originally on top of the low coral walls. These courtyards contained dwelling houses whose respective floor areas were perhaps 355 and 300 square feet. An approximately 16-inch-high terrace or bench engaged most of the interior walls of Kinyeir Fulat.

Insru and Inol

Primarily a mortuary compound, part of the Insru group probably also functioned as a sacred compound related to funeral practices. The enclosing 15-to-17-foot-high walls are constructed of stacked prismatic basalt. Several of these walls contained a unique cap of truncated coral. The reconstructed drawing presents Insru and Inol as a single architectural entity, viewed from the southwest. Together, Insru, Inol 1, and Inol 2 contain approximately 58,850 square feet, an area larger than a football field.

A narrow service entrance and a large main entry portal give access to Insru from the canal. Due to the sacred nature of Insru, access probably was limited to priests, the king, members of the Kosraean nobility, and their servants. Directly in front of the main entry is a large area paved with rectangular basaltic stones. Here was located a funeral feast house containing possibly 5,000 square feet, one of the two largest wooden structures in ancient Leluh. Its dimensions were perhaps 56 × 89 feet. Nearby are two *saka* pounding stones, one of which measures 4 feet in diameter and is the largest pounding stone in Leluh. Also nearby are the remains of earth ovens that were used to prepare food during royal funeral ceremonies. Insru's forecourt contains about 14,000 square

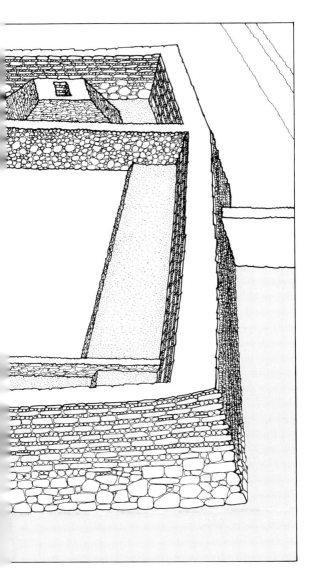

feet, an area slightly smaller than Lurun or Kinyeir Fulat.

The forecourt is mostly paved with flat coral. A 20-inch-high terrace or bench engages part of the southeast and southwest walls. A low coral wall encloses a small courtyard in the forecourt's south corner shown to the lower right in the perspective. Here probably was located a temporary priest's house, perhaps 590 square feet in area (Cordy, 1981).

In the center of the Insru group is a unique 20,400-square-foot mortuary compound containing twin royal tombs. The 7-foot-high surrounding wall has no entrance. The compound's floor is paved with flat coral and

The crypt of the Inol wall tomb is lined with stacked prismatic basalt of alternating header and stretcher courses carefully fitted together.

some basalt. Shaped like truncated pyramids, both tombs have small central crypts lined with small stacked prismatic basalt.

Southeast of Insru's central mortuary compound is an 11,880-square-foot sacred compound related to mortuary practices. The floor of this compound probably was originally paved. The floor shows no evidence of house foundations or pounding stones and very little shell food remains. Along the canal wall is a roughly 20-inch-high terrace that diminishes in width from about 20 to 15 feet.

A 200-foot-long street leads from Insru to Inol along the northwest side of the Insru mortuary compound. To the left is the dwelling compound of Bat. The roughly 10-foot-wide street terminates at the unusual Inol tomb built in part on top of the Inol and Insruun walls.

Like the other royal tombs in Leluh, Inol's wall tomb is shaped like a truncated pyramid and contains a small central crypt lined with small stacked prismatic basalt. Apparently, this was the last tomb to be constructed at Leluh. It may have been a replacement for the Insruun tomb that the typhoon of 1800 destroyed.

Inol's wall tomb lacks an enclosing wall and seems to have been constructed hastily. Flat coral paving stones apparently were removed from the nearby walls of Insruun to build the wall tomb. This would have been the least labor intensive method of constructing a traditional royal tomb, an important factor in view of Kosrae's dramatic population decline shortly after 1800. Utilizing the corner of existing walls substantially reduces the quality of stones required to construct a traditional tomb.

The mortuary compound of Inol is about 7,360 square feet in area. Its now unpaved floor consists mostly of old reef sand. The floor contains no remains of house foundations, earth ovens, shell food, or pounding stones, clearly suggesting Inol's role as a mortuary compound.

The east end of Inol contains the fourth royal tomb of the Insru group. In the center of the approximately 3,900-square-foot walled enclosure is a truncated pyramid. It has a central crypt similar in size and features to the other royal tombs of Leluh. The enclosing wall contains no entrance.

Little is known of burial practices in old Leluh. In 1852 the Reverend Luther Gulick observed a Kosraean burial and noted: "Their burial custom is: after death to anoint the body with cocoanut oil, then to carefully wrap it with mats and bind it from head to foot with colored cordage. Within two or three days it is buried in a grave and left for about three months when it is dug up, the bones are carefully washed and tied together and then sunk in a particular spot in the harbor" (Gulick, 1861, in Cordy, 1981:131). Gulick did not indicate where the body was buried initially or where in the harbor the final interment occurred.

Most likely, only the kings were buried temporarily in one of the royal tombs (saru), while their wives and relatives were buried in Posral. Chiefs and commoners probably were buried within their own compounds. Understanding that the nobility was separated from the lower echelons of society during life, it seems unlikely that all were interred finally in the same part of the reef hole north of Yenasr Islet, where the kings' remains probably were placed. The remains of low chiefs and commoners probably were interred in another part of the Yenasr reef hole or elsewhere in the waters around Leluh (Cordy, 1981).

The central crypt of the Inol wall tomb is typical of the crypts in all four of Leluh's royal tombs. The long axis of the crypt is oriented from northeast to southwest. Carefully laid, stacked prismatic stones line the crypt. These remain today in excellent condition, unlike most of Leluh's surviving stone walls. The alternating basalt headers and stretchers were skillfully fitted and laid without mortar.

The crypt is about 3 feet wide by 8 feet long and 7 feet deep. The floor of the crypt is perhaps 18 inches above the level of the paving around the tomb. The bones of a dog were found with the remains of an adult male in one of the royal crypts (Hambruch, 1919). The last interment apparently occurred after European contact and the last

royal remains never were transferred to the Yenasr reef hole.

The nature of possible funeral ceremonies on Yenasr Islet is unclear. Today the islet is heavily eroded. Paved with flat coral, the islet seems to have been originally rectangular in plan, perhaps about 80 × 110 feet. Ross Cordy (1981) found no internal walls or house foundations on Yenasr. He noted, however, fire-burnt rock, rectangular blocks of *Tradacna* (large bivalve shells), shell food remains, and moderate amounts of turtle carapace, all of which are thought to have been related to some type of mortuary ceremony.

Insruun, Bat, and Fanana/Sremuta

Shortly after 1600 the high chiefs' dwelling compounds of Insruun, Bat, and Fanana/Sremuta were added to Central Leluh. Evidently, Insruun later was converted into a mortuary compound by adding the tomb and funeral feast house. Insruun was built on the tidal sand of the original island, while Bat and Fanana/Sremuta were constructed on artificial fill in the shallow lagoon. They were the last high-wall compounds built at Leluh.

Primarily of round basalt construction, the Bat and Fanana/Sremuta walls rose up to 17 feet in height above the canal level. The roughly 3-foot-high wall between Bat and Fanana/Sremuta was constructed of coral. Exterior wall portals and corners were reinforced with stacked prismatic basalt.

One of Leluh's largest compounds, Insruun was roughly square in plan and contained an area of some 68,900 square feet, second in size only to Posral. The Insruun royal tomb may have been the largest in Leluh. Its surrounding wall created a mortuary compound with an entrance facing the Fanana/Sremuta portal. An entrance through the northeast wall of Insruun gave access to Insruun Lan. To the southeast a third portal opened into Inol 3.

Between Insruun's tomb and the Fanana/Sremuta entrance was a funeral feast house containing perhaps 5,000 square feet, one of the two largest wood structures in old Leluh. Its dimensions and size were similar to those

of the Insru funeral feast house. Both measured about 56 × 89 feet, and both had floors paved with basalt. Three *saka* pounding stones were found in the basalt paving at Insruun. A temporary priest's house of possibly 470 square feet may have been located in the south corner of the compound where flat coral paving has been found. The remaining large area of Insruun may have been used for special sacred activities.

The dwelling compound of Bat contains an area of some 33,500 square feet, more than twice the size of Kinyeir Fulat, but less than half the area of Insruun. Two entrances along the canal gave access to Bat. A feast house that may have been located near the southern canal entrance probably measured about 23 × 59 feet and contained perhaps 1,360 square feet. Basalt prisms form the border of the feast house floor, while basalt stones of various shapes pave the floor.

A wall about 4 feet high and 3 feet wide formed an approximately 3,840-square-foot enclosure near the center of the Bat compound. The enclosure was open toward the southeast. A private house of possibly 340 square feet apparently was located in the enclosure, while a second residence may have been situated between the enclosure and the canal wall. Most of Bat was paved with coral and some basalt. Along the Fanana/Sremuta wall was an unpaved garden area. Several other private houses probably were located near the Insruun wall, away from the canal and feast house.

The dwelling compound of Fanana/Sremuta contained an area of about 25,600 square feet, somewhat less than Bat. Three of Fanana/Sremuta's entrances faced the canal. A fourth entry opened into Insruun to the northwest, where the threshold is raised the thickness of one basalt stone. The threshold forms a step up as visitors enter into the mortuary compound.

Stacked prismatic basalt reinforces the wall opening. Here the stones turn slightly upward, increasing the wall height at the portal. At the entry the wall is 18 feet high and 15.3 thick at its base.

The Fanana/Sremuta canal walls are about 17 feet thick at their bases and 18 feet high

Aerial view of Insruun, Bat, and Fanana/
Sremuta from the southwest. The central canal
appears in the foreground; to the right, royal
tomb compounds of Inol and Insru.

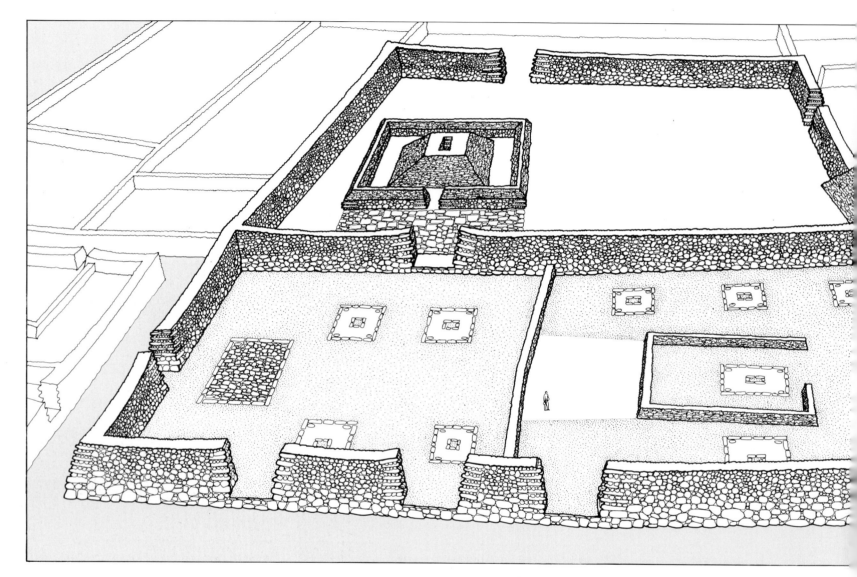

at the west corner. The walls are constructed
of round basalt with horizontal ledges of flat
coral inserted as required to secure the stones
structurally. The light color of the bleached
coral contrasts sharply with the dark color
of the basalt stones. The resulting texture
and scale impart a distinctive architectural
character to Fanana/Sremuta's walls compared, for example, to the massive and som-
ber stacked prismatic basalt walls of Kinyeir
Fulat and Lurun. The walls of Fanana/Sre-
muta are in immediate need of stabilization
and restoration.

The floor of Fanana/Sremuta is almost entirely paved with flat coral today, although
the paving has been disturbed in several

places. Little evidence remains of the activities that originally took place in the compound. Fanana/Sremuta probably once had
a feast house near the northwest canal
entrance and perhaps four private houses
located away from the feast house (Cordy,
1981).

WALL CONSTRUCTION

In 1824 Captain Duperrey observed that
the island city of Leluh "probably would be
invaded by the sea if the natives who had
chosen this locality as their principal residence had not taken the precaution to raise
the level of the soil . . . above sea level and
to develop the entire island with a belt of

walls, capable of offering an insurmountable
dike against the periodic phenomena of the
tides. The village was thus protected against
floods by the industry of the inhabitants and
criss-crossed in various directions by canals
which canoes could easily navigate when the
tide was high. The walls which encase the
canals, as well as those which surround
the island, are composed of fragments of basalt and coral, chiseled with great care
and placed, with absolutely no cement, one
on top of another. The natives constructed
them by using large ropes and levers, and
they gave them a rather considerable slope,
such that they could resist the upward thrust
of the earth which they are destined to sup-

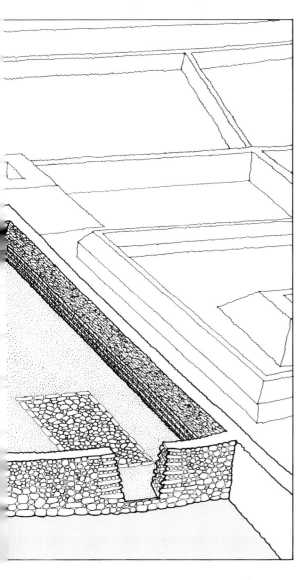

port" (Duperrey, 1828, in Ritter and Ritter, 1982 : 14).

Natural basalt outcroppings occur in a number of places on the main island of Kosrae and on the original island of Leluh. Likely sources for the building stones of Leluh were quarries in the vicinity of Utwe Harbor, along the north shore of Kosrae, in several locations around Leluh Harbor, and at several inland sites near the coast of the main island. Geochemists and archaeologists presently are comparing stone quarry samples with samples taken from specific structures in Leluh. Matching the samples would identify the quarry source of material for particular structures and would make possible rea-

Typical wall sections in central Leluh: *left,* Lurun and Kinyeir Fulat; *center,* Bat, Fanana/Sremuta, and Insruun; and *right,* the Inol wall enclosing the twin royal tombs (after Cordy, 1981 and 1986).

sonable estimates of the amount of labor required for construction.

The quarries contain basalt in its natural state. After prolonged exposure to the weather, stones break away from their outcrops along their lines of natural cleavage. Some of the stones are rounded or multilateral in shape. The log-shaped stones used in stacked prismatic construction are columnar basalt. The prisms, usually with four, five, or six sides, range in size from a few inches to several feet in diameter and vary widely in length.

Where the columnar basalt had not weathered free of the outcrop, the ancient Kosraeans may have detached the column

by building a fire at the base and applying water to quickly cool the stone, thus producing a transverse fracture (Bath, 1986). Fire also seems to have been used as a quarrying technique in Pohnpei, the Mariana Islands (Spoehr, 1957), and elsewhere in Micronesia.

The most likely method of moving megaliths from the quarries to Leluh was by means of rafts. At high tide the lagoon is sufficiently deep in most places to float heavily laden rafts, and the reef around the island afforded protection against the heavy surf and swells of the open sea. Transporting large stones by raft apparently was subject to accidental loss of stone, for basalt stones can be seen lying

on the bottom of the shallow lagoon in several places near Leluh.

Foundations seem to have been constructed by first placing large block basalt stones around the perimeter of the artificial islet to be filled. Large pieces of coral were placed on the lagoon bottom inside the perimeter foundation. Additional coral and sometimes small quantities of basalt were added until the desired level of fill was attained. Basalt stones continued to be placed on the perimeter foundation as the filling operation proceeded.

Coral was taken from the extensive, shallow reef around Leluh. A Kosraean legend tells of the building of Pisin Islet by the

108

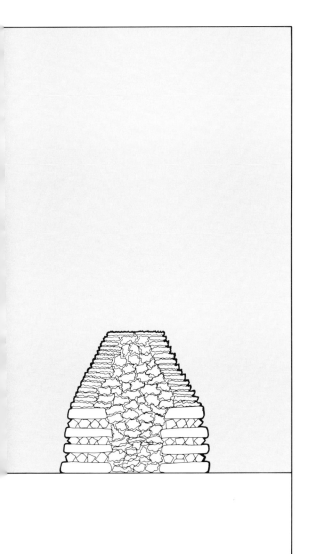

people of Tofol who "formed a long chain across the reef and passed pieces of coral from hand to hand" (Sarfert, 1919:44). This procedure seems to be entirely plausible. Sand fill also appears to have been used, for example, in areas used for gardens. Flat coral often served for paving the surfaces of the artificial islets.

One Kosraean legend tells that Leluh's walls were built by magic. When certain words were spoken, "the stones quickly piled themselves on top of each other" (Sarfert, 1919, in Cordy, 1981:465). Attractive as this prospect is, it seems clear that an alternative was available within Kosrae's neolithic technology. Unfortunately, the al-

ternative required the employment of considerable skill and effort.

Three separate reports (Sarfert, 1919: 252–253) suggest that large stones were lifted into place by pulling or rolling the stones up inclined planes from one level to another by use of ropes and levers. The inclined planes may have been made of logs or stones. Similar methods for moving heavy objects are used elsewhere in Micronesia. For example, heavy logs for canoes are moved by skillfully manipulating ropes and levers in Yap and Palau (Sam, 1984).

Pulleys and other modern construction devices were not required for building the walls of ancient Leluh. Kosraean construction techniques were entirely adequate for building the magnificent stone structures. The work force may have consisted of a relatively small group of men working for an extended period of time, or a larger number of workers for a shorter period of time. A key factor in building the ancient city appears to have been the organization of labor and requisite logistical support within the framework of a highly structured society. As the power of the king and high chiefs waned, the building and maintenance of ancient Leluh ceased.

Wall Types

The stone walls of Leluh were constructed of basalt and coral without the use of mor-

tar. Posral's 21-foot-high walls were built of huge blocks of basalt and measured up to 10 feet across and sometimes weighed several tons. These were Leluh's highest walls and probably the most magnificent. Today almost nothing remains of them, and they lie mostly beneath the modern city. The ancient residence of the king has given place to modern princes of commerce.

Several types of walls can be seen today in the central area of the ancient city. All of the walls have rubble-filled cores of coral and some basalt. All have flat coral tops. The structural damage to the walls that is occurring today is attributable to the rupturing effect of tree roots and vegetation or to the removal of facing stones in recent times, rather than to a lack of skill during original construction. The ancient builders seem to have understood the importance of developing adequate resistance to shear, of minimizing bending, and of eliminating tension. Basalt, coral, and other types of stone are naturally strong in compression. Leluh's walls are interlocked and slope inward as they rise, taking maximum advantage of their inherent strength.

The exterior face of the Kinyeir Fulat and Lurun walls consists of block basalt in the lower courses and stacked prismatic basalt in the upper courses. The interior wall is built of stacked prismatic basalt throughout. Here the stones are larger toward the base

109

and smaller toward the top. The interior stones are smaller in size than the exterior stones. The scale of the compound's interior was more refined than its exterior.

Apparently, each layer of the coral core was placed at the same time that the corresponding courses of facing stones were laid. In this way the entire wall assembly could be structurally interlocked in order to sustain the weight of the upper wall through the centuries. The wall was almost as wide as it was high, not counting the additional basal width of Kinyeir Fulat's interior wall terraces or benches.

The construction used in the walls of Bat, Fanana/Sremuta, and Insruun was similar. Bat was built perhaps a century after Kinyeir Fulat and their structures differ accordingly. The facing stones of Bat are round basalt. They graduate from larger sizes in lower courses to smaller sizes in upper courses, and the stones of the interior walls are smaller than those of the exterior walls. The lower courses of the wall are vertical, while the upper part of the wall slopes inward on both sides. The width of the base is well less than the height.

Typical round basalt stones weigh 100 to 200 pounds, much less than the major facing stones in Kinyeir Fulat, Lurun, or Posral. The newer walls were smaller in volume and required less labor than their predecessors. Horizontal wedges of flat coral were laid beneath many of the round basalt stones of Fanana/Sremuta. They may have served to increase friction in the wall facing and thereby reduce the tendency of the round stone to roll down and out of the wall. The resulting structure is less stable than a stacked prismatic basalt wall.

The Insru wall is vertical and is faced with relatively small stacked prismatic basalt. Its core is filled with coral and is capped with flat coral. A unique truncated coral cap crowned the walls around Insru's twin royal tombs and between Insru and Bat. The truncated coral wall cap recalls the shape of the truncated royal tombs. The base of this wall is of small stacked prismatic basalt.

Other types of walls found in Leluh are dominant coral mixed with some basalt, such as the internal walls of Insru and the wall between Bat and Fanana/Sremuta. Walls of mixed flat and round coral also were built in Leluh.

The outside corners and entryways of the high-wall compounds were built consistently of stacked prismatic basalt. Here additional strength was required. The basalt stacks were tilted upward, imparting an upward sweep to the wall's corners and entries. The configuration may recall the prows of double-ended canoes or the high gable ends of crescent-shaped roofs. Although the walls step inward slightly as they rise, they create the visual illusion of thrusting outward. The corners and entries of Lurun and Kinyeir Fulat vividly demonstrate this architectural phenomenon.

The appearance of Posral's immense block walls, which were built very early in the city's building sequence, is without precedence in Leluh's ancient architecture. The largest structures that had been built previously were the unsophisticated foundations and modest compound walls of the earliest islets filled. No high or massive compound walls at all had been built when Posral's walls appeared. The ability to perfect, perhaps in four or five generations, the knowledge and skill of quarrying, transporting, and placing immense basalt stones was a remarkable achievement. A major factor in building the immense walls seems to have been the unification of Kosrae's several societies under Leluh's leadership about 1400.

The population of Leluh at the time of Posral's construction was possibly about six hundred, of whom presumably only one-fifth at most would have been available or suitable for heavy construction labor. This assumes a typical family size of five persons: a father, mother, two children, and a fifth family member, such as grandparent, invalid, or baby. Since the father presumably was responsible for such tasks as building houses or canoes, heavy clearing, and certain types of fishing, his remaining time was limited. An additional work force from the main island probably was available, but even so the organization of the labor force and its logistical support would have required very efficient

Front and side elevations of King John's model of a traditional residence for a nobleman, an exhibit in Leluh's public library.

planning and management. This suggests that the society was by then firmly under some form of centralized leadership, quite likely the king and high chiefs.

The walls that were built after 1650 seem to have been smaller, less labor intensive, and less sophisticated in construction than those built in the preceding two and a half centuries. The emphasis seems to have shifted to increased quantity of artificial islet fill and decreased quality of wall construction.

Through the centuries the building traditions of Leluh continued to change. Lurun probably was built during the fifteenth century. One of its canal entry walls measures 18.3 feet in width and is 15 feet high. Perhaps a century later Insruun was added. Its portal wall toward Fanana/Sremuta measures 15 feet in width and is 18.3 feet high, the opposite dimensions from Lurun. The later wall was higher but less stable.

Leluh's population had increased to perhaps nine hundred when Insruun was built, but its construction quality had declined. By 1800 the population may have reached about fifteen hundred, but none of the newer construction rivaled the magnificent architecture of the king's and high chiefs' com-

pounds. This may suggest a relatively stable number of high chiefs, an increasing number of low chiefs, and a proportionately large increase in the number of commoners.

STRUCTURES OF WOOD

In 1827 Friedrich von Kittlitz observed: "From these wall-enclosed compounds loom the high, half-moon shaped, scalloped roofs with their graceful gables of thin poles woven together; the woodwork of these gables, especially on those buildings which serve the chiefs as dwellings, is painted red like the canoes with pleasing white decoration. Thus, a compound forms a miniature city, cut off from the rest of the world by walls" (Kittlitz, 1858, in Cordy, 1984:102–103).

The original wood structures of Leluh perished generations ago. The modest wood structures of present-day Kosrae employ imported building materials, such as metal roofing, reinforced concrete, plywood, millsawn lumber, nails, and bolts. The best information presently available on Leluh's original wood structures is found in the accounts and engravings of early visitors (Ritter and Ritter, 1982), the photographs and drawings of the South Sea Expedition (Sarfert, 1919),

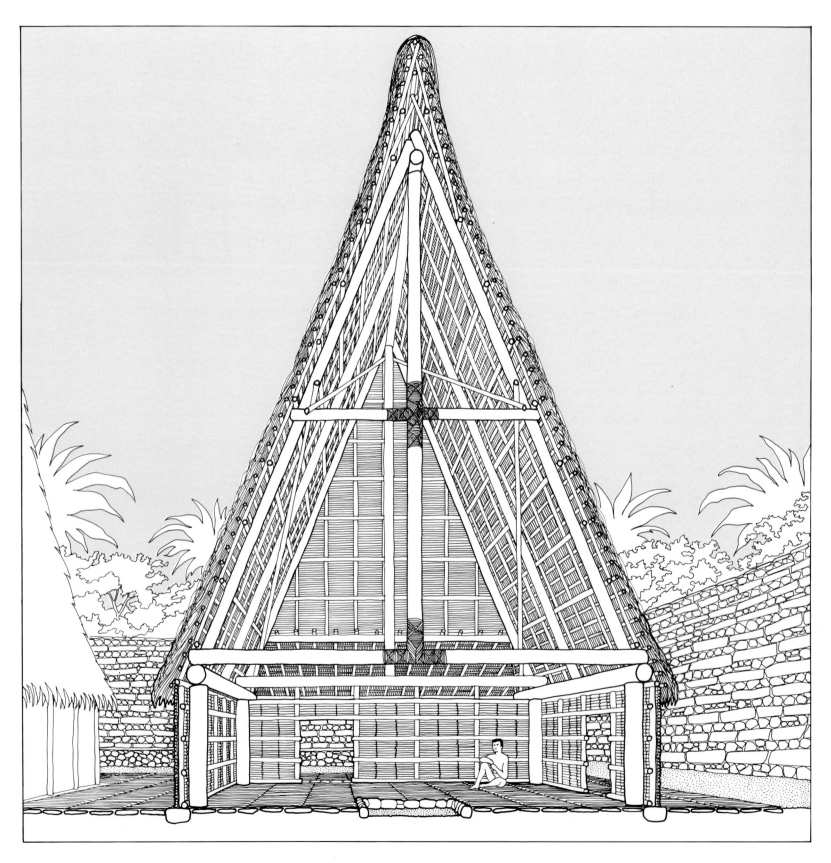

The cord bindings of posts, beams, and rafters at Kosrae's Community Development Office are characteristic of traditional wood structures in ancient Leluh.

The cord bindings of the end bay, Community Development Office.

a model of an ancient dwelling in Leluh's public library, and the traditional construction methods sometimes used in contemporary buildings on Kosrae.

The model illustrated here is an approximately 12-inch-high replica of a traditional dwelling house for a nobleman in old Leluh. The model was built by King John, the last *tokosra,* whose Kosraean name was Awane Noa. He lived through the German and Japanese administrations and died in the 1950s (John, 1984). Although the height of the model's walls seems exaggerated in proportion to the height of its roof, the model appears to be accurate in many details.

The crescent-shaped roof is thatched and curves upward at the gable ends of the house. The wall structure consists of exposed wood posts at all four corners and at convenient intervals on each side. Horizontal wood timbers run on the interior side of the wall posts to which they are lashed with cord, while woven mats fill in the wall between the posts. The interior floor is level with the exterior grade. Woven mats cover the interior floor and extend outside.

The door of the model has been removed to reveal interiors of the dwelling, which is clean and uncluttered. A wooden tray is suspended from rafters. The interior walls consist of a network of small vertical and horizontal wood members bound together with cord. No diagonal wall braces are used. The

scale of the interior walls is smaller than that of the exterior walls—the same shift of scale that the stone walls of compounds exhibit. The model's details correspond closely to the accounts of early observers.

The photographs shown here illustrate the binding that connected the posts, beams, and rafters of the present-day Community Development Office in Kosrae. The connections are typical of the structural joints traditionally used in old Leluh. The binding cords are continuous, no knots appear, and the woven joints firmly secure the structural wood members together without internal pegs or notches. The triangles of each binding are painted with yellow and red colors to draw attention to the weaving of the joint.

The bindings permit the wood members to yield slightly during temporary stresses, such as gusts during windstorms. Less elaborate cord bindings joined smaller building components, such as rafters, purlins, and roof thatch. Similar cord bindings are used in the traditional wood structures of Yap, Pohnpei, and other Micronesian islands.

The use of color was important in Kosraean architecture. During his 1824 visit, René Primevère Lesson observed that "the islanders built their houses with the greatest care, and the chiefs' residences, although built on the same model, are more spacious, better finished, and never show a piece of wood that is not painted either red, black,

yellow, or white" (Lesson, 1839, in Ritter and Ritter, 1982:62).

He also noted that the Kosraeans' "main dye color, as in paint, is a dark red which they get from a big woody root, called *mahori,* which they steep in water in sunlight. They place, for several days, the threads which they want to dye in this bath, which no mordant that I know can brighten. . . . The other principles of color which they possess are: a very brilliant black whose source I am ignorant of, a very bright golden yellow furnished by the bark of *morinda citrifolia,* a precious wood dye which grows in abundance in all the islands which I visited in the South Pacific" (p. 66).

The source of black pigment on Yap is charcoal. Perhaps the source is the same on Kosrae. The source of white pigment is white lime powder produced by firing coral.

Concerning the feast house of Posral, the residence compound of the *tokosra,* Jules Sébastien César Dumont d'Urville noted in 1824, "It was a large house surrounded completely by mats. . . . The interior was only a large room entirely open, bare of furniture, and in it the only noticeable thing was a partition at the lower end, like all the others that we have seen" (d'Urville, 1835, in Ritter and Ritter, 1982:31–32). The following day d'Urville recorded that "there are two beautiful and large houses which are bigger, and better maintained than those

Fyedor Lütke's Plate 18 shows residences in Leluh as they appeared during the Russian sea captain's visit of 1827–1828 (Lütke, 1971).

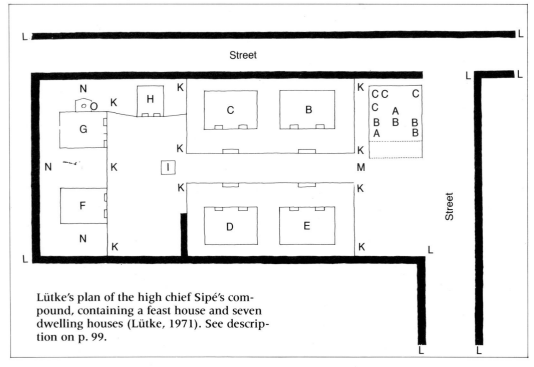

Lütke's plan of the high chief Sipé's compound, containing a feast house and seven dwelling houses (Lütke, 1971). See description on p. 99.

114

of the king. The majority of these houses contain two or three large canoes on beams five or six feet above the ground" (p. 32).

A Reconstructed Wood Structure

The perspective drawing presented in this section suggests a possible reconstruction of a 20-foot-wide feast house, one of Leluh's larger wood structures. The reconstructed house proposed here is only an initial suggestion pending improved information in the future. Near the center of the floor is a 5-foot-square fire pit. Mats cover the stone-paved interior floor and extend to the exteriors. A row of rectangular basalt lines the perimeter of the building. The ridge is 30 feet above the floor at the center of the building and is almost 40 feet high at the gable end.

Corner posts are placed in deep holes and braced at ground level with stones to provide horizontal resistance to wind. Intermediate wall posts reduce the spans of lintel beams. Horizontal beams rest on the lintels and span between parallel walls. Elevated center posts support the ridge beam. A second horizontal beam braces the center post and roof halfway up the center post; the tips of this beam are diagonally braced to the corner post so that the main structure does not move while the roof is being placed.

Purlins are placed at equal spaces between the ridge beam and the wall lintels. These cantilever beyond the end walls to form the gables. Rafters are lashed at right angles to the purlins, while additional short rafters are placed above the ridge, varying in length and angle of rise to form the upward sweep of the ridge toward the gable end. Sections of thatch are laid progressively up the roof in the manner of overlapping shingles.

After the roof is in place, horizontal wall stringers are bound to the structural wall posts. Vertical posts are placed outside the stringers, and woven mats are tied to the wall stringers between the exposed exterior posts. Doorways are formed by omitting horizontal stringers and mats between exterior posts. Open woven mats close in the gables and permit air circulation for ventilation. Favorable orientations for gable ends on Kosrae are toward the northeast and southwest. Pleasant trade winds blow from the northeast six months of each year, and intermittent winds come from the southwest at other times.

The degree of ridge curvature may have been related to social rank in Kosrae (John, 1984). More modest buildings were reported to have had flat ridges. The highest sweeping roofs of Leluh may have been reserved for the high chiefs and the king. The building of wood structures on Kosrae seems to have been largely a matter of weaving and binding, apparently employing techniques sometimes used in canoe construction.

The elevated center posts of Kosraean houses permitted clear span interiors. Similar construction apparently characterized the houses of prehistoric Pohnpei. In traditional Yapese houses, however, rows of center posts extend down to the floors and divide the interior spaces longitudinally into right and left halves.

Traditional Palauan houses had horizontal ties above the walls to resist the outward thrust of roofs, but no center posts at all were used. The structural principles of ancient houses in the Marianas is unclear, although it seems likely that they more closely resembled the houses of Palau than those of Pohnpei or Kosrae. The distinctive crescent-shaped roofs of ancient Kosrae were unique in prehistoric Micronesian architecture.

SUMMARY

Among the most impressive examples of traditional architecture in Oceania are the remains of Leluh, the ancient ceremonial and administrative center of Kosrae. Well known to Western mariners in the nineteenth century, the island city consisted of more than one hundred walled enclosures. Remarkable stone walls up to 21 feet high surrounded many of the compounds and amazed early French (1824) and Russian (1827) visitors.

The complex hierarchical Kosraean society consisted of the king, high chiefs, low chiefs, and commoners. Residing in the royal dwelling compound of Posral, the king apparently occupied both sacred and secular positions in the island's society. The maximum prehistoric population of the island probably was in the range of five to six thousand people of whom perhaps one quarter lived in Leluh. About two thirds of the population were commoners, most of whom lived on the main island.

Like Nan Modal on Pohnpei, Leluh was constructed on artificial fill in a shallow lagoon along the east coast of the main island. The building process seems to have begun around A.D. 1250 and to have continued for some six centuries, reaching its pinnacle of development about the time of European contact. The great walls of Posral, Kinyeir Fulat, and Lurun probably were completed between 1400 and 1600. Major portions of these extraordinary walls survive today, serving as magnificent examples of Kosrae's ancient architecture.

By 1600 three distinctive elements of the city plan were in place: compounds with high walls, a canal through the center, and paved streets interconnecting compounds and boat landings. At the time of Western contact Leluh extended half a mile to its western terminus at Pisin Islet. Surrounded by a protective seawall 5 to 6 feet high, the ancient center contained three royal tomb compounds, seventeen sacred enclosures, numerous walled dwelling compounds, and an unknown number of unwalled areas where commoners lived.

Canoes daily transported tribute of food and goods from the main island to boat landings on the more than 3,000-foot-long canal. Early visitors described the graceful saddle-shaped roofs of hundreds of dwellings and feast houses. Some roofs curved upward as high as 40 feet above their courtyards. A typical residential compound contained within its walls a feast house near the main entry, several residences in more secluded locations, stone pavings, earth ovens for cooking, pounding stones, and often a small garden.

Ancient builders employed rafts to transport natural prismatic basalt stones to Leluh from quarries at various locations around Kosrae. Islet construction began by carefully placing often immense basalt boulders around the perimeter of the area to be filled. Large pieces of coral then were placed inside the basalt foundation, and upper stones were added until the desired heights of perimeter walls and coral fill were attained. While coral usually was light enough in weight to be lifted by hand, the ancient workers are reported to have moved the sometimes huge basalt stones by a system of inclined planes, ropes, and levers.

Particularly impressive are the skillfully constructed, stacked prismatic basalt walls surrounding Lurun and Kinyeir Fulat. Thicker at their bases than they are high, the remarkable walls have graceful, upward-sweeping corners and portals. The basalt prisms generally have from four to six sides, range in diameter from a few inches to several feet, and vary considerably in length and weight.

The mortuary compounds of Insru, Inol, and Insruun contain distinctive royal tombs shaped like truncated pyramids, each having a small crypt lined with walls of stacked prismatic basalt. Some of the compounds' walls have unique truncated coral caps. During Leluh's later phases of construction wall heights gradually diminished, and more rapid methods of wall construction appeared. These included walls of medium to small round basalt, flat and round coral, and various combinations of these stones. Leluh's ancient walls characteristically had rubble-filled cores of coral and perhaps some basalt, and caps of flat coral.

Traditional Kosraean houses had distinctive crescent-shaped roofs of thatch, graceful gables with sometimes colorful decorations, and structures of wood members woven and lashed together with often intricate bindings. The structures rested on perimeter bearing walls anchored to their foundation by sturdy corner posts. Typical residences ranged in area from 150 to 300 square feet, while feast houses were much larger. The funeral feast houses of Insru and Insruun, the largest wood structures recorded on Kosrae, contained some 5,000 square feet each.

Although the wood structures of Kosrae perished long ago, the spectacular remains of Leluh's ancient walls continue to amaze visitors today. The distinctive stone monuments nobly recall one of the most remarkable achievements of ancient Micronesian architecture.

5. THE MARIANA ISLANDS

The megalithic columns and capitals of the Marianas silently recall the once splendid architecture of northern Micronesia. At the time of Magellan's arrival in the Marianas in 1521, the first European contact with Micronesia, the native Chamorros were building impressive structures on megalithic foundations called *latte*. The *latte* consisted of two rows of stone columns supporting hemispherical capstones. They are believed to have supported structures of wood. As social complexity and competition for limited resources increased, the height and size of the *latte* apparently increased. At the time of Western contact the stone columns and capstones of the House of Taga on Tinian rose to the height of 16 feet, and an even larger structure had been started on Rota. Today the magnificent stone remains are the most visible symbols of the ancient Chamorro people.

The Marianas consist of fifteen volcanic islands in a curving arc that extends 420 miles from Guam in the south to Uracas (also Farallon de Pajaros) in the north. Located in the northwestern extremity of the Micronesian culture area, the Marianas lie between the Pacific Ocean to the east and the Philippine Sea to the west. The largest of the islands are Guam, Rota, Tinian, and Saipan, all toward the south of the group. These probably always were the centers of population in the Marianas (Spoehr, 1957). Prehistoric architectural sites have been found on all four islands. Primarily superimposed limestone terraces resting on volcanic bases, the islands contain major areas of flat or gently sloping terrain suitable for human occupation.

Based on linguistic similarities, the Philippines or the islands of southeast Asia seem to be fairly widely accepted as the most likely place of origin for the early settlers, who may have arrived in the Marianas about 1300 B.C. Existing evidence suggests that the early settlers may have had an effec-

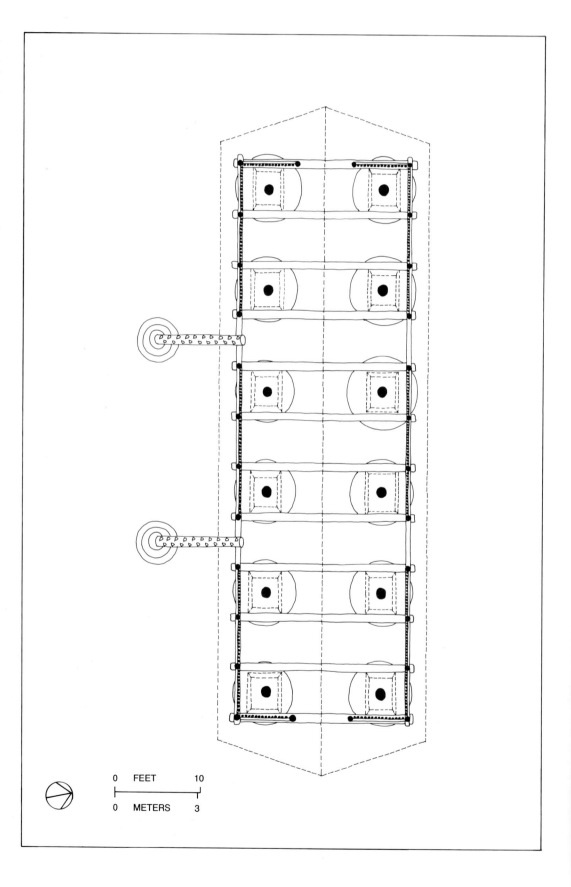

Reconstructed House of Taga, Tinian, plan.

0 FEET 10

0 METERS 3

Ancient megaliths have been reconstructed to form an eight-column *latte* more than 7 feet high in a public park of Agana, Guam.

Guam.

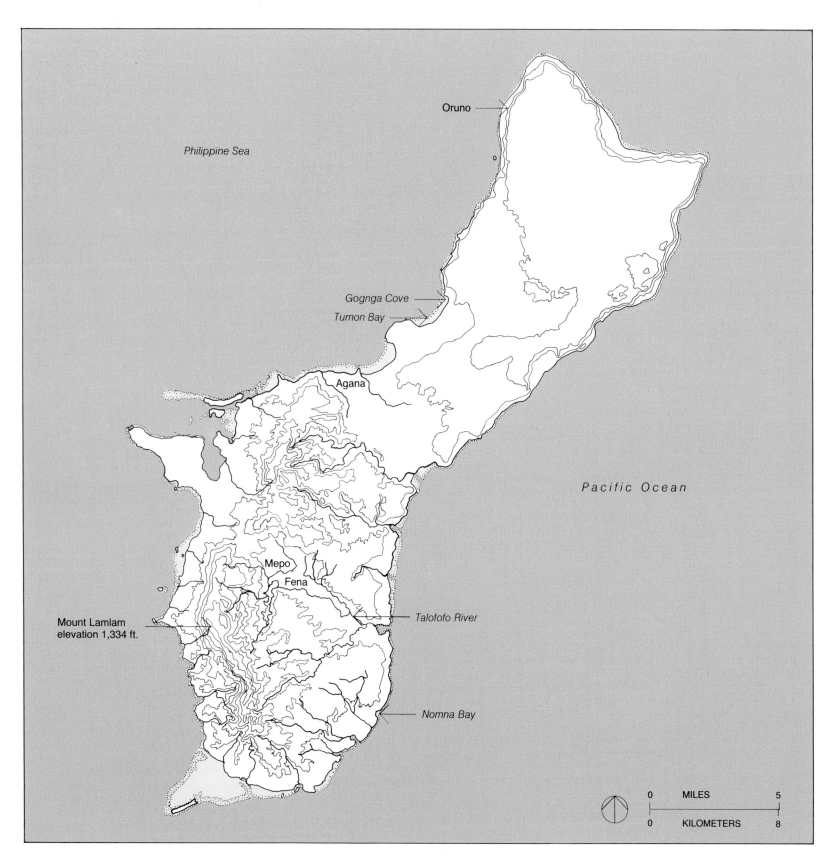

Oruno

Philippine Sea

Gognga Cove
Tumon Bay

Agana

Pacific Ocean

Mepo
Fena

Mount Lamlam
elevation 1,334 ft.

Talofofo River

Nomna Bay

0   MILES   5

0   KILOMETERS   8

tive sailing technology, and that they may have engaged in return voyaging to the islands of their origins.

Concerning the *latte,* Peter Bellwood (1979*a*:283) observes: "These structures give every appearance of being indigenous developments in the Marianas, and the only outside similarities lie in reports of stone pile houses in the Palau Islands and possibly on Yap. In basic principle, the form is simply a translation of the raised pile houses of Island Southeast Asia."

Larger houses in Palau and probably the Marianas were built on wood platforms raised above the ground on stone piers, while the major structures of Yap had solid stone platforms elevated above grade. The plans of major structures on all three island groups were based on regularized proportions. Typical large meeting houses of Micronesia, such as the *pebaey* of Yap and the *bai* of Palau, were rectangular or nearly so in plan and had high roofs thatched with palm fronds or pandanus leaves. Their ridgepoles, rafters, and plates were lashed together with cord bindings, except on Palau, where certain main structural joints were mortised and fitted. Yapese and Palauan houses often were elaborately decorated.

Early European observers noted that the Chamorros built and sailed outrigger canoes with great skill. The boats of the Marianas seem to have been somewhat similar to those elsewhere in Micronesia. Called "flying proas" (Walter, 1974), their main hulls were double ended for sailing in either direction, and they employed single outrigger floats with a lateen sail. The technology required for building these graceful craft suggests the level of technology available for planning and constructing the prehistoric architecture in the Marianas.

THE *LATTE* PHASE
OF THE MARIANAS

Perhaps as early as A.D. 1000, *latte* houses began to be built in the Marianas. The group of columns and capstones that together comprise a single foundation structure is referred to as a *latte* set. The number of stone columns with capstones observed in a *latte* set varied

from six to fourteen. The piers almost always were erected in two parallel rows that varied from three to seven columns in length.

Near the ancient houses, food probably was prepared, cooked, and stored, and tools were manufactured, maintained, and stored. Both extended and secondary burials consisting of collections of bones are found under or near the houses. Brown-stained teeth found in Chamorro graves attest to the antiquity of betel nut chewing in the Marianas.

Latte often were grouped together, sometimes in a series of rows, and were located inland from nearby beaches, where canoe sheds or club houses may have been located. Village alignments usually were parallel to the nearest coastline or river and may have been oriented to take advantage of prevailing breezes. Chamorro villages frequently were located near the sea, their principal source of protein, and near a source of fresh water and areas suitable for farming. Even inshore villages were not so far removed from the sea as to eliminate it as a food resource.

Latte building in the Marianas seems to have continued until about 1650, and sites on Guam apparently continued to be occupied until perhaps 1750. Large bones of pelagic fish appeared in the Marianas during the *latte* building phase, suggesting off-shore fishing and canoe building, but probably not trade or contact with islands outside the Marianas.

It seems unlikely that a single person owned or controlled a particular *latte* house. More likely, a household or larger kin group was responsible for building and maintaining the structure. A senior member of the household or kin group may have been awarded certain rights of use, but the control of the house probably was retained by the larger group.

Megalithic foundations may have had symbolic meanings that related enduring stone to enduring social position. One reason for building elevated structures may have been related to the idea that increased height once symbolized increased authority and importance in much of Oceania. As the height and number of columns per *latte* increased, size and social rank apparently gained in im-

portance. Foundation size may have been related to wealth and the power to control labor.

The height of *latte* varies widely in the Marianas, but the maximum is about 8 feet, with the exceptions of the 16-foot-high House of Taga on Tinian and the unfinished structure in the quarry at As Nieves on Rota that would have been perhaps 18 feet high. The significance of these exceptionally high structures is the subject of differing interpretations by scholars. One view holds that the House of Taga probably represents the emergence of a third level in the Chamorro society about the time of European contact. Thus, the superordinate height of the House of Taga's foundation would suggest the emergence of a single paramount chief above all the lesser chiefs of Tinian. Similarly, the unfinished megaliths of the quarry at As Nieves might suggest the emergence of a supreme ruler on the island of Rota.

Another scholarly interpretation of the significance of the unusually high House of Taga *latte* is that it represents the presence of one of two competing factions on Tinian. Historical documents of 1660 to 1680 indicate that no supreme ruler existed on the island at that time. Instead, two alliances existed, one dominated by Makpo Village in the southeast area of the island and the other by the Taga area on the west side. Both interpretations see *latte* as symbols of ranking but disagree on the social organizations they represent.

A 1565 diary entry by a member of the Miguel de Legaspi expedition, commissioned by the Spanish crown to sail from Mexico to the Philippines, offers this description of the Chamorro housing: "Their houses are high, well kept and well made. [They] stand the height of a man off the ground, atop large stone pillars, upon which they lay the flooring. . . . These are the houses in which they sleep. They have other low houses, on the ground, where they cook and roast food. . . . They have other large houses which are used for boathouses. These are not dwellings, but communal [houses] in which they store the large proas [double-ended sailing canoes with a single outrigger] and [which] shelter [their] canoes. In each barrio [a group of dwellings forming a distinctive unit] there is one of these boathouses" (Plaza, 1973:7).

The diary entry clearly mentions three types of structures: residences built on *latte*, small cookhouses built on grade, and large community houses not necessarily associated with *latte*. A communal house may have served purposes other than canoe storage, such as a men's clubhouse, a community storehouse, a meeting place, or other public functions. For example, in 1671, Padre Diego Luis de Sanvitores noted that "the bachelors have some public houses . . ." (Barrett, 1975, in Cordy, 1986). While some *latte* may have served other purposes as well, they apparently were primarily residences.

Coral-pebble paving has been found adjoining and beneath *latte* houses at Objan, Lau Lau, and Unai Bapot on Saipan, Nomna Bay on Guam, Tachognya on Tinian, and other sites. This suggests that work areas may have been located near or below the raised floors of *latte* houses. Earth ovens found near many *latte* houses indicate the same manner of cooking that is used widely in Micronesia. Separate frame cookhouses in Saipan and elsewhere in the Marianas suggest that *latte* houses originally may have had frame cookhouses nearby.

THE ANCIENT CHAMORROS

The Chamorros were prolific potters who are not known to have employed highly decorative designs. Their cutting tools were made more frequently from shell than from stone. Other tools were made of bone and wood, but metal was unknown prior to Western contact. The Chamorros used hooks and nets for fishing and ate seals and turtles. Pigs were unknown in the Marianas until Europeans introduced them. The Chamorros' subsistence economy was based on agriculture, fishing, gathering mollusks from the reefs, limited hunting for birds, bats, and crabs, and gathering wild vegetable products. Coconuts, yams, breadfruit, several types of taro, bananas, and sugarcane were important crops. The Chamorros appear to have been the only people in Micronesia who grew rice. Digging sticks with stone blades were the primary agricultural implements.

Men's work seems to have included clearing land, planting, cultivating, and harvesting, cooking large quantities of food in earth ovens for special feasts, building houses and canoes, and manufacturing tools. Women apparently fished on the reefs with small hand nets and sometimes stored part of their catch in stone-lined holding ponds along the shore. They also prepared daily meals by boiling food in locally manufactured pots, wove baskets and mats from pandanus, made pottery, prepared medicines, performed domestic chores, and probably assisted in agricultural production.

Laura Thompson (1945) suggested that Chamorro households were extended families usually based on some form of matrilineal descent. According to Ross Cordy (1983c), two strata existed in Chamorro society, chiefs and commoners. Early Spanish observers reported that *latte* houses were occupied by members of the chiefly class rather than by commoners.

The larger islands of the Marianas traditionally seem to have been divided into several alliances of independent villages, each influenced by the highest-ranking chief within the alliance. Smaller islands may have been under the control of a single alliance or village. The alliances were not consolidated into large, well-knit political units. As representatives of lineages, the chiefs controlled all or most of the village land and fishing grounds.

Warfare, feuding, and shifts in alliances were common. Not subject to a high degree of organization, warfare was conducted primarily by stealth and ambush. The weapons of the Chamorros included barbed spear points, made from human bones or wood, and sling stones. Competition for status and rank probably was as constant in the Marianas as elsewhere in Micronesia.

The art of the Marianas probably was expressed primarily in perishable materials that have long since disappeared. Ornaments that have been found include highly decorative carvings, beads, bracelets, and pendants. Burial artifacts generally are lacking.

WESTERN CONTACT

In 1521, Antonio Pigafetta recorded the first contact between Europeans and the people of Micronesia; he described the following incident as Magellan's three ships approached what may have been the coast of Guam: "On Wednesday, the sixth of March, we discovered a small island in the northwest direction, and two others lying to the southwest . . . The captain general wished to touch at the largest of these three islands to get refreshments of provisions; but it was not possible because the people of these islands entered into ships and robbed us, in such a way that it was impossible to preserve oneself from them. Whilst we were striking and lowering the sails to go ashore, they stole away with much address and diligence the small boat called the skiff, which was made fast to the poop of the captain's ship, at which he was much irritated, and went on shore with forty armed men, burned forty or fifty houses, with several small boats, and killed seven men of the island; they recovered their skiff" (Pigafetta, 1969, in Alkire, 1977:1).

In the years immediately succeeding Magellan's initial contact with the Marianas, the islands remained in relative isolation. During the seventeenth century, however, Spain established a prosperous trade route between Acapulco and Manila, and Guam became an important base for galleons plying the sea lanes. The people of the Marianas suffered from the severity of seventeenth-century colonialism, not because of the economic value of their islands but because they were situated strategically on the Acapulco trade route and the Spanish at that time considered it essential to missionize and convert.

In 1668, Padre Diego Luis de Sanvitores established a mission on Guam. Within two years the missionaries became caught up in political enmities, and the Chamorros began to resist forced conversion and the missionaries' efforts to disband community clubs. The Spanish introduced European diseases, such as measles and smallpox, to which the Chamorros had no immunity.

After three decades of epidemics, warfare, and two disastrous typhoons, the Chamorro

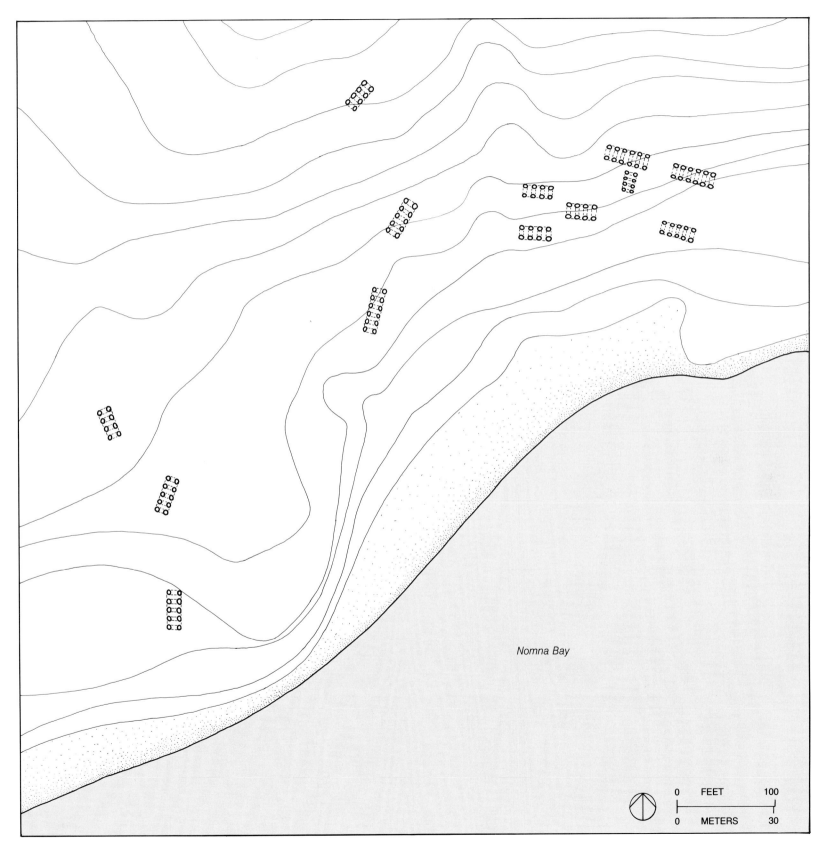

Nomna Bay

0   FEET   100

0   METERS   30

Plan of the Gognga Cove site, Guam.

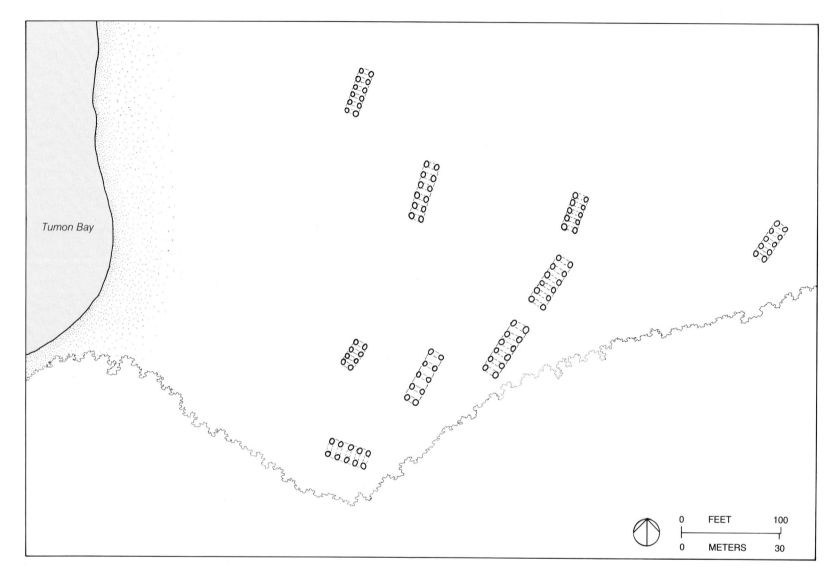

Tumon Bay

0 FEET 100

0 METERS 30

population declined sharply. The maximum population of the islands before European contact has been estimated in the range of 50,000 (Spoehr, 1954). By 1710, the year of the first Spanish census, the number of surviving Chamorros had been reduced to 3,439 (Cordy, 1983*c*).

To improve political control after severe depopulation, the Spanish concentrated all of the Chamorros in the Marianas on Guam during the late seventeenth century, except for a small group on Rota and a few on Tinian. The Chamorros were required to change their traditional settlement patterns to European models. The present-day population of the Marianas is thoroughly mixed with Spanish, Filipino, American, Chinese, Japanese, and others.

After the Spanish-American War, Spain ceded Guam to the United States and sold the other islands of the Marianas to Germany. In 1914 Japan occupied the former German possessions in Micronesia, relinquishing the islands at the conclusion of the Second World War to the United States according to the provisions of a United Nations mandate. During the latter 1970s, the Mariana Islands north of Guam became a commonwealth of the United States. Guam continues to be a possession of the United States.

Unlike most of the other islands of Micronesia, Guam, Tinian, and Saipan suffered ex-

tensive destruction as a result of the Second World War. The disappearance of prehistoric architectural sites in the Marianas is a result of both the construction of military installations and the destruction during battles for control of the islands. Urban expansion on Guam in recent decades also has resulted in the loss of many ancient sites. Fortunately, most of the remains on Rota have been spared the ravages of war and subsequent developments.

GUAM

Having 215 square miles of land area, Guam is the largest island in Micronesia. It also is the southernmost island of the Ma-

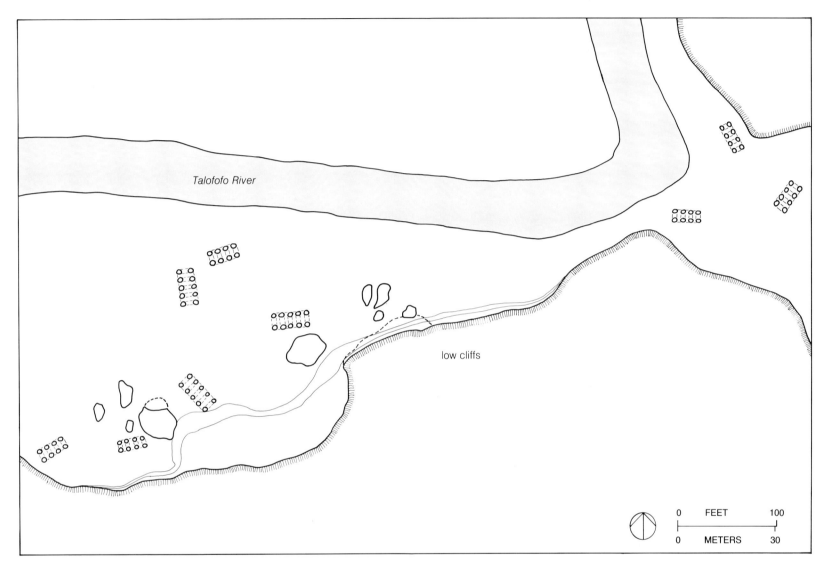

Talofofo River

low cliffs

| 0 | FEET | 100 |
| 0 | METERS | 30 |

riana archipelago. The Yap Island group is 530 miles to the southwest, and Truk Atoll lies 630 miles to the southeast. The highest point on Guam is 1,334-foot-high Mount Lamlam. Fringed by coral reefs, the 30-mile-long island ranges from 4 to 12 miles wide.

Southern Guam is basically volcanic with an elongated mountain range dividing the inland valleys from the coastline. Central and northern Guam are primarily limestone plateaus uplifted 300 to 600 feet. Near the north end of the island sheer cliffs drop precipitously into the sea. Although the island is much larger than Rota and Tinian, the area between the escarpment and the beach that is suitable for human occupation on Guam is relatively limited. Chamorro village sites on Guam apparently were more numerous, but on the average probably smaller, than those on Rota and Tinian.

Guam's maximum prehistoric population may have been at most thirty thousand Chamorros. Prehistoric settlements in the central and northern areas of the island generally were located in coastal areas, where springs occur at regular intervals at the base of the limestone uplifts. Southern Guam has clayey soils. Here rain water runs off quickly and areas suitable for human occupation are limited except near streams.

Six to twenty *latte* sets per settlement are the standard for most sites on Guam, except in the southern area, where two or three sets are the norm. An exception is the Nomna Bay site in southern Guam where seventeen *latte* are located. Many sites were in low-lying areas within a few hundred feet of the nearest beach or near inshore streams, although a site at Tumon lay 1,500 feet from the shore, and such sites as Mepo and Fena are found near the center of southern Guam. In 1668, Sanvitores counted 180 villages on Guam. Of these, only 7 villages remained in 1698.

Comparative *Latte* Site Plans

All of the *latte* site plans presented in this section are drawn at the same scale to as-

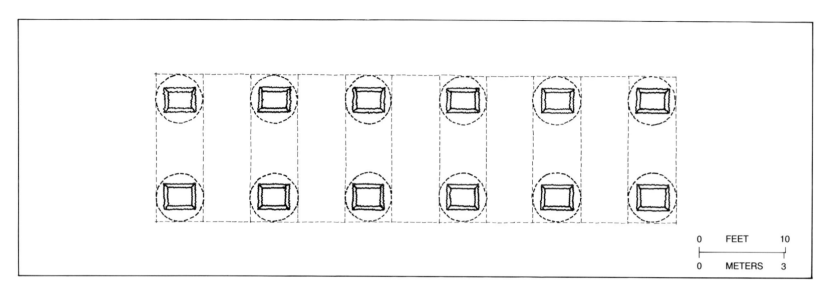

0   FEET   10

0   METERS   3

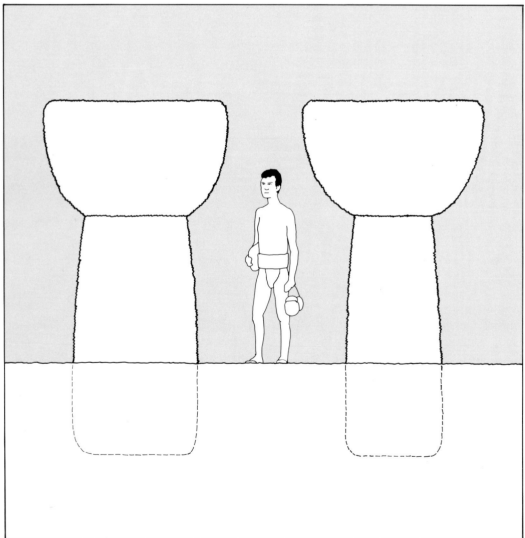

sist the reader in comparing spatial arrangements and relative sizes. Each site is oriented with north toward the top of the page. Three prehistoric sites on Guam illustrate the differences in planning on the northwest and southeast coasts and in an interior river valley.

Nomna Bay

Seventeen *latte* are located within 400 feet of Nomna Bay on the southeast coast of Guam. The plan shown here shows thirteen structures, but four others were found about 350 feet to the southwest (Reinman, 1977). The foundations are generally parallel or perpendicular to the bayshore and are spaced at irregular distances from each other. The northernmost structure is elevated 30 feet above the bay on the hillside sloping down to Nomna Bay.

The largest structure was located near the center of the eastern group. Its columns were truncated reef rocks that rose about 3.5 feet above grade; they originally supported limestone capstones measuring about 3 feet in height and diameter. The main structure was some 15 feet wide, 43.6 feet long, and 6 to 7 feet high on the downslope side. Immediately south of this structure and perpendicular to it was an eight-column *latte* that was at most 3 feet high. The T-shaped plan of these two structures is a very unusual architectural grouping for the Marianas.

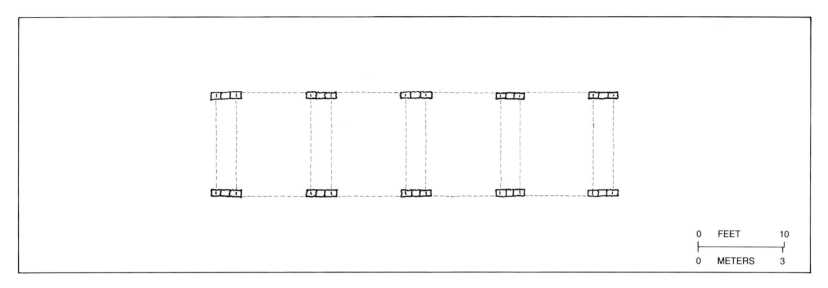

Near the Nomna Bay houses were fire pits that contained heavy concentrations of pottery, stone, and faunal remains. Ash deposits indicated that fires were made repeatedly in the pits. Numerous stone mortars for processing food were found near the foundations. Excavations beneath the structures revealed numerous burials and evidence of coral-pebble floor paving.

Several of the foundations had been so badly disturbed that the original orientations of the houses no longer could be discerned clearly. Radiocarbon dates indicated occupation of some of the *latte* between 1360 and 1675 (Reinman, 1977).

Gognga Cove

Gognga Cove, also referred to as Faifai Beach or Gun Beach, is located at the north end of Tumon Bay on the northwest coast of Guam. The plan shown here is based on a map prepared by Douglas Osborne, who recorded nine *latte* sets, with possibly three others located from 250 to 600 feet to the north and west. The upland area contained a residential group that lacked *latte*.

The group shown here lay between 260 and 680 feet from the beach. Like most of the prehistoric sites on Guam's northwest coast, the long axes of all but one of the structures lay parallel to the shore and had almost identical compass orientations. The single exception was the southernmost *latte*.

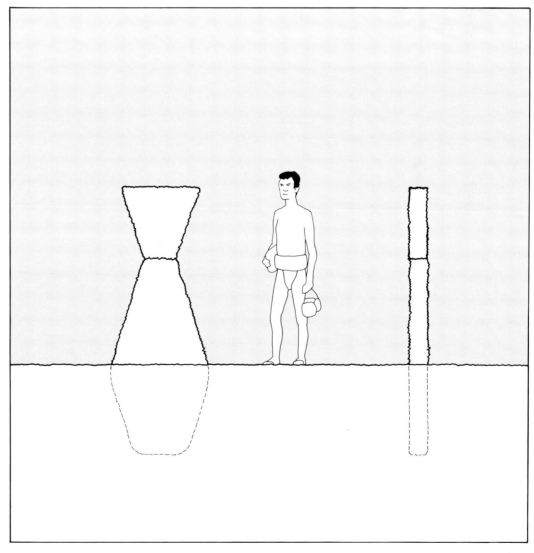

125

Plan and elevation of a *latte* at Tumon Bay, Guam.

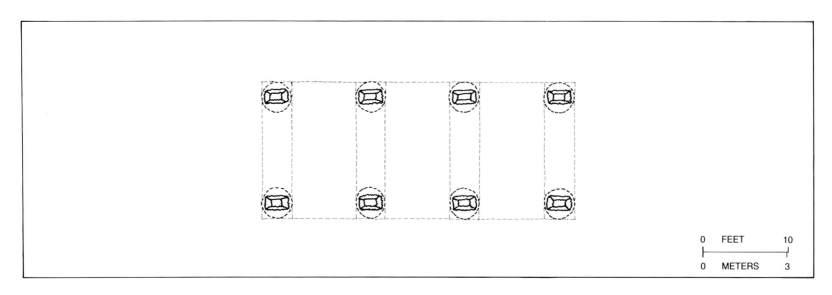

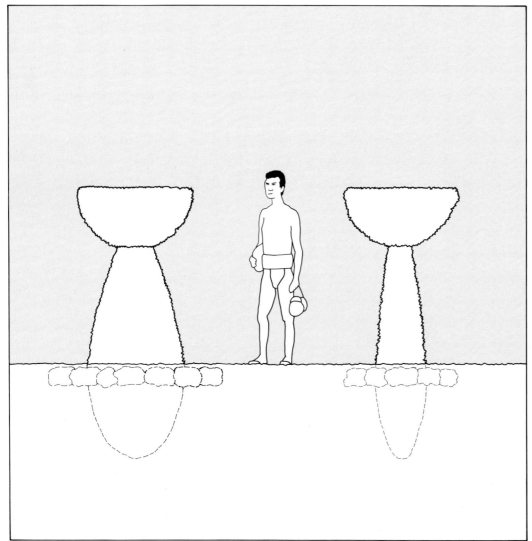

The structures varied in length from about 26 to 54 feet. Four of the nine foundations had twelve columns and four contained ten columns. Only one had eight columns. Although the Gognga Cove site is more orderly than the Nomna Bay site on the opposite side of the island, it lacks the classical end-to-end alignment of all *latte* that characterized the more architecturally disciplined sites on Tinian and Rota. Most of the prehistoric sites along Tumon Bay were destroyed during the building boom on Guam that followed the Second World War.

Talofofo River

The Talofofo River and its tributaries drain a large area of southcentral Guam. The *latte* site shown here lies between the south bank of the river and a line of low cliffs that define the valley. The site contains nine house foundations, two rock shelters beneath overhanging cliffs and rocks, and a cave 20 feet above the valley floor in the face of the cliff toward the western end of the site.

The only burial at the site was found in one of the rock shelters. Pottery and stone tools were found, but evidence for prolonged or extensive occupation of the site was lacking. Radiocarbon dating indicated human occupation as early as 210 B.C. (Reinman, 1977). Several large rocks occupy the site; long ago they fell down from the cliffs and came to rest on the valley floor.

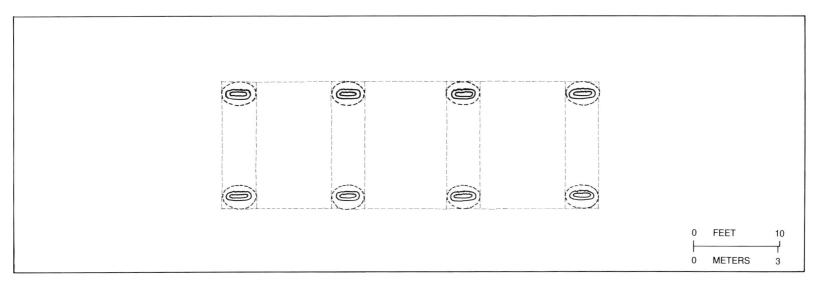

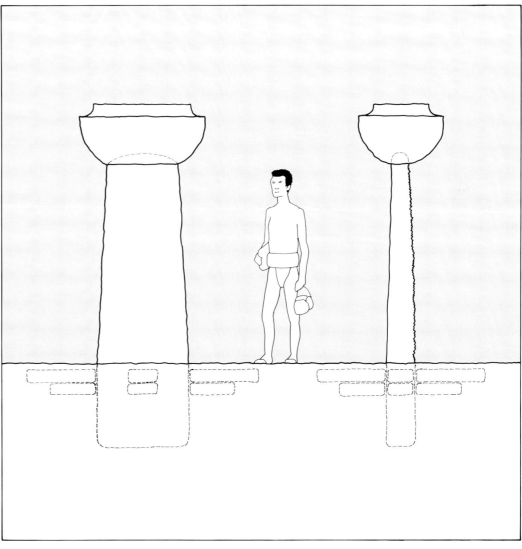

Three *latte* sets lie in a cluster 370 feet east of the main group. All the structures of this site seem to be oriented orthogonally with respect to the river bank and cliffs. The site shown here contains the largest number of *latte* found in the Talofofo River valley. Most of the sites in this area are smaller and their structures typically are separated by substantial distances, unlike Guam's larger and more compact coastal sites.

Comparative *Latte* Plans and Elevations

The elevation drawings for *latte* presented here are prepared at identical scales with the view of assisting the reader in comparing the structures visually. The human scale figure in each elevation drawing is 5 feet 6 inches tall, the assumed height of a typical adult male Chamorro about the time of European contact. In each drawing the elevation parallel to the longitudinal axis of the *latte* set is shown to the left; the end elevation, to the right. The scale of the plans is one-fourth the scale of the elevations. Typical dimensions and areas appear in the text.

Mepo

The Mepo *latte* set originally consisted of two parallel rows, each of six stone columns and capitals. The foundation probably once supported a wooden platform whose outermost dimensions were perhaps 16 × 60 feet, an area of some 960 square feet. The long axis of the structure was parallel to a nearby branch of the Talofofo River. The top of the capstone was more than 7 feet above the ground level, one of the highest *latte* found on Guam. The limestone quarry for the columns and capitals was at least a mile from the site.

After the Second World War, the Mepo site was incorporated into the United States Naval Magazine. Six of the original *latte* columns and capstones were removed from Mepo and reconstructed in a public park in the city of Agana. The reconstruction involved casting concrete foundations around the bases of the columns, obviously not original features. The sizes and proportions of the seventh and eighth columns and capstones suggest that they probably were not part of the original group.

Compared with other *latte* on Guam, the capstones at Mepo are unusually large in proportion to the height of the columns. The columns are almost square in plan and lack the more truncated appearance of typical Guamanian *latte*. Some of the columns display a slight degree of entasis, an outward bulging in the profile of the column that visually suggests increased strength and bearing capacity.

Fena

Like the Mepo site, Fena is an inland site located in southcentral Guam on the banks of the Talofofo River. The *latte* consists of ten columns arranged in two parallel rows of five columns each. The longitudinal axis of the composition is parallel to the river some 50 feet to the north. The maximum plan dimension of the original wood platform probably was about 11.5 × 46 feet, an area of approximately 530 square feet.

The columns and capitals of the Fena *latte* were carefully cut from 6-inch-thick slabs of coral limestone according to a distinctive, uniform pattern. Both the column and the capital were carved into the shape of truncated pyramids that fit together when the capstone was inverted. The overall height of the original foundation was about 5 feet.

All of the capitals had fallen to the ground when Thompson (1932) recorded the site.

The Fena *latte* is unusual in that the width of the column base exceeds the width of the capital, an exception to the general rule for *latte*. Truncated capital and column slabs were reported for a limited number of foundations on Guam, but not on other islands of the Marianas.

Tumon Bay

Located on the northwest coast of Guam, Tumon Bay had an extensive *latte* site consisting of eight stone columns and capstones about 5 feet high. The original wood platform may have measured at most 15 × 36 feet, suggesting an area of perhaps 540 square feet. The long axis of the plan, columns, and capstones is parallel to the shoreline to the northwest, a typical orientation of *latte*.

Thompson (1932) noted that the columns were roughly cut limestone and that the capstones were rough, natural coral heads. The columns extended 36 to 41 inches above the ground and about 32 inches below the surface. In plan the truncated piers measured 30 to 39 inches in length by 8 to 11 inches in width. Bracing stones were placed just below the ground surface around each column base, apparently to keep them upright. The hemispherical capstones were 36 to 45 inches in diameter and 16 to 28 inches in height.

Between the column rows seventeen extended burials were found at depths of 12 to 39 inches below the surface. The skeletons lay on their backs with their feet pointing toward the sea and their heads toward the interior of the island. Of different ages and sexes, the adults were buried deeper than the children. Six other burials were located nearby.

Oruno

Oruno (also Uruno) lies north of Tumon Bay on the northwest coast of Guam. The structure illustrated here consisted of eight stone columns and capitals that were originally about 7 feet high. The wood platform supported by the *latte* may have measured perhaps 14 × 43 feet and contained an area of about 600 square feet. Like most coastal

latte, the long axis of the structure was parallel to the nearest seashore.

The Oruno foundation differed markedly from the Tumon Bay *latte* in shape, size, and method of support. The columns were carefully cut from slabs of a conglomerate stone formed by coral, worm tubes, and mollusks. The material probably was taken from the beach 220 feet to the west. The stone slabs tapered from 10 × 34 inches at their bases to 6 × 22 inches at their tops. Carefully laid stone blocks 16 and 24 inches long braced the column foundations on all four sides to hold the uprights in their vertical positions. The smooth surfaces of the columns faced seaward; the rough surfaces, inshore. In plan the distance between pairs of columns varied slightly.

The capstones, all of the same species of brain coral, were elliptical in plan. They measured 29 × 35 inches and were 20 inches high. A 6-inch groove was incised into the perimeter of each capital, and slots about 4 inches deep were carved into the capitals' bases to receive their columns. The Oruno columns and capstones were much more uniform in size and shape than those of Tumon Bay. Burials with grave artifacts typical of *latte* sites also were found at Oruno. Thompson (1932) reported a limited number of similar *latte* for other sites on the north and northwest coasts of Guam and in the southern interiors.

TINIAN

The *latte* stones of the House of Taga on Tinian are some 16 feet high, about twice the height of the next highest stone foundation in the Marianas. Located some 100 miles northeast of Guam, Tinian is separated by a 3-mile-wide channel from Saipan to the northeast. The coastal area of the island is mostly suitable for villages and contains a high percentage of productive land. Inland Tinian, like inland northern Guam, is a limestone plateau with no potable water and thus is unsuitable for human habitation.

The 12-mile-long island is at most 6.5 miles wide and encompasses a land area of 39.3 square miles. The highest point of land is 614-foot-high Kastiyu Hill, well less than half the height of Mount Lamlam on Guam. No streams are found on Tinian. Here water collects in pools at the foot of high ridges or in wells.

The island consists of two major raised limestone plateaus separated by the fertile Makpo Valley near the southern end of the island. The coastline largely consists of limestone cliffs dropping abruptly into the sea, but several beaches and sandy coves interrupt the rocky coast. Of particular importance is the Tinian Harbor area on the southwest coast, the principal landing area on the island and the local center of population since prehistoric times.

The three major areas of *latte* sites on the island are Tinian Harbor represented by the Tachognya and Taga sites in this study, Makpo Valley, and Unai Dangkulo along the northern east coast. Alexander Spoehr (1957) found three *latte* sites near the fresh water swamp of Makpo Valley. The largest of these sites consisted of two *latte* located 40 feet apart. The northern set contained ten stone columns and measured 13.5 × 45 feet. The best preserved of the shafts was trapezoidal in shape and rose 3 feet above the ground. In 1984 Darlene Moore found more than twenty *latte* in a single large coastal site at Unai Dangkulo (Graves, 1986).

Tachognya

The Tachognya site contains the relatively intact remains of an entire prehistoric village. The site also is known as the Blue Site, a synonym derived from its designation as Blue Beach by U.S. invasion forces in 1944. The area was bombarded but no invasion occurred at Blue Beach, thus sparing the remains of the village from destruction. The Chamorro name for the area is Tachognya.

The site consists of ten *latte* houses placed end to end in a 730-foot-long alignment parallel to the sandy beach and about 200 feet from the coastline facing the Philippine Sea. The site is well located to take advantage of fishing along the coast and soil suitable for farming inshore. Heavy concentrations of shells and sherds were found within 50 feet of the houses. The site is level, but to the west the ground slopes down toward the beach.

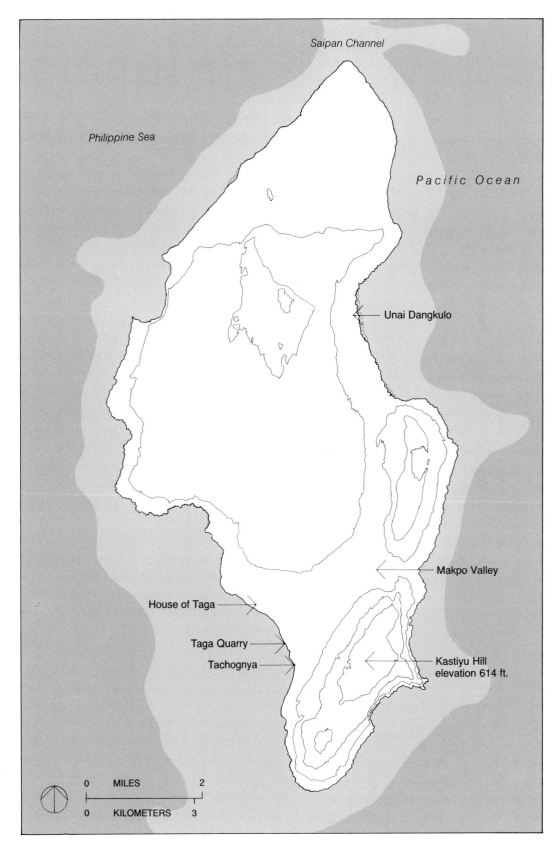

Plan of the Taga site, Tinian (based on the un-published notes of Hans G. Hornbostel in the archives of the Bernice P. Bishop Museum).

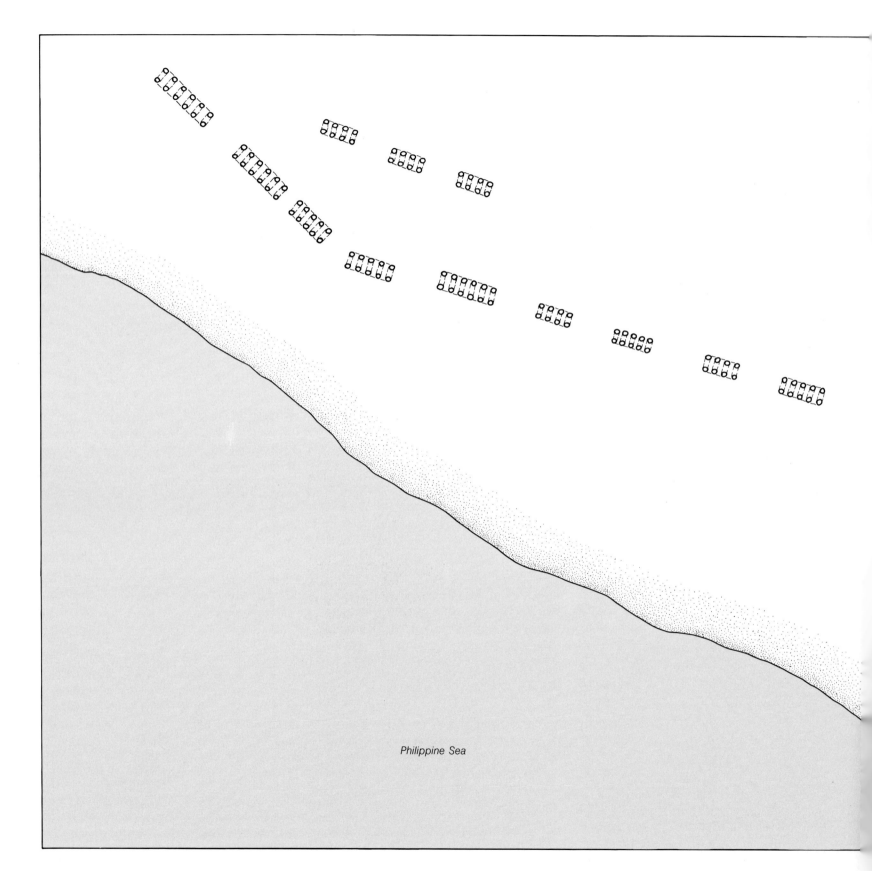

Philippine Sea

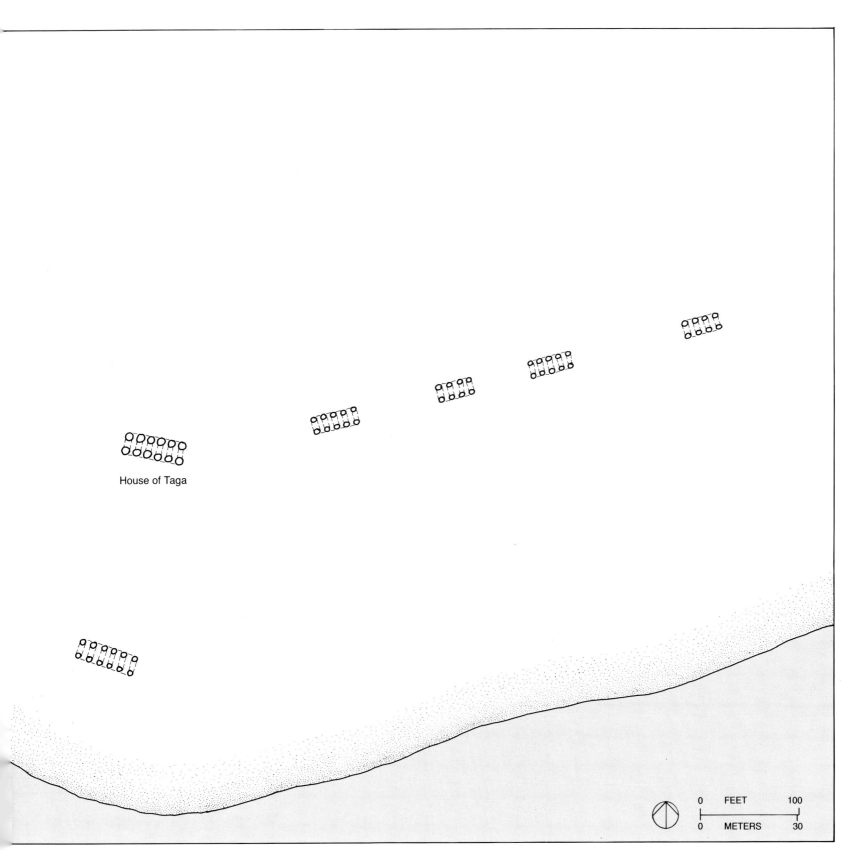

House of Taga

0   FEET   100

0   METERS   30

Plan of the Tachognya site, Tinian.

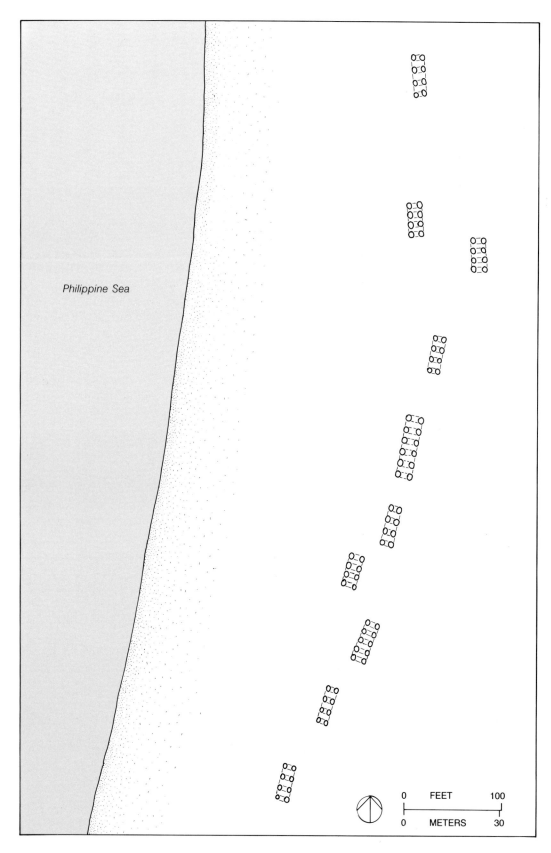

Philippine Sea

0   FEET   100

0   METERS   30

Middens contribute to the leveling of the site's surface.

Typical of *latte* sites, the largest house is near the center of the group, perhaps reflecting the social organization of the community. The site lies along the edge of an abandoned sugarcane field. Quite likely, wood houses and additional *latte* have disappeared from the site since prehistoric times. The largest foundation had twelve columns and measured 14 × 58 feet, suggesting an area of 812 square feet. This may have been the residence of the chief or the highest ranked person in the village.

All of the columns and capstone remains were coral limestone. The markedly trapezoidal piers tapered from 2.5 × 4.1 feet at their bases to 1.5 × 1.6 feet at their tops and rose 5.2 to 5.8 feet in height. Stones were packed around the columns' bases to keep them upright. The capstones appear to have measured at most 4 feet in diameter and were 1.8 to 2 feet in thickness. The top of the capstone originally would have been about 7.5 feet above the ground level. Burials were found in the direction of the sea west of the centerline of the *latte*, and coral-pebble paving formed a floor on grade beneath the house. Both of these features are characteristic of *latte* sites.

North of Tachognya's largest structure were four house foundations, each having eight columns. They ranged from 31 to 34 feet in length and from 372 to 416 square feet in area. The dimensions given are measured to the outermost faces of the stone columns rather than to their centerlines. The columns also were markedly trapezoidal and proportionately smaller in size than the twelve-column structure. The houses of the northern group were placed 50 to 100 feet apart.

South of the central *latte* were five houses, four with eight columns and one with ten columns, which ranged from 30 to 41 feet in length and from 360 to 513 square feet in area. Of sizes proportionately smaller than the twelve-column foundation, the houses to the south were spaced only 25 to 50 feet apart.

The widths of houses at Tachognya were 11 to 14 feet at most, typical of Marianas *latte.* The long dimensions of the columns in plan were parallel to the longitudinal axis of the house foundations, the axis of the village alignment, and the coastline.

Taga Site

The Taga site was a lineal arrangement of eighteen *latte* in a curving 1,600-foot-long arc parallel to the coastline of Tinian Harbor at the time of Hans G. Hornbostel's visit in 1924. During the Second World War the nearby town of Tinian was completely destroyed. Subsequently, the harbor area was altered substantially and the shore was expanded into the lagoon in the process of building a large military installation. Fortunately, the largest stone foundation at the site and the highest in the Marianas, the House of Taga, escaped destruction. The reconstruction shown here is based largely on the notes of Hornbostel in the Bernice P. Bishop Museum, the field work of Alexander Spoehr (1957), and my personal observations.

The structures of the Taga site lay 130 to 350 feet from the original shoreline, according to Hornbostel's notes. Fourteen *latte* lay along the primary axis of the site, three were inshore toward the northwest, and one was near the center of the group and about 130 feet from the shore. The House of Taga was located near the center of the site, some 160 feet from its closest neighbor.

Of the nine foundations closest to the coast and northwest of the House of Taga, three had twelve columns, four had ten columns, and two had eight columns. The structures were spaced 20 to 60 feet apart. The westernmost *latte* was the largest of the north group. It had twelve columns and measured 10.9 × 61.6 feet, an area of about 670 square feet. Its columns rose about 5 feet above the ground level, suggesting an original height to the top of the capstones of almost 8 feet.

The inshore group to the northwest had three stone foundations with possibly eight columns each. All three structures were in ruins, according to Hornbostel. The column heights were about 3 feet. The foundations in this group were spaced about 40 feet apart.

The four-*latte* group east of the House of Taga had two structures with ten columns and two with eight columns. The structures were spaced from 65 to 125 feet apart, and all were in ruins. Columns in the east group were at most 5.3 feet high. The structure closest to the shore was second in size only to the House of Taga. Its columns rose about 5.4 feet above the ground, and its capstones were approximately 5.3 feet in diameter. Its plan dimensions were about 12.7 × 54.5 feet, an area of almost 700 square feet.

The House of Taga was first recorded by Lord Anson (Walter, 1974) during his voyage around the world, 1740–1744. When he arrived on Tinian in August of 1742, the island was inhabited only by a small foraging band of Chamorros and a Spaniard, all of whom he took prisoner. The original inhabitants of Tinian had been removed to Guam less than fifty years before Anson's visit. Concerning the *latte* of Tinian, he observed:

. . . there are, in all parts of the Island, a great number of ruins of a very particular kind; they usually consist of two rows of square pyramidal pillars, each pillar being about six feet from the next, and the distance between the rows being about twelve feet; the pillars themselves are about five feet square at the base, and about thirteen feet high; and on the top of each of them there is a semi-globe, with the flat part upwards; the whole of the pillars and semi-globe is solid, being composed of sand and stone cemented together, and plaistered over. This odd fabrick will be better understood, by inspecting the view of the watering place inserted above, where an assemblage of these pillars is drawn, and is denoted by the letter (a). If the account our prisoners gave us of these structures was true, the Island must indeed have been extremely populous; for they assured us, that they were the foundations of particular buildings set apart for those *Indians* only, who had engaged in some religious vow; and monastic institutions are often to be met with in many Pagan nations. However, if these ruins were originally the basis of the common dwelling-houses of the natives, their numbers must have been considerable; for in many parts of the Island they are extremely thick planted, and sufficiently evince the great plenty of former inhabitants. (Walter, 1974:293–294)

Lord Anson's engraving shows all twelve of the original columns and capstones of the House of Taga standing erect. He gave us the first account of prehistoric architecture in Micronesia, describing the remarkable House of Taga in unmistakable detail although he did not mention its name. Anson also noted larger numbers of ancient sites elsewhere on Tinian.

In 1818, Jacques Arago found only seven columns still standing at the House of Taga, and by 1900 only five were erect (Spoehr, 1957:86–87). Hornbostel observed two standing columns in 1924, the same two that I saw thirty years later. The columns originally were buried 1.7 to 3 feet into sandy soil and had no underlying bearing strata. Their foundations were not adequate to maintain most of the columns upright, particularly during the seismic disturbances that occur frequently in the Marianas. Bracing stones that may have been packed around the bases of the columns to keep them erect apparently were not adequate in size or number. The *latte* is placed on a slight rise about 2 feet above the surrounding grade.

The overall dimension of the House of Taga platform may have been about 21 × 64.3 feet or 1,350 square feet. The remarkable dimension of the stone foundation is not its plan area but its exceptional height of 16 feet. The columns range from 12.9 to 14.1 feet in length, from 3.5 to 5.8 feet in width, and from 3 to 3.9 feet in thickness. The capstones vary from 6.9 to 8.1 feet in diameter and from 4 to 5.1 feet in thickness. Both the columns and the capstones are limestone coral. The columns were less trapezoidal in elevation and more nearly square in plan than most *latte* piers.

Near the center of the House of Taga's south side, and about 11.5 feet from it, Spoehr (1957) found an isolated capstone 3.5 feet in diameter. The stone appeared to have been carved to form three steps. Spoehr speculated that it may have served as the base of a ladder that gave access to the house originally. If this is true, the main entry would have been from the direction of the sea into the house's long side. Large amounts of pottery on and below the surface of the House of Taga site suggest human occupation of the site over an extended period of time.

Lord Anson's engraving illustrating the House
of Taga *latte* in 1742 shows all twelve columns
erect with capstones in place (Anson, 1748:pl.
37, upper right, in Walter, 1984).

The method of erecting the House of Taga megaliths remains a matter of speculation, although Spoehr suggested the possible use of earth ramps. We know that the wheel and its uses were unknown in Micronesia. Noting the apparent method of lifting *latte* stones from quarries, I would offer the possibility that levers, successive layers of earth fill, quite likely ropes, and log rollers may have been used in erecting the foundation stones of the House of Taga. I estimate the weight of a typical stone column to be in the range of fourteen tons, assuming a 14-foot column length, 4.5 × 3.4-foot average plan dimension, and a coral limestone density of perhaps 130 pounds per cubic foot.

During my visit to the site in 1954 the site was largely cleared of underbrush. The remains of the House of Taga were in a rectangular opening bordered by dense trees along the perimeter. The edge of the preserve was defined by a small, stone-lined drainage channel, perhaps installed during the Japanese administration. The presence of a clearing in the otherwise dense jungle underbrush and the monumental megalithic remains imparted a memorable sense of place.

The stone columns and capstones of the House of Taga came from a coastal quarry about 4,000 feet south of the site, one of several prehistoric quarries found on Tinian. Here a limestone formation terminates ab-

ruptly in a cliff facing the Philippine Sea to the west. A small cove with a sandy beach divides the limestone formation into two parts. It seems plausible that the quarried stones were moved to the beach, loaded onto wooden rafts or floats, transported by sea northwesterly to a landing point as close as possible to the final destination, and moved several hundred feet inland to the erection site.

The quarrying operation seems to have consisted of cutting a small trench around the stone column or capital and then deepening the trench until the stone was undercut and freed from its matrix. The excavation may have ceased at a depth where a softer

vein occurred. Pecking with harder stones into the softer vein may have assisted in dislodging the megalith. An alternative method would have been to drive wooden wedges into the stone around the perimeter of its base to produce a fracture and permit extraction. Wetting the wood wedges would have caused the wood to expand, increasing the stresses on the stone and producing a fracture.

Some stones apparently broke during the quarrying operation. Stones seem to have been lifted vertically from the quarry, capstones being removed with their flat tops up. In some places tool marks up to 4 feet long and 2 inches deep were found, probably made by adzes or chisels. The quarry yielded smaller stones as well as the megaliths for the House of Taga.

ROTA

Like Tinian, the island of Rota was densely inhabited in prehistoric times and today yields some of the most notable remains of prehistoric architecture in the Marianas. A 1980 survey of the island identified 46 separate *latte* sites containing some 113 individual structures (Gordon, Hanson, and Thomas, 1982). The stone columns and capstones in the As Nieves Quarry seem to have been intended for a foundation even higher than the House of Taga on Tinian. The largest number of *latte* in a single site was found at Mochong (also Mochon or Muchon) on the north coast of Rota. The site contained at least 47 structures in a single large settlement (Ward and Craib, 1983).

Rota, which lies about 30 miles northwest of Guam in the direction of Tinian, is approximately 12 miles long and 5 miles wide and contains a land area of 32.9 square miles. Composed of calcareous rock, Rota is dominated by 1,627-foot-high Mount Savana near its center. Five freshwater streams along the southcentral coast and numerous wells supply fresh water to the island. Today dense tropical vegetation covers much of Rota, but no large trees are found.

Plan and elevation of the House of Taga *latte*,
Tinian.

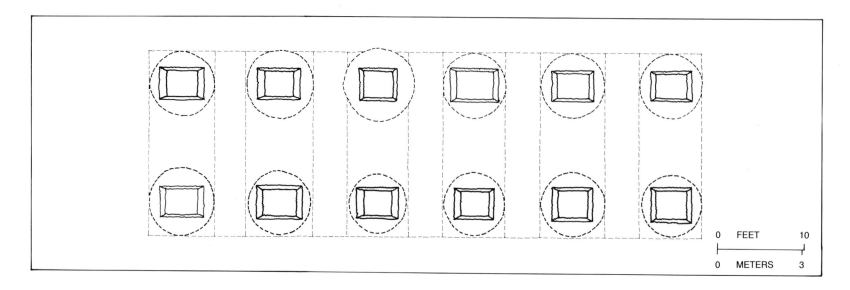

Latte sites on the island generally are found along the north coast and on the east end well away from the escarpment of Mount Savana. Rota's main settlement today is the town of Songsong, the Rotanese word for village. The town is located on a peninsula that extends out from the southwest end of the island, the probable location of the earliest prehistoric settlement on Rota (Ward and Craib, 1983). Rota's population in 1984 was perhaps 1,100. Although the island's prehistoric sites have been disturbed considerably over the years, particularly by a Japanese coastal trenching system during the Second World War, Rota has more *latte* sites intact today than do Guam, Tinian, or Saipan.

The earliest European contact with Rota probably occurred when the Spanish ship *Santa Margarita* struck a reef on the island in 1601 (Driver, 1983). Rota became a center of Chamorro resistance against the Spanish, but a Sergeant-Major Quiroga subjugated the island in the last uprising of 1684. Most of the Chamorros were relocated to Guam in 1696, but part of the population was permitted to remain on Rota "and thus maintained a continuity with the prehistoric past unclaimed by others of the Marianas" (Ward and Craib, 1983:8).

As Nieves Quarry

The quarry at As Nieves, also spelled Niebes, rivals in impressiveness the Taga site on

Tinian. Here within a 120 × 180-foot area lie the remains of an unfinished *latte* that would have been perhaps 18 feet high, some 2 feet higher than the House of Taga foundation. The quarry contains nine columns and seven capstones surrounded by trenches excavated into the limestone. The trenches were 2 to 4.3 feet deep, except for a 4-inch-deep depression around one capstone that today is filled with surface soil. Only one capital had been lifted about 3 feet out of its pit. The megalith presently rests on soil apparently placed as it was lifted by levers.

The plan of the quarry at As Nieves shown here is based on the map prepared by Hornbostel during his 1925 survey and on the plan subsequently published by Spoehr (1957:fig. 44). Hornbostel found considerable lime and fired rock particles in the soil along the trenches. He observed that the trenches apparently had been fired in order to convert the stone into lime and successively scraped out with a stone adze until the megalith was isolated and could be removed. The prehistoric Chamorros were betel nut chewers and hence familiar with firing coral to obtain lime for combining with betel nut. This seems to be an example of transferring a trait associated with chewing a narcotic to the quarrying of stone.

During my visit to the site in 1984, I measured several of the megaliths. The columns ranged from 16.3 to 16.9 feet in length and

from 4.9 to 7.7 feet in width. The sides of some of the columns were straight, but others showed entasis of up to 3 inches. I also had observed slight, but inconsistent, entasis on some of the columns of the House of Taga. My guess would be that the Chamorro builders probably were not consciously attempting to employ the visual subtlety of entasis, although they seem to have understood clearly the improved stability achieved by making columns bigger at their bases than at their tops.

The columns were not quarried side by side, although this procedure would have minimized the quantity of trenching required. Perhaps this would have hampered the process of lifting the megaliths to the level of adjacent grade, or it may refer to some symbolic or ritualistic meaning in the quarrying process that has been lost. Ritual during construction was important in all of the islands of Micronesia. The quarrying operation may have been deliberately labor intensive, by way of reinforcing the class distinction associated with *latte* building. Another possibility might be that the quarry workers lacked the experience required to evolve more efficient quarrying procedures.

The As Nieves capstones that I measured were not precisely circular in plan. For example, the diameter of the easternmost capital varied from 9.5 to 10 feet. The northwesternmost capital was about 10 feet in di-

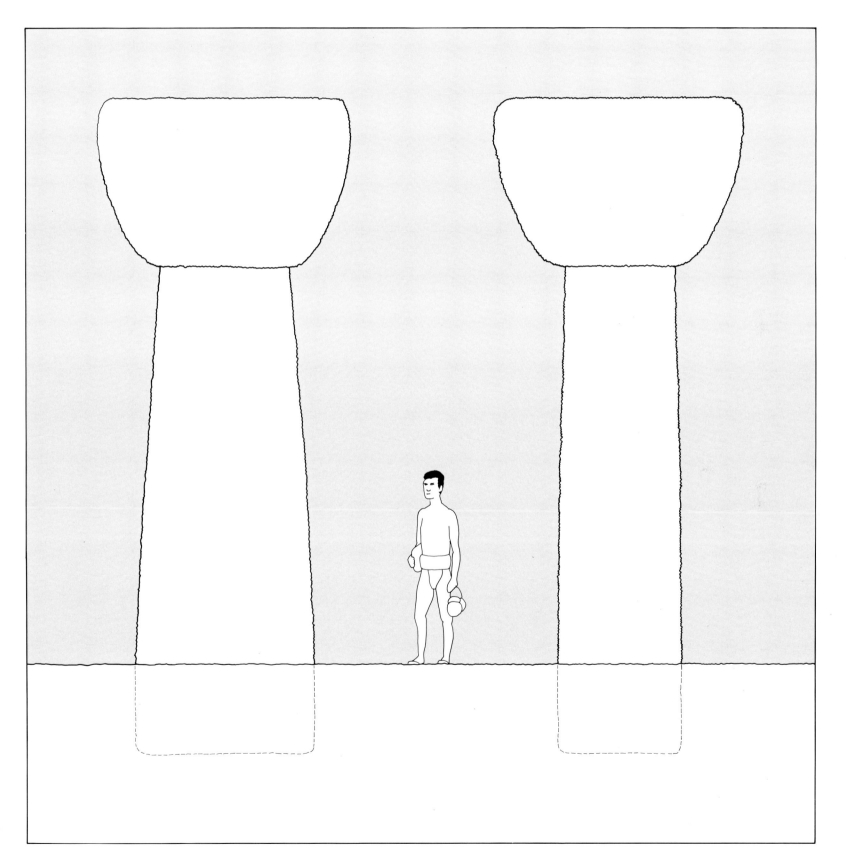

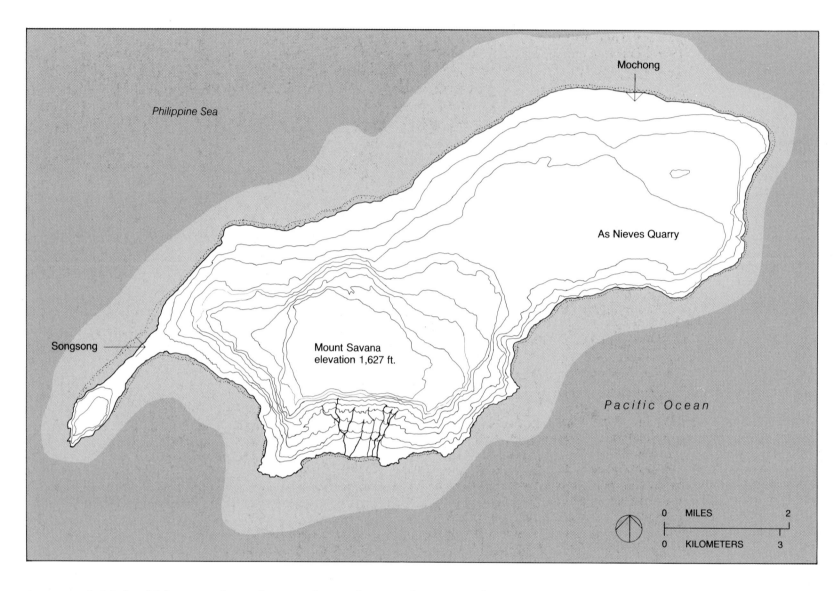

Mochong

Philippine Sea

As Nieves Quarry

Mount Savana
elevation 1,627 ft.

Songsong

Pacific Ocean

| 0 | MILES | 2 |
| 0 | KILOMETERS | 3 |

ameter and 5.3 feet high. My estimate for the weight of a typical column at As Nieves would be in the range of 27 tons, almost twice the weight of a typical column of the House of Taga *latte*. This estimate is based on a 16.9-foot-long column with an average 4 × 6.3-foot section and an assumed limestone density of 130 pounds per cubic foot. I noticed that some of the columns were cracked although they had not been moved. When weathered, the coral limestone changes in color from ochre to gray.

Mochong Site

The site of the largest group of *latte* found in the Marianas, Mochong is located on the rocky north coast of Rota near the eastern end of the island. The prehistoric remains extend some 1,480 feet along the shore and up to 900 feet inshore, encompassing an area of about 30 acres. Of the 53 foundations shown in the site plan presented here, 47 were recorded and 6 more were reported to have existed until recently. The site plan is based on a well-recorded survey in 1983 by a field crew under the direction of Drs. Graeme K. Ward and John L. Craib. The earliest radiocarbon date for Mochong indicated human occupation within eighty-five years of 640 B.C. (Takayama and Intoh, 1976).

During my visit I observed more than a dozen separate structures and others that dis-

appeared into the dense undergrowth, for the jungle had reclaimed much of the site since the clearing and surveying operation of the previous year. I measured the two unusual structures shown on these pages, one incorporating a wall in lieu of the usual second row of columns and capstones, and the other containing fourteen columns, the largest number of shafts for any *latte* reported in the Marianas. All of the Mochong capitals had fallen from their original positions. Characteristic of most *latte* sites, the structures were parallel to the nearby coastline and generally were arranged in long rows with end-to-end alignments.

The exceptional Mochong wall *latte*, desig-

nated ML-1 by the 1983 survey, consisted of six columns in a row parallel to five abutting stone slabs that formed a solid wall 54.3 feet long. The column row was 11.6 feet from the wall. Originally, six capstones placed on top of the wall aligned with the capitals on the six free-standing columns. If the capstones were restored to their original positions, the structure would measure about 6.7 feet in height and some 14.4 feet in width.

The foundation could have supported a wooden platform with an area of perhaps 950 square feet. The columns rose 4.3 feet above the grade and tapered from 2.7 feet in width at their bases to 2 feet at their tops. In 1984 all of the wall slabs and five of the

six columns remained erect. The fallen capstones lay near the bases of the wall and columns and showed relatively little evidence of weathering or fracturing. No other combined wall and column foundations have been reported in the Marianas.

Radiocarbon dating for the Mochong wall *latte* indicates that it probably was constructed sometime after 1335 and remained in use until within eighty years of 1780 (Takayama and Egami, 1971). Takayama found several burials beneath the structure and noted that stones were packed around the column and wall bases to keep them erect. Soil on the site was 2 feet deep. Below this depth lay beach sand.

A second extraordinary structure at Mochong is the fourteen-column foundation located between the wall *latte* and the coastline. It was designated ML-4 by the 1983 survey. Structures having as many as fourteen columns rarely have been reported in the Marianas. The plan dimensions are about 15.8 × 72.8 feet, measuring to the outermost surfaces of the capitals.

Mochong's fourteen-column structure could have supported a wooden platform perhaps 1,150 square feet in area, somewhat smaller than the 1,350-square-foot platform of the House of Taga with twelve columns. Although it was more than 8 feet longer than the House of Taga, the fourteen-column

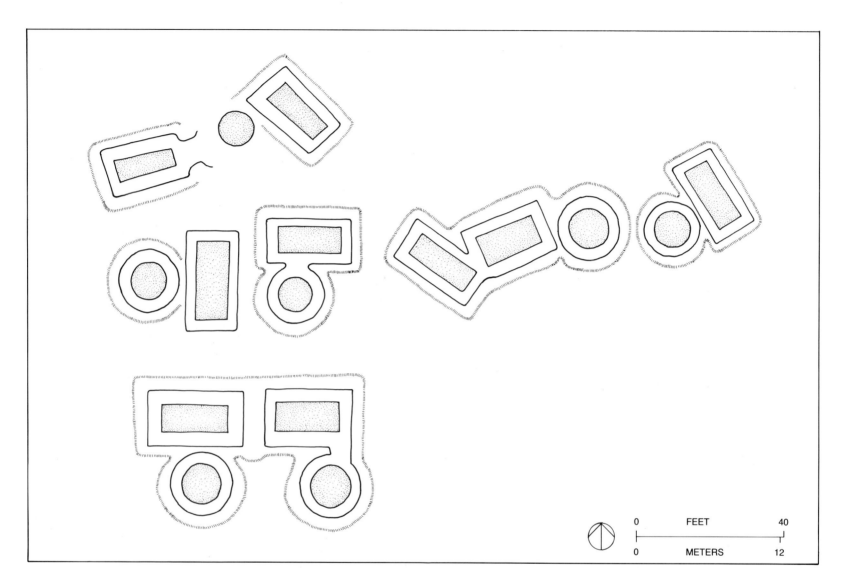

```
                              0        FEET         40
         ◍                    ├─────────────────────┤
                              0       METERS        12
```

structure's wood platform was about 5 feet narrower. The differences in width for the two *latte* are due partly to the distances between the column rows and partly to the variations in capstone diameters.

The fourteen columns rose slightly more than 5 feet above grade, varied from 2.7 to 3.6 feet in width, and measured about 2 feet in thickness. The capstones varied in diameter from 4 to 5 feet and were approximately 3 feet high. If the megaliths were restored to their original positions, the *latte* would be about 8.2 feet high.

LATTE HOUSE ALTERNATIVES

The perishable wood superstructures of the Marianas' *latte* houses disappeared centuries ago. Lord Anson found only the surviving megaliths of the House of Taga foundation during his visit in 1742, although the Chamorros had left Tinian less than fifty years before. Various configurations for structures have been proposed in recent centuries.

Carano and Sanchez (1964) proposed a hip roof built over the stone columns and capstones with a floor on grade. Their hip roof model terminated possibly 3 or 4 feet above grade. A number of problems arise with this proposal. Hip roofs lack gables, the traditional roof type for all of the important houses on Yap, Palau, Pohnpei, and Kosrae. The perimeter below the roof would have been open all around. No "small windows" (Abella, 1965) would be present, although a member of the Legaspi expedition recorded these features in 1565. Another problem would be that braces would be required to keep the lower extensions of the rafters from sagging in larger structures.

A third problem with the pyramidal model would be encountered in placing this structure on very uneven terrain, such as the Nomna Bay site where a floor on grade would be all but useless. Another question arises in the case of relatively low *latte*, such as those

only 3 or 4 feet high. Headroom would be totally inadequate. Carano and Sanchez apparently derived their model from Louis de Freycinet (1829), who about 1818 proposed a similar structure, almost three centuries after initial Western contact with the Marianas. In my view the pyramidal roof seems to be a very unlikely configuration for a *latte* superstructure of wood.

Alejandro Lizama (1983), a Guamanian artist and chief technician to the territorial archaeologist who has studied many *latte* sites, proposes a modified A-frame superstructure with main rafters exposed to the weather and extending to grade. This proposal also has a number of problems. One is the

exposure of main structural members to the weather in Micronesia, where unprotected wood deteriorates very quickly. Roof and wall thatch is intended to be replaced periodically, but main structural wood members can be replaced only with great difficulty. Frequent wetting and drying in tropical rainstorms would require frequent replacement of exposed rafters extending to grade.

A second question about the A-frame proposal for a *latte* superstructure would be the lack of precedent for structures of this type anywhere in Micronesia. Stone bases of widely differing types occur throughout Micronesia. All of the important wood structures of Micronesia have vertical enclosing

walls or wall posts defining vertical planes. An A-frame would lack vertical walls on its two long sides.

Another problem with the A-frame model involves the lengths of wood members required. The length of a roof beam for an 8-foot-high *latte* would be about 40 feet from ridge to grade, plus perhaps 2 feet embedded into the ground. The 16-foot-high House of Taga foundation suggests roof beams perhaps 50 feet long in an A-frame configuration. The longest structural timbers I have found in Micronesia are the 34-foot-long central posts of the *pebaey* in Bechiyal Village. Their base diameters are in the range of 24 to 30 inches. Trees capable of yielding long, rela-

141

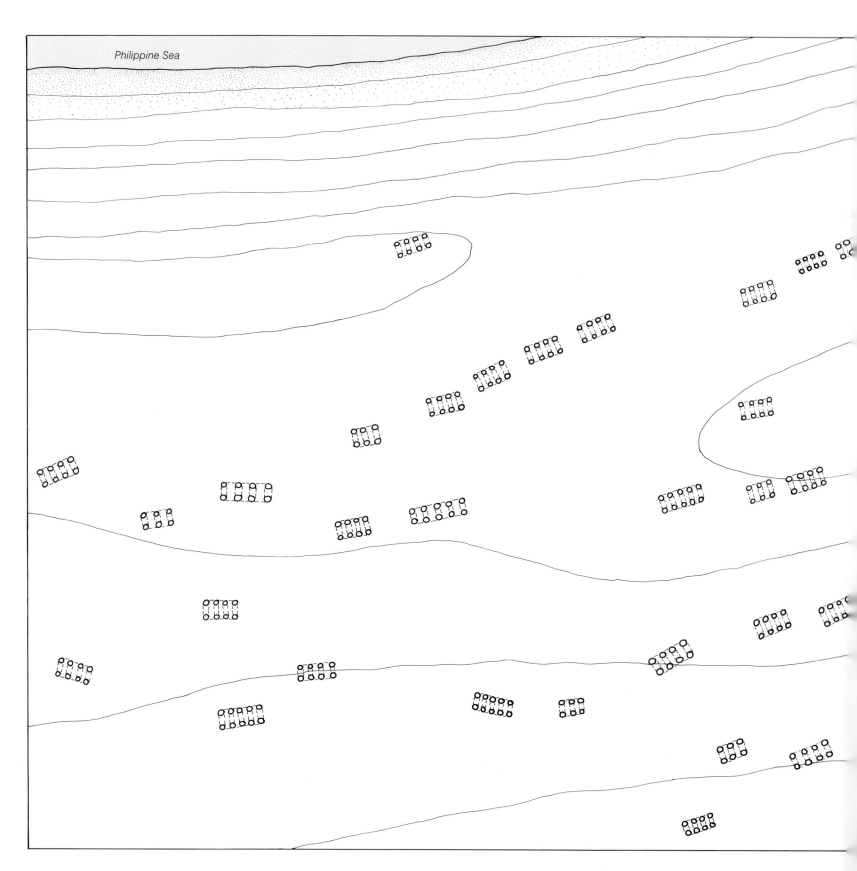

Plan of the Mochong site, Rota (after Ward and Craib, 1983).

Philippine Sea

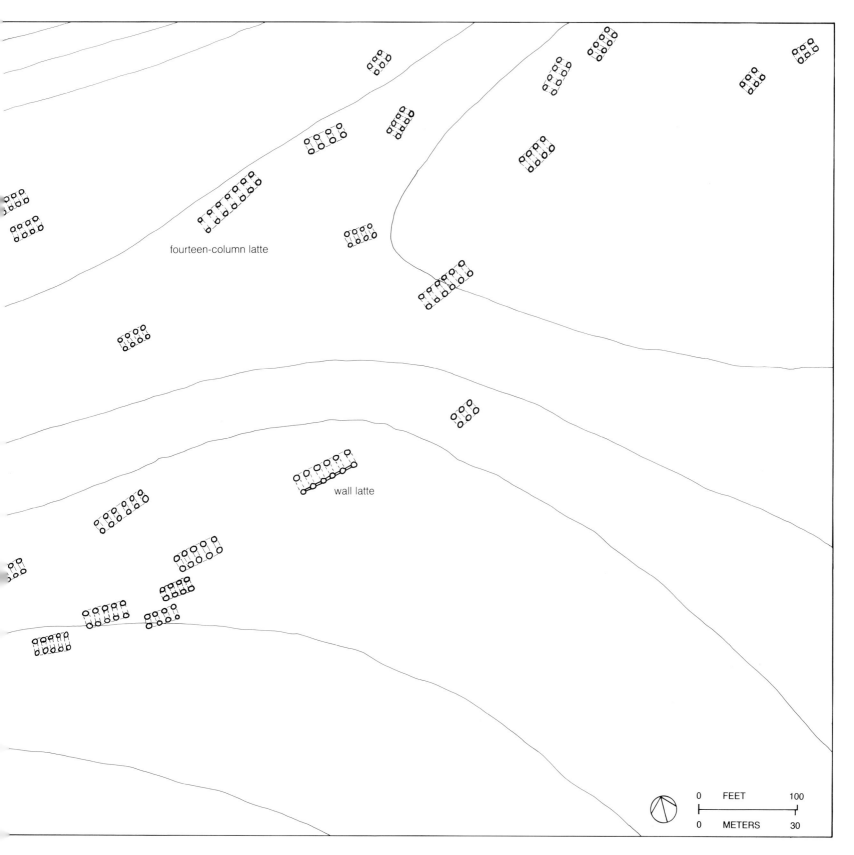

fourteen-column latte

wall latte

0   FEET   100

0   METERS   30

Plan and elevation of the Mochong wall *latte*.

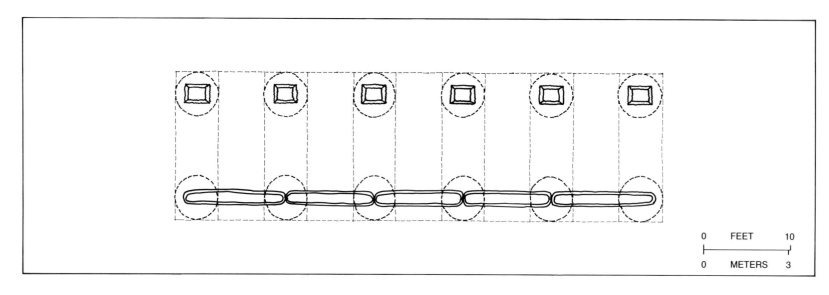

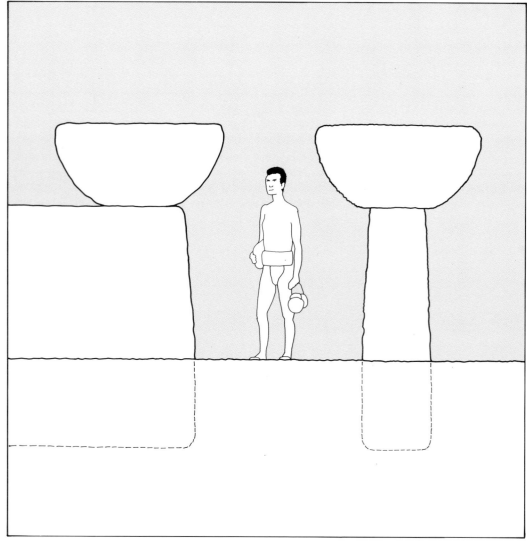

tively straight roof beams in the required quantities seem to be problematical in the Marianas.

Ventilation is another question for the A-frame model. Abella (1965) noted that "the chambers have small windows," an arrangement not possible in the two long sides of the A-frame structure. Lizama (1983) proposes that the "windows" may have been in the floor, but again no precedent for this arrangement exists elsewhere in Micronesia. Throughout Micronesia the typical ventilation system is a series of small windows or portals, frequently with flaps or shutters of some sort, in the vertical walls of structures.

Another question arises with respect to entrance into an A-frame structure through one of the two gable ends. We know that *latte* often were located parallel to a nearby shoreline or watercourse. Thus entry into an A-frame could not have been from the direction of the sea. We also know that burials were found near the seaward side of many *latte,* that smooth sides of stone columns faced the sea at Oruno, and that Spoehr suggested an entrance from the seaward side of the House of Taga.

I suggest that the seaward orientation may have held a special significance for the ancient Chamorros, and that this was likely the direction of the major entrance. Abella (1965) noted "rooms and quarters on either side of the living room" (Plaza, 1973:7).

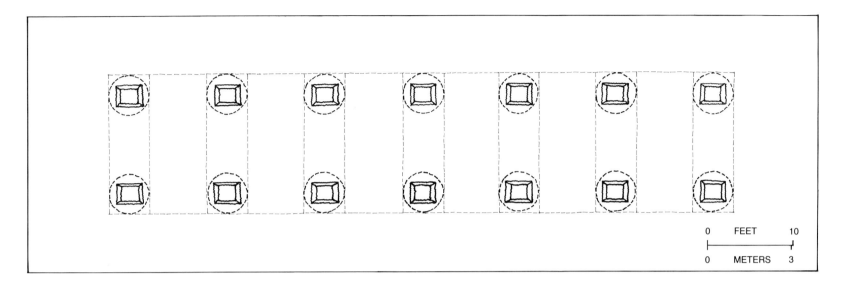

It seems likely that the elongated plan of the typical *latte* house was partitioned transversely, and that entering into the center compartment would afford access to flanking rooms without traversing the entire length of the platform.

One reason for proposing pyramidal or A-frame configurations over the centuries may have been a mistranslation of the original Spanish account of "long column-like stones in the shape of pyramids" (Plaza, 1973:6). The improper translation suggests that the wood structures were in the shape of pyramids, not the columns supporting the houses. Without further exploration of problems with pyramidal or A-frame models, I would seek a more plausible alternative.

A third possible configuration for *latte* house superstructures might be along the lines of traditional wooden structures found on Truk (Le Bar, 1964). Here secondary rafters extend beyond the main roof rafters to form perimeter spaces supported by exterior posts. The posts and beams are of wood and are protected from the elements by thatched roofs. While this model may be plausible for some *latte* structures, it seems most unlikely for columns and capstones lower than head height or for structures located on very uneven terrain, such as those at Nomna Bay. A further problem with the perimeter post proposal is that to my knowledge no perimeter post molds have been recorded to date for

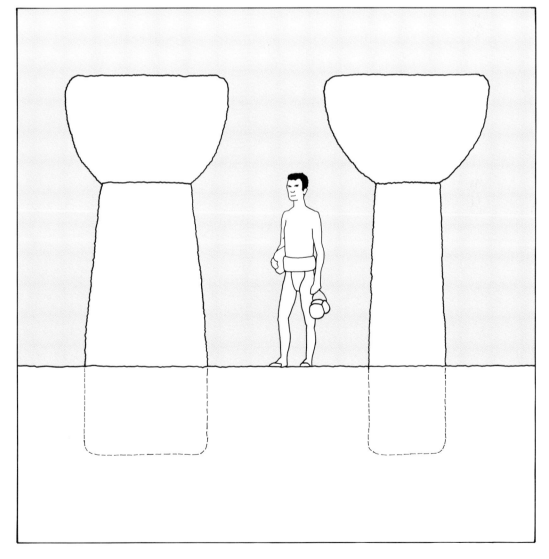

Alternative configurations for *latte* house superstructures.

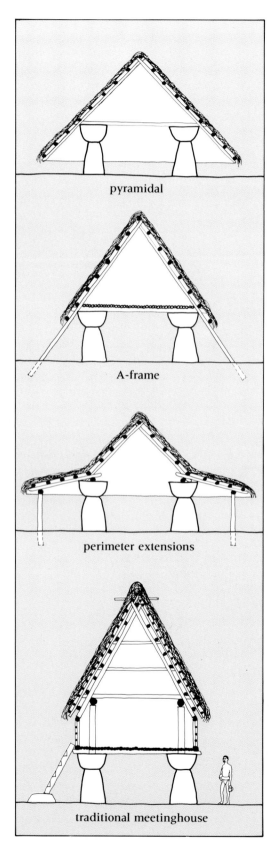

pyramidal

A-frame

perimeter extensions

traditional meetinghouse

any *latte* set. Thus, the Trukese model appears to be unlikely for *latte* superstructures.

Proposed Reconstruction

A more plausible configuration of *latte* superstructures was suggested by Laura Thompson (1932:463), who wrote, "It is likely that the ancient twelve stone pillared house of the Marianas resembled the Pelew *keldok-bai* in structure." Her text referred specifically to Kubary's (1895) illustration in his Volume 2, Plate 29. We know that the languages of Palau and the Marianas, unlike other Micronesian languages, seem to have come from the direction of the Philippines or perhaps islands southeast of Asia. Perhaps the architecture of Palau and the Marianas had origins similar to their languages. In any event, the House of Taga reconstruction proposed here is based on Kubary's illustration, Spoehr's (1957) site plan, and my own speculations.

The reconstruction shows transverse beams of wood bearing on pairs of capstones, a wood-framed superstructure, plaited split bamboo walls, and a steep roof thatched with pandanus. Six wall portals provide access and ventilation, two on each long side and one on each end. Two wall posts flank each portal on the long sides; thus, three infilled panels flank each portal in a well-resolved architectural composition.

As in Kubary's Plate 29, the reconstructed wood structure above the platform consists of two distinctly separate components. The primary structure is made up of the main posts, roof beams, purlins, and tie beams at three levels. The secondary structure is associated with the external surfaces of the house, the roof thatch, and the wall infill.

The roof gable projects outward for protection from the rain, and no porches or verandahs are used. While interior partitions occasionally were used elsewhere in Micronesia, they often tended to be little more than temporary screens that were removed when no longer required. I propose that the interior partitions of Chamorro houses probably resembled temporary screens more closely than compartmentalizing walls associated with European houses.

Beyond this point the reconstruction departs from Kubary's *keldok-bai* model. Because the House of Taga columns were placed more than 11 feet apart, I suggest that each capstone may have supported two floor beams to reduce the span of the flooring. The paired beams may have been placed 5 to 6 feet apart. Lashing cords may have secured the floor beams to the capstones to prohibit either horizontal movement or vertical uplift during windstorms.

Thus, the main beams of the wood platform would have served to stabilize the capstones, helping to keep them in position on their stone columns. The disappearance of wood platforms may help to account for the rarity of capstones on the top of their columns today. A floor consisting of bamboo poles covered with woven mats is suggested rather than the hewn planks characteristic of Palau. I propose that the Marianas' *latte* house probably employed wood logs and cord-bound joints rather than hewn planks and posts or carefully interlocking joinery. Perhaps notched log ladders of the type used widely in Micronesia provided access to the platform. A three-stepped stone is shown at the base of the ladders, following Spoehr's suggestion.

At this point the reader may find it helpful to refer to the reconstructed platform plan proposed for the House of Taga. Comparing this plan with the previously presented floor plan of the existing Bai-ra-Irrai, Palau, one observes that both structures are about 20 feet wide. However, the 64-foot-long *latte* platform is some 4 feet shorter than the floor of the *bai*. Six wall portals appear in both structures, one at each end and two on either side. Note that the main posts of the Taga plan are located in the centers of their supporting capstones and columns. These components would have transferred the superimposed weight of the roof structure directly to the ground with no unbalancing vertical forces. The wall weight on one side of each capstone seems to balance the midspan weight of the platform floor, contributing additional stability to the structure.

My further speculation would be that the *latte* house was generally less sophisticated

A reconstructed perspective of the House of Taga on Tinian shows 16-foot-high stone columns and capstones supporting a traditional wood frame house.

Reconstructed House of Taga section in perspective, Tinian Island. In all some 45 feet high, the structure rests on the tallest *latte* in the Marianas.

architecturally than major wood structures found elsewhere in Micronesia. The Chamorro builders presumably understood the problem of keeping water from standing on the flat tops of capstones in view of the vulnerability of wood beams to rot caused by repeated wetting and drying. Roof overhangs would have been essential to the preservation of the *latte* house.

The House of Taga reconstruction proposed here would require more than thirty large timbers at most 20 feet long for use as floor, roof, and tie beams. Presumably, longer longitudinal members were composed of several timbers spliced end to end. Roof purlins and the ridge beam may have consisted of bundled bamboos, such as those used elsewhere in Micronesia.

Large native timbers are exceedingly rare in the Marianas today, although Michael Graves (1986) suggested that trees yielding large timbers may have been more common in the Marianas prehistorically. An example is the *Eugenia reinwardtiana* tree, of which a few rare specimens survive on Guam today.

No fire pits are shown in the proposed House of Taga reconstruction. Fire pits were used widely throughout prehistoric Micronesia for illumination at night, to deter mosquitoes, and to prepare or warm food, but fire pits present a special problem for wood platform structures raised above grade. On Palau, free-standing stone structures were built to support fire pits in the floors of traditional *bai*. No evidence exists for elevated fire pit structures in the Marianas, although earth ovens and food preparation areas on grade frequently are found near *latte*. It seems likely that the ancient Chamorros cooked their food near their houses and relied on other means, perhaps a type of lamp or lantern, for illumination and for insect deterrence.

The reconstructed House of Taga proposed here suggests a structure perhaps 43 feet high, measured from the gable peak to the ground level. The roof pitch is similar to the roofs of important buildings elsewhere in Micronesia. Presumably, the original structure would have been an exceptional achievement in the eyes of the ancient Chamorros.

SUMMARY

The megalithic columns and capstones of *latte* sites in the Mariana Islands are the most visible remains of a distinctive type of ancient architecture not found elsewhere in Oceania, although other types of stone foundations have been found widely throughout Micronesia and Polynesia. *Latte* seem to have appeared first in the Marianas sometime between 1000 and 1100 and continued to be built and used until sometime after European contact. Large prehistoric sites were found in important Chamorro population centers on Guam, Rota, Tinian, and Saipan. *Latte* probably were the foundations of houses occupied by members of important families or groups in the Chamorro society.

Prehistoric houses often were grouped in end-to-end alignment parallel to nearby coastlines, watercourses, or other features of the natural terrain. In plan, the structure invariably was rectangular. So far as is known, the columns per *latte* varied in number from six to fourteen and were arranged in two parallel rows usually spaced between 10 and 14 feet apart. Larger plan areas were achieved by adding pairs of columns rather than by increasing the distances between columns. The megaliths were carved from locally available island sources of stone or reef rock.

Capstones usually were hemispherical in shape and sometimes were notched to fit on the heads of their supporting columns. Columns usually were rectangular in plan and trapezoidal in elevation and often were buried several feet in the ground. Smaller stones sometimes were packed around the bases of columns to keep them erect. Coral-pebble pavings on the ground below and near *latte* suggest the presence of work areas at many sites.

Stone foundations seldom exceed 8 feet in height, with the notable exception of the 16-foot-high structure of the House of Taga on Tinian. A structure that would have been some 18 feet high lies abandoned in the quarry at As Nieves on Rota. Increasing height seems to have represented increasing power and social prestige among the Chamorros. The largest number of *latte* in a single site is found at Mochong on Rota, where at least forty-seven have been located. As the number of structures at a site increased, the variations in foundation heights increased. This may be an indication of increased social complexity.

Less is known about the prehistoric architecture of the Mariana Islands than about the ancient monuments of Palau, Yap, Pohnpei, or Kosrae where Western contact occurred later and less severely impacted the respective native cultures. The ancient Chamorros had no administrative or ceremonial center, such as Nan Madol or Leluh, and no single ruler held power over the Mariana Islands. The prehistoric architecture of the Chamorros, like their culture, seems likely to have been somewhat less complex than the ancient architecture of other Micronesian Islands.

The perishable wood structures of the Chamorros appear to have included houses built on *latte*, smaller cookhouses built on grade, large community houses, and probably other types of structures. The megalithic ruins of the House of Taga today mutely recall one of the most remarkable examples of prehistoric architecture in Micronesia and suggest the possibility of similar achievements in structures of wood whose original appearance we may never know exactly.

OBSERVATIONS

Considering their substantial technical limitations and comparatively small numbers, the ancient people of Micronesia seem to have been among the world's most resourceful and creative people. The character of their architecture suggests multiple and exceptional sources of inspiration. Perhaps each island had its own particular motivation, such as a highly respected paramount in the case of the *saudeleur* on Pohnpei. Absent the *saudeleur*, the succeeding regional chiefs, the *nahnmwarki* and *nahnken*, seem to have been either unable or unwilling to carry forward their predecessors' centuries-old tradition of creating magnificent architecture. The foremost achievements of the ancient Pohnpeians seem to have been associated with the rule of the *saudeleur*.

Creative architecture makes statements that subsume the ideas, concerns, and ambitions of its period and culture. It is difficult to imagine the evolution of Gothic cathedrals without the religious concern of reaching heavenward toward divine benevolence. At the Acropolis in Athens one becomes aware of the Greek ideal of measured perfection. The extraordinary engineering achievements of ancient Rome, such as the arches of great aqueducts and the vaults of the public baths, mutely attest to the extraordinary ambitions of their builders.

Similarly, the architecture of prehistoric Micronesia reflects the preferences, ideas, and aspirations of its creators. The magnificent stone city of Leluh seems to have been a manifestation of ancient Kosrae under the supreme rule of the *tokosra*. On Yap closely knit clans or village groups appear to have taken pride in creating often ornate and always impressive meeting houses, residences, boat houses, and other structures. Competing clans or groups on Palau apparently expressed their cultural ambitions in the form of handsome *bai*, sculpted megaliths, and often immense earthworks. In the Marianas the height of a *latte* house above the ground seems to have been an indication of its social status relative to its neighbors; the higher the building, the greater its prestige.

COMMITMENT OF RESOURCES

The construction of many of Micronesia's monuments required the commitment of substantial manpower and material. The House of Taga, with its dozen megalithic columns, each weighing perhaps 14 tons, was the most ambitious completed project in the prehistoric Marianas, while the unfinished megaliths of the As Nieves quarry would have been even larger. The organization of quarry activities, coastal barge operations, and the erection sequence of the House of Taga suggests skillful and well-coordinated workers.

Considerable resources also were required to erect Nan Madol, where major construction apparently continued for several centuries. Basalt prisms weighing up to 5 tons and boulders up to 50 tons were taken from quarries in various locations around Pohnpei. Few of the quarries were near the construction site. Many megaliths had to be moved first down to the shore and then by rafts around the island for distances of sometimes several dozen miles. A very substantial motivation must have existed for succeeding generations to continue to expend major resources in creating their magnificent monuments.

The stone city of Leluh on Kosrae is another example of the considerable dedication required to create the extraordinary architecture of ancient Micronesia. A similar expression of ideas important to the community appears in the architecture of Palau and Yap, although on scales different from Leluh and Nan Madol. Highly skilled craftsmen carved and painted the exuberant ornamentations of the *bai* at Irrai and the *pebaey* of Bechiyal. Built with great patience and expertise, these structures recall architectural traditions that have been central concerns of the islanders for centuries.

TRADITION AND INVENTION

Efficiency in erecting a traditional house on Yap gives way to the magic of erecting certain posts or beams before others. Only if the customary sequences are followed will the building be beautiful and last a very long time, the Yapese explain. The people who use the structure will be healthy and live long lives. A propitious spirit for the place is vastly more important than expediency in construction.

The Palauans devised a particularly ingenious method of protecting a house from the winds of a destructive typhoon. They are able to lower the roof of a *bai* like a sail. The two roof planes are lashed together at the ridge and are tied to the main structural frame at a limited number of points. When the bindings are released, the planes slide down to ground level while the structural frame remains in place. The main rafters and beams offer comparatively little wind resistance—the winds simply blow through the structural frame.

Yapese canoe sheds (*sipal*) demonstrate an exceptional degree of resourcefulness within the limits of neolithic technology. The double-ended sailing canoe of prehistoric Micronesia is in itself a remarkable feat of naval architecture. To house the graceful canoe of Bechiyal the Yapese devised a method of eliminating several central posts required for typical structures. The posts otherwise would have prohibited the outrigger from entering the shed. A combination of curving wood posts cantilevering up from the ground and a network of roof rafters and beams resolves the problem structurally.

Understanding that all of the original settlers were of Asian origins and that the isolated high islands they inhabited had generally similar environments, one might expect that the islanders would develop generally similar ideas about architecture. However, the opposite is more frequently the case. Their architectural ideas are in fact richly diverse.

DENSITY AND ACCOMMODATION

An unusual aspect of Micronesia that may have influenced its architectural evolution is the relatively very high population densities of the islands. Table 1 illustrates this phenomenon, assuming the prehistoric population of Micronesia, excluding Guam, to have been about what it is today.

Several centuries ago the populations of the six continents would have been much smaller, and consequently their densities would have been much lower. By contrast, prehistoric Micronesia's density was exceptionally high. Much of the land area of the islands is infertile, such as major inshore portions of Babeldaob, Yap, and Guam. Thus, the areas suitable for human habitation and food production are exceedingly limited and quite highly prized. Our guides on Yap and Pohnpei were able to recite the names of the owners of each individual tree, shrub, and plant. Fishing rights in the bountiful lagoons and reefs surrounding the islands, the main protein food source, also were carefully apportioned. The same sensitive regard for limited resources seems to pervade the prehistoric architecture of Micronesia.

Like densely concentrated people elsewhere, the ancient Micronesians required high degrees of cooperation and discipline in order for their communities to survive and prosper. Their skillful plans, sometimes on comparatively large scales, such as those of Leluh and Nan Madol, reflect the discipline of their buildings. Similarly, their works of architecture are accommodated in special places while celebrating particular purposes.

A unique characteristic of traditional Micronesian architecture is its quality of being precisely special, just as the *pebaey* of Bechiyal is not replicated elsewhere on Yap or anywhere else in Micronesia, for that matter. The design of the *pebaey* in Okau Village on Yap is distinctly different from the functionally comparable edifice in Bechiyal.

ARCHITECTURAL EVOLUTION

Information presently available on prehistoric Micronesia points to several phases in the evolution of its traditional architecture. The phases occurred at different times on various islands and not at all on others, thus defying generalization. Although the Marianas appear to have been settled first, perhaps about 1300 B.C., *latte* houses did not appear until about A.D. 1000, some two millennia later.

At first the *latte* stone foundations may have been of modest heights, but in time many were built up to 8 feet in height. The unique House of Taga *latte* rose 16 feet, and the unfinished As Nieves structure probably would have been about 2 feet higher. The latter project may have been abandoned about the time of Magellan's discovery of the Marianas in 1521. *Latte* continued to be built until perhaps 1650. During the six and one-half centuries of *latte* building, increasing height seems to have been an important factor, apparently an indication of increased prestige.

Perhaps first settled not long after the Marianas, Palau apparently began to produce huge earthen terraces and stone-columned meeting houses during the fifth century A.D. Thus, monumental architecture seems to have appeared on Palau some five centuries earlier than in the Marianas. The *bai* at Badrulchau apparently represents an early stage in the evolution of Palauan community houses. Here the primary roof beams seem to have been built parallel to the longitudinal axis of the structure, the floor apparently rested directly on the ground, and a central row of columns supported the ridge beam. Traditional *bai* recorded by early European observers some fifteen hundred years later were of a different design indeed. Without exception they had wood platform floors elevated several feet above grade on stone piers and lacked central rows of columns.

The earliest time for the beginning of architecture on Yap is presently unknown, although a chronology roughly similar to Palau's would be a reasonable possibility. Also lacking is information on the origin of the hexagonal-shaped, elevated stone foundations of traditional Yapese community houses, residences, and other structures. Elevated stone foundations with hexagonal plans occur nowhere else in Micronesia. My speculation would be that the shape may have evolved from rectangular platforms in response to the projection of roof peaks above gable ends. The central row of columns unique to traditional Yapese architecture would have facilitated the evolution of hexagonal plans.

Following several centuries of modest building activity at Nan Madol, elaborate megalithic architecture seems to have begun in the thirteenth century and continued until perhaps the early seventeenth century. The roughly four centuries of major construction correspond with the unification of the island under the *saudeleur*. Thereafter, comparatively little building occurred at Nan Madol. Thus, the prehistoric architecture of Pohnpei had been in a state of decline for about two centuries by the time sustained contact with the West began in the 1820s.

The island city of Leluh apparently was built over the six-century period immediately preceding Western contact. The city's largest and most impressive walls probably were erected in the fifteenth and sixteenth centuries, but building activity continued until about 1800, when Leluh appears to have reached the pinnacle of its development. Thus, monumental architecture seems to have appeared about two centuries later on Kosrae than on Pohnpei. Leluh's evolution over a period of centuries can be seen in its remaining walls, some built stoutly on grand scales while those built subsequently were more hurriedly assembled and more modest in size. As conditions in the life of the city changed in the course of time, so did its architecture.

SPANNING SOLUTIONS

Wood frame houses with thatched roofs probably were found throughout prehistoric Micronesia, but the methods of supporting the roofs seem to have varied widely. The spanning of the roof refers to the system employed for extending the roof structure from one bearing wall, beam, or post to another. As the distance between the points of support increases, the structural problem increases and the spanning solution often becomes more complex.

The simplest method of spanning a roof is by means of a beam resting on two posts. In a roof structure the beam may serve as a rafter, spanning from the central ridge down to the wall. Sheds, such as the copra drying houses (*toorba*) on Yap, are examples of these basic structures.

Table 1. Comparative Population Densities

Area	Population*	Square Miles	Persons/Square Mile
Asia	2,696,082,000	16,998,000	159
Africa	471,769,000	11,688,000	40
North America	366,628,000	9,366,000	39
South America	240,818,000	6,885,000	35
Europe	684,824,000	4,017,000	171
Australia	14,588,000	2,966,000	5
Micronesia	135,000	708	191
Truk	40,000	49.2	813
Yap	27,000	30.6	882

SOURCE: Based on data from *Atlas of the World* (Washington, D.C.: National Geographic Society, 1981, 1983), p. 234.
*1985 estimate.

A variation of the simple shed roof may be found in the traditional *pebaey* of Yap. One of the unique features of Yapese houses is the row of posts through the center of the structure below the ridgeline. The ridge beam is a simple post-and-beam arrangement. The rafters on either side of the ridge also act like simple beams. They bear on the side wall at one end and on the ridge at the other end. Apparently, the *bai* at Badrulchau represents a similar type of structure very early in the evolution of architecture in Palau. None of the more recent Palauan *bai* have central rows of columns.

While the Yapese seem to have preferred rows of posts through the centers of their buildings, the people elsewhere in Micronesia devised methods of eliminating central supports. On Pohnpei and Kosrae a type of king post truss was introduced to permit the roof structure to span from one bearing wall to the other with no interior post. This was accomplished by introducing a horizontal beam between two bearing walls and placing a vertical post in the middle of the beam so that it supported the ridge beam.

The extent to which the king post assembly actually worked like a truss is unclear. The joints, for example, would have to firmly attach adjoining structural components in order to act as a truss. It seems possible that, once the roof planes were in place, they could take all of the gravity forces down to the bearing wall. Thus, the king post could

have supported the ridge beam during construction but thereafter may have played little or no role in supporting the roof. The horizontal beam on which the king post rested, however, served the important function of resisting the outward thrust of the roof planes by tying them to each other.

A different method of attaining column-free interiors was employed traditionally in Palau and quite likely in the Marianas. Here the spanning solution was a matter of triangulation. The roof rafters formed two sides of the triangle, and one or more horizontal ties through the interior of the house served as the third side of the triangle. In the Bai-ra-Irrai, three horizontal ties, one several feet above the other, bind opposing rafters to each other.

LELUH AND NAN MADOL COMPARED

Although some early observers attributed the stone cities of Kosrae and Pohnpei variously to Japan, China, or other highly developed civilizations, these notions have been discredited for some time. Nan Madol was under construction about the same time that the largest walls in Leluh were erected. During the early sixteenth century, Kosraean warriors are said to have conquered Nan Madol and to have imposed a new political order on Pohnpei. Occasional trade for turmeric and other goods is known to have been conducted between the islands. Architec-

tural ideas also may have been exchanged between the people of Pohnpei and Kosrae, although they developed their respective architectural traditions quite independently.

Like Nan Madol, Leluh was built on artificial fill over a shallow lagoon within the reef on the eastern shore of the main island. Leluh extended from the original small island of Leluh, while Nan Madol was built out from Tenwen Island. Both cities had stacked prismatic basalt walls, often on foundations of huge basalt blocks in places where the walls served as seawalls. Both city plans contained residences of a king and high chiefs, royal tombs, and sacred areas. In size, the two cities are almost identical, although the total area of artificial fill is slightly greater in Leluh. Building construction apparently was underway in both cities during the fourteenth century. Beyond these similarities, however, there were many differences.

While Nan Madol's walls were built dominantly of basalt prisms or boulders, the types of walls in Leluh varied widely. Many of the latter were constructed of round basalt, mixed coral and basalt, or stacked round and flat coral. Leluh's highest walls were associated with residential compounds; Nan Madol's, with mortuary areas. House foundations at Nan Madol were raised, while at Leluh they were level with the surrounding grade. The major tombs of Leluh were truncated pyramids of coral with small central crypts lined with basalt. Those of Nan Madol were rectangular structures of stacked prismatic basalt with large interior vaults.

Kosraeans apparently interred the remains of their kings and high chiefs at sea, but similar remains on Pohnpei stayed ashore in tombs. Waterways surrounded most of the islets of Nan Madol, while a central canal system and a network of walled streets provided access at Leluh. Entryways through stone walls always were open to the sky at Leluh, but stone lintels and walls sometimes extend over wall entries at Nan Madol. In Leluh, mortuary and sacred compounds are located near the middle of the city and are surrounded by residential compounds. Nan Madol's sacred and mortuary areas are located in the northeastern half of the city, and residential areas are grouped in the southwestern half.

These and other features clearly illustrate the independent development of architectural ideas in Leluh and Nan Madol. The two island centers do seem to have been sister cities (Cordy, 1981), perhaps like Florence and Venice during the Italian Renaissance at about the same time in Europe.

HOUSES AND DECORATION

The large and impressive meeting houses of Micronesia usually were rectangular in plan and always had high roofs thatched with pandanus or palm fronds. Their posts, beams, rafters, and plates were held together solely by sennit lashings except in Palau, where major structural components were carefully mortised and fitted. The houses were built on wood platforms elevated above grade in Palau and the Marianas, on elevated stone platforms in Yap and Pohnpei, and apparently directly on the ground with stone-paved floors covered by mats in Kosrae.

Ordinary residences were smaller than meeting houses but similarly constructed. Regularized proportions seem to have been maintained. Increasing the height of a platform above grade may have indicated a higher status of the resident or owner.

Traditional house decorations were more elaborate on Palau and Yap than on Pohnpei, Kosrae, and quite likely the Marianas. Incised and painted or lime-inlaid geometric designs decorated the *bai* of Palau and the *pebaey* of Yap. The most elaborate were Palauan motifs, including figures and scenes from oral histories and traditional legends. Nevertheless, wood carving in Micronesia was less elaborate and varied than that of Melanesia (Alkire, 1977).

PREHISTORIC MASONRY WALLS

Gracefully upward-swept corners and portals of stacked prismatic basalt are distinctive architectural characteristics of many walls in Nan Madol and Leluh. The walls slope inward for roughly the lower two-thirds of their heights and then corbel outward to their tops. The inward batter and upward tilt of the corners serve to stabilize and strengthen the structure. The masonry mass leans inward and downward, in effect locking the stones together by compression.

An interesting parallel exists in the prehistoric masonry walls of Egypt, for instance, in the Third Dynasty Pyramid of Sekhemkhet at Saqqara (Gideon, 1981:300–313). The unfinished corner of the pyramid tilts inward at an angle of about 75 degrees and curves upward to stabilize the structure. This engineering knowledge helped the Egyptians to build enduring pyramids. Apparently, the ancient Micronesian masons independently developed a similar masonry technique for their structures.

An unusual feature not found in Egyptian walls is the pronounced outward corbel of the upper courses of stone, such as those projecting from the upper walls of Lurun and Nandauwas. Apparently, the Micronesians discovered the inherent compressive strength of basalt prisms when they are stacked like logs. The bases of the elongated stones were locked firmly into the wall by the weight of upper stones bearing down. The Egyptian stones tended to be more cube shaped. If the Egyptians had projected their stones too far out of their walls, the stones would have become unstable and fallen from the wall. The Egyptians did use corbel vaults, of course, for the roofs of certain interior chambers and passageways. Their architectural expression, however, is quite different from that of Micronesian masonry walls.

ORIGINS OF IDEAS
IN ARCHITECTURE

The origins of ideas in architecture have been the subject of theoretical conjecture since at least the time of the Roman architect Vitruvius (Rykwert, 1984). Information presently being generated by archaeologists provides new insights into the probable beginnings of architecture. For example, architectural theorists have assumed for centuries that tools, such as an axe to fell a tree, were required to construct the earliest structures of humankind. However, more recently developed information casts substantial doubt over this set of assumptions. Data from pre-historic sites as far removed from each other as the eastern United States and the remote islands of Micronesia suggest that the earliest works of architecture were created by placing together materials commonly found in nature, such as shells and stones. These materials were employed without modification by tools.

Thus far the earliest architecture in the eastern United States appears to have been the sometimes immense shell rings along the Atlantic coast from South Carolina to northeast Florida (Morgan, 1980). The remarkable structures began to appear some 4,200 years ago and continued to be built for several centuries. Occasionally large enough in diameter to encircle a modern-day football field, the rings were constructed by carefully placing discarded seashells in circular mounds over extended periods of time, perhaps involving several generations. The builders undoubtedly were ancient Americans who apparently had no previous experience in creating enduring architectural monuments. What purpose the shell rings served, if any, is unknown.

Micronesia provides other examples of assembling unmodified natural materials to create architecture. Coral and basalt boulders and naturally formed basalt prisms are carefully stacked and interlocked to form walls on Pohnpei and Leluh. In some instances the walls exceed 20 feet in height and 15 feet in thickness. Mortar is not used, and the stones retain their natural shapes.

These very early structures appear to have evolved as their builders gained experience. They seem to illustrate LeCorbusier's (1926: 54) observation that "great architecture is at the very origins of humanity . . . it is the immediate product of human instinct . . . Geometry is the measure of the mind." The earliest act in creating architecture may well have been the act of placing natural materials in relation to each other, rather than the act of converting natural materials to more usable forms, such as firing clay to produce bricks, shaping stones to fit into walls, or producing an axe to fell a tree.

OVERVIEW

The examples of prehistoric architecture presented in this study illustrate the rich diversity of design ideas that evolved in Micronesia during the many centuries preceding Western contact. The skill and knowledge necessary to create the traditional architecture of the islands were handed down from parents to children for many generations. In some places, such as Bechiyal Village in Yap and Irrai Village in Palau, young artisans presently are being instructed in the ancient skills by those few craftsmen who still remember the traditional Micronesian methods of building. Today the fragile remains of many of the ancient monuments are in danger of being destroyed by nature, on the one hand, and by humans, on the other. Many of the prehistoric sites continue to be very impressive, including the remains of Leluh and Nan Madol, the restored structures of Bechiyal and Irrai, the sculpted terraces of Babeldaob, and the enigmatic *latte* sites of the Marianas.

The emerging states of Micronesia have no resources more important than their people and their ancient architectural heritages. Properly preserved and where possible restored, the prehistoric monuments would serve as a living record of the islanders' ancient and venerable traditions. At the same time research efforts should continue in the interest of expanding our presently limited understanding of human experience in the remote islands of the South Seas.

The ancient architecture of Micronesia is one of the most remarkable and impressive cultural achievements of any prehistoric people. It is a source of continuing inspiration for architects, designers, and other people who search for meaning in our present-day environment.

154

BIBLIOGRAPHY

Abella, Domingo. 1965. "Legaspi Claims Marianas for Spanish Throne." *Pacific Profile* 3(1):18–36. [A 1565 diary.]

Advisory Council on Historic Preservation. 1981. *Termination of the U.S. Trusteeship of the Islands of Micronesia.* Report to the President and Congress of the United States. Washington, D.C., 25 August.

Alkire, William. 1977. *An Introduction to the Peoples and Cultures of Micronesia.* 2d ed. Menlo Park, Calif.: Cummings.

Anson, Lord George. 1748. *A Voyage around the World in the Years 1740–1744.* [*See* Walter, 1974.] London: John and Paul Knapton.

Athens, J. Stephen. 1981. *The Discovery and Archaeological Investigation of Nan Madol, Ponape, Eastern Caroline Islands.* Micronesian Archaeological Survey Report, no. 3. Saipan: Office of Historic Preservation, Trust Territory of the Pacific Islands.

———. 1983. "The Megalithic Ruins of Nan Madol." *Natural History* (American Museum of Natural History) 92(12):50–61.

———. 1984. "Surface Artifact Distributions at the Nan Madol Site: A Preliminary Assessment of Spatial Patterning." *New Zealand Journal of Archaeology* 6:129–153.

———. 1986a. *Archaeological Investigations at Tarague Beach, Guam.* Report submitted to Base Civil Engineering, 43rd Strategic Wing. Andersen Air Force Base, Department of the Air Force, APO San Francisco.

———. 1986b. "Nan Madol: Archaeology of a Pohnpeian Chiefdom Center." Manuscript on file, Office of Historic Preservation, Trust Territory of the Pacific Islands, Saipan.

Ayres, William S., and Alan E. Haun. 1978. *Ponape Archaeological Survey, 1977 Research.* Micronesian Archaeological Survey Report, no. 1. Saipan: Office of Historic Preservation, Trust Territory of the Pacific Islands.

———. 1982. "Ponape Archaeological Survey, 1979 Research." Manuscript on file, Office of Historic Preservation, Trust Territory of the Pacific Islands, Saipan.

Ayres, William S., Alan E. Haun, and Craig Severance. 1981. *Ponape Archaeological Survey, 1978 Research.* Micronesian Archaeological Report, no. 4. Saipan: Office of Historic Preservation, Trust Territory of the Pacific Islands.

Ballendorf, Dirk. 1977. "Historic and Cultural Preservation in Micronesia." *Guam Recorder* (University of Guam) 7:30–32.

Barrett, Ward, trans. 1975. *Mission in the Marianas: An Account of Fr. Diego Luis de Sanvitores and His Companions, 1669–1670.*

Minneapolis: University of Minnesota Press.

Bath, Joyce E. 1984. *Sapwtakai: Archaeological Survey and Testing.* Micronesian Archaeological Survey report, no. 14. Saipan: Office of Historic Preservation, Trust Territory of the Pacific Islands.

———. 1986. Personal communications over a four-year period.

Bath, J. E., and K. Shun. 1982. "Archaeological Salvage on Waterline C, Lelu, Kosrae, Final Report." Manuscript on file, Office of Historic Preservation, Trust Territory of the Pacific Islands, Saipan.

Bellwood, Peter S. 1979a. *Man's Conquest of the Pacific.* New York: Oxford University Press.

———. 1979b. "The Oceanic Context." In *The Prehistory of Polynesia,* ed. Jessie D. Jennings. Cambridge, Mass.: Harvard University Press.

Berg, Mark L., trans., and Robert D. Craig, ed. 1982. *The Palau Islands in the Pacific Ocean,* by Karl Semper. Mangilao: Micronesian Area Research Center, University of Guam.

Bernart, Luelen. 1977. *The Book of Luelen.* Trans. and ed. John L. Fischer, Saul H. Riesenberg, and Marjorie G. Whiting. Pacific History Series, no. 8. Honolulu: University Press of Hawaii.

Campbell, Dr. 1836. "Island of Ascension." *The Colonist* (New South Wales) 2(78):193–194. [Republished with minor revisions in Ward, 1967.]

Carano, Paul, and Pedro C. Sanchez. 1964. *A Complete History of Guam.* Rutland, Vt., and Tokyo: Charles E. Tuttle.

Carucci, James. 1983. *Archaeological Survey of the "Bai-ra-Irrai," Airai State, Republic of Palau.* Koror: Belau National Museum and the Division of Cultural Affairs, Republic of Palau.

Cheyne, Andrew. 1852. *A description of islands in the Western Pacific Ocean, north and south of the Equator, with sailing directions together with their productions, manners and customs of the natives, and vocabularies of their various languages.* London: J. D. Potter.

———. 1866. "Journal aboard the Brigantine Acis. November 1863–February 1866." [Private journal in the possession of Sir Joseph Cheyne, Rome.]

Christian, F. W. 1899. *The Caroline Islands: Travel in the Sea of Little Islands.* London: Methuen.

Clune, Francis J. 1981. "Truk Islands, Eastern Caroline Islands, Trust Territory of the Pacific, Archaeological Investigations." Manuscript on file, Micronesian Archaeological Survey, Office of Historic Preservation, Trust Territory of the Pacific Islands, Saipan. Produced at the

Department of Anthropology, State University of Hawaii, Honolulu.

Cordy, Ross. 1979. "Archaeological Survey in Ngersung and Ngerdiull Villages on Palau." Manuscript on file, Office of Historic Preservation, Trust Territory of the Pacific Islands, Saipan.

———. 1981. "The Lelu Stone Ruins, Kosrae, Micronesia." Social Science Research Institute, University of Hawaii, Honolulu.

———. 1982a. "Lelu, the Stone City of Kosrae." *Journal of the Polynesian Society* (Auckland) March: 103–119.

———. 1982b. *A Summary of Archaeological Work in Micronesia since 1977.* Indo-Pacific Prehistory Association Bulletin, no. 3. Canberra: Australian National University.

———. ed. 1983a. *An Archaeological Survey of Innem, Okat and Laol, Kosrae Island.* Micronesian Archaeological Survey Report, no. 7. Saipan: Office of Historic Preservation, Trust Territory of the Pacific Islands.

———. 1983b. *Leluh Ruins: Short Walk/Interpretive Guide.* Kosrae: Historic Preservation Office.

———. 1983c. "Social Stratification in the Mariana Islands." *Oceania* 53(3): 272–276.

———. 1984. "Preliminary Archaeological Report: 1984 Leluh Ruins Jobs Bill Project." Manuscript on file, Office of Historic Preservation, Trust Territory of the Pacific Islands, Saipan.

———. 1985. "Anthropological Investigations at the Leluh Stone Ruins, Kosrae, Micronesia." National Geographic Research, Washington, D.C.

———. 1986. Personal communications over a three-year period.

Craib, John L. 1983. "Micronesian Prehistory: An Archaeological Overview." *Science* 219: 922–927.

Darwin, Charles. 1901. *The Structure and Distribution of Coral Reefs.* 3d ed. New York: Appleton.

Davidson, Janet M. 1967. "Preliminary Archaeological Investigations on Ponape and other Eastern Caroline Islands." *Micronesia* 3: 81–97.

Dixon, Robert. 1981. "The Mathematical Daisy." *New Scientist* 17 December: 792–795.

Driver, Marjorie G., trans. 1977. "The Account of a Discalced Friar's Stay in the Island of the Ladrones." *Guam Recorder* (University of Guam) 7: 19–21.

———. 1983. "Notes and Documents: Fray Juan Pobre de Zamora and His Account of the Mariana Islands." *Journal of Pacific History* 18 (3): 198–216.

Duperrey, Louis Isidore. 1828. "Mémoire sur les Opérations Géographiques faites dans las Campagne de la Corvette de S. M. Coquille, pendant les années 1822, 1823, 1824 et 1825." *Annales Maritimes et Coloniales* (Paris) pt. 2, vol. 1.

d'Urville, Jules Sébastien César Dumont. 1834–1835. *Voyage Pittoresque autour du Monde.* Vols. 1 and 2. Paris: Chez L. Tenré, Libraire-Éditeur, and Chez Henri Dupuy. Furne and Co., Publishers.

Edwards, Julie Olsen, and Robert L. Edwards. 1978. "Fauba, a Past Waiting for a Future: Tol Island, Truk Lagoon, Micronesia." Manuscript on file, Office of Historic Preservation, Trust Territory of the Pacific Islands, Saipan.

Fischer, John L., Saul H. Riesenberg, and Marjorie G. Whiting. 1977. *Annotations to the Book of Luelen.* Pacific History Series, no. 9. Honolulu: University Press of Hawaii.

Force, Roland W. 1960. *Leadership and Cultural Change in Palau.* Chicago Natural History Museum, Fieldiana Anthropology, vol. 50. Chicago.

Force, Roland W., and Maryanne Force. 1972. *Just One House: A Description and Analysis of Kinship in the Palau Islands.* Bulletin no. 235. Honolulu: Bishop Museum Press.

Freycinet, Louis de. 1829. *Voyage autour du Monde . . . exécute sur les corvettes de S. M. L'Uranie et La Physicienne, pendant les années 1817, 1818, 1819, et 1820.* Part 2: *Historique,* vol. 2. Paris: Pillet Aine.

Gideon, Sigfried. 1965. *Space, Time, and Architecture.* 4th ed. Cambridge, Mass.: Harvard University Press.

———. 1981. "The Beginnings of Architecture." Part 2 of *The Eternal Present.* Bollingen Series, no. xxxv-6-11. Princeton: Princeton University Press.

Gifford, E. W., and D. S. Gifford, 1959. "Archaeological Excavations in Yap." *Anthropological Records* 18(2): 149–224.

Gilliand, Cora Lee C. 1975. *The Stone Money of Yap.* Smithsonian Studies in History and Technology, no. 23. Washington, D.C.: Smithsonian Institution Press.

Gordon, C. C., D. B. Hanson, and M. R. Thomas. 1982. "Phase One Report on the Cultural Resource Survey of Rota." Pacific Studies Institute, Agana. Report to the Historic Preservation Office of the Commonwealth of the Northern Marianas, Saipan.

Gosda, Raymond. 1958. "Notes on Archaeological Specimens from Truk Atoll Sent to the U.S. National Museum on July 8, 1958—Brief Description of Sites." Manuscript on file, Micronesian Archaeological Survey, Office of Historic Preservation, Trust Territory of the Pacific Islands, Saipan.

Graves, Michael W. 1982. "An Annotated Bibliography of Prehistoric and Protohistoric References Pertaining to the Mariana Islands and Micronesia." Manuscript on file, Research Council, University of Guam, Mangilao.

———. 1983. "Archaeological Correlates of Ranking in the Mariana Islands: Architectural Variation in Latte Sets." University of Guam, Mangilao. Paper presented at the 15th Pacific Science Congress, Dunedin, New Zealand.

———. 1985, in press. "Organization and Differentiation within Late Prehistoric Ranked Social Units in the Mariana Islands of the Western Pacific." *Journal of Field Archaeology.*

———. 1986. Personal communications over a three-year period.

Gulick, L. H. 1857. "The Ruins on Ponape, or Ascension Island of the Pacific Ocean." *The Friend* n.s. 6(8): 57–60.

———. 1861. "The Ruins on Kusaie." *The Friend* n.s. 10(8): 59.

Gumerman, George J., David Snyder, and W. Bruce Masse. 1981. *An Archaeological Reconnaissance in the Palau Archipelago, Western Caroline Islands, Micronesia.* Southern Illinois University Center for Archaeological Investigation Research Papers, no. 23. Carbondale.

Hambruch, Paul. 1919. "Die Ruinen von Lolo." In *Kusae,* by E. Sarfert. Hamburg: Friederichson and Co.

———, trans. 1929. *Elf jahre in Australien und auf der insel Ponape: Ergebnisse eines irischen matresen in den jahren 1822 bis 1833,* by James F. O'Connell. Berlin: August Scherl. [Originally published in 1836.]

———. 1936. "Ponape: Die Ruinen." In *Ergebnisse der Sudsee-Expedition 1908–1910,* ed. G. Thilenius, II, B, VII, 3. Hamburg: Friederichson and Co. [English translation from HRAF Microfilm Collection of Micronesia, Reel 50, no. 1006. The translations were made at Yale University about 1942–1944. Human Relations Area Files, Yale University, New Haven.]

Hezel, Francis X. 1983. *The First Taint of Civilization: A History of the Caroline and Marshall Islands in Pre-Colonial Days, 1521–1885.* Honolulu: University Press of Hawaii.

Hornbostel, Hans G. 1921–1925. Unpublished notes and manuscripts on archaeology in the Marianas. On microfilm at the library of the

Bernice P. Bishop Museum, Honolulu.

Hunter-Anderson, Rosalind L. 1981. "Yapese Stone Fish Traps." *Asian Perspectives* 24(1): 81–90.

———. 1983. *Traditional Yapese Settlement Patterns: An Ethno-archaeological Approach.* Guam: Pacific Studies Institute.

———. 1984. "Recent Observations on Traditional Yapese Settlement Patterns." *New Zealand Journal of Archaeology* 6: 95–105.

———. 1985. Personal communications over a three-year period.

Intoh, Michiko. 1984. Annotated site plan of Bechiel Village Map Island, Yap. University of Otago, Dunedin, New Zealand.

Intoh, Michiko, and Foss Leach. 1984. *The Pottery Traditions of the Yap Islands: Preliminary Report of the Survey Work Conducted in the Yap Islands from May 1983 to January 1984.* Dunedin, New Zealand: Department of Anthropology, University of Otago.

Jennings, Jesse D., ed. 1979. *The Prehistory of Polynesia.* Cambridge, Mass.: Harvard University Press.

Jensen, John Thayer. 1977. *Yapese-English Dictionary.* PALI Language Texts: Micronesia. Honolulu: University Press of Hawaii.

John, Teddy [Kosrae Preservation Officer]. 1984. Personal communications incident to the author's visit to Kosrae.

Keate, George. 1789. *An Account of the Pelew Islands, situated in the western part of the Pacific Ocean, composed from the journals and communications of Captain Henry Wilson and some of his officers who in August 1783 were there shipwrecked in the Antelope.* London: G. Nicol.

King, T. F., and P. L. Parker. 1984. *Pisekin Noomw Noon Tonaachaw: Archaeology in the Tonaachaw Historic District, Moen, Truk.* Micronesian Archaeological Survey Report, no. 18. Carbondale: Center for Archaeological Investigations, Southern Illinois University.

Kirch, Patrick V. 1978*a*. *Archaeological Reconnaissance of the Proposed Yap Airport Alternate Sites, Yap District, Western Caroline Islands.* Honolulu: Bernice P. Bishop Museum.

———. 1978*b*. *Archaeological Reconnaissance of the Proposed Babeldaob-Koror Airport Site, Palau District, Western Caroline Islands.* Honolulu: Bernice P. Bishop Museum.

Kobayashi, Shigeki. 1978. *Structure and Process of Erection of the Yapese House.* Nagoya, Japan: Little World Museum of Man.

Kramer, Augustin. 1917. "Palau." In *Ergebnisse der Sudsee Expedition, 1908–1910,* ed. G. Thilenius, II, B, III, i. Hamburg: Friederichson and Co.

———. 1919. "Palau." In *Ergebnisse der Sudsee Expedition, 1908–1910,* ed. G. Thilenius, II, B, III, ii. Hamburg: Friederichson and Co.

———. 1926. "Palau." In *Ergebnisse der Sudsee Expedition, 1908–1910,* ed. G. Thilenius, II, B, III, iii. Hamburg: Friederichson and Co.

———. 1929. "Palau." In *Ergebnisse der Sudsee Expedition, 1908–1910,* ed. G. Thilenius, II, B, III, iv. Hamburg: Teilband, Friederichson and Co.

Kubary, Jan Stanislaw. 1874. "Die Ruinen von Mamnatol auf der Insel Ponape (Ascension)." *Journal des Museums Goddefroy* 6(23): 3.

———. 1889 and 1895. *Ethnographische Beiträge zur Kenntnis des Karolinen Archipels.* Leiden: Verlag von P. W. M. Trap.

Kugfas, Andrew [Yap Historic Preservation Officer]. 1984. Personal communications incident to the author's visit to Yap.

Labby, David. 1976. *The Demystification of Yap.* Chicago: University of Chicago Press.

LeBar, Frank M. 1964. *The Material Culture of Truk.* Yale University Publications in Anthropology, no. 68. New Haven: Department of Anthropology, Yale University.

LeCorbusier, [Charles-Edouard Jeanneret]. 1926. *Vers une architecture.* Paris.

Lessa, William A. 1956. "Myth and Blackmail in the Western Carolines." *Journal of the Polynesian Society* (Wellington) 65.

———. 1975. *Drake's Island of Thieves: Ethnological Sleuthing.* Honolulu: University Press of Hawaii.

Lesson, René-Primevere. 1838–1839. *Voyage autour du monde entrepris par ordre du gouvernement sur la corvette la Coquille.* Vols. 1 and 2. Paris: Porrat.

Lingenfelter, Sherwood G. 1975. *Yap: Political Leadership and Cultural Change in an Island Society.* Honolulu: University Press of Hawaii.

Lizama, Alejandro. 1983. An 18 × 24 inch annotated drawing illustrating a proposed A-frame superstructure for *latte.* Historic Preservation Section, Department of Parks and Recreation, Government of Guam. 10 February.

Lucking, Laurie J. 1980. "Final Report: Babeldaob-Koror Airport Mitigation Project." Manuscript on file, Office of Historic Preservation, Trust Territory of the Pacific Islands, Saipan.

———. 1981. "Archaeological Salvage Investigations at Irrai Quarry, Proposed Palau Airport." Manuscript on file, Office of Historic Preservation, Trust Territory of the Pacific Islands, Saipan.

———. 1984. "An Archaeological Investigation of the Prehistoric Terraces of Palau." Manuscript on file, Office of Historic Preservation, Trust Territory of the Pacific Islands, Saipan.

Lütke, Frederic [Fyedor]. 1971. *Voyage autour du Monde: Exécute par Ordre de sa Majesté l'Empereur Nicolas 1st, sur la Corvette Le Seniavine.* Paris: Firmin Didot, 1835. Reprinted *Bibliotheca Australiana,* nos. 58 and 59. New York, Amsterdam, and N. Israel: DaCapo.

McCoy, Patrick C. 1979. "Easter Island." In *The Prehistory of Polynesia,* ed. Jesse D. Jennings. Cambridge, Mass.: Harvard University Press.

McManus, Edwin G., et al. 1976. *Palauan-English Dictionary.* Honolulu: University Press of Hawaii.

Malone, Mike. 1983. "Micronesia's Star Path Navigators." *Glimpses of Micronesia* (Agana, Guam) 24(4): 12–19.

Marck, Jeffrey. 1975. "The Origin and Dispersal of the Proto Nuclear Micronesians." M.A. thesis, University of Iowa.

Morgan, William N. 1980. *Prehistoric Architecture in the Eastern United States.* Cambridge, Mass.: MIT Press.

Morison, Samuel Eliot. 1974. *The European Discovery of America: The Southern Voyages, 1492–1616.* New York: Oxford University Press.

Mueller, Wilhelm. 1917. "Yap." In *Ergebnisse der Sudsee Expedition, 1908–1910,* ed. G. Thilenius. Hamburg: Friederichson and Co.

O'Connell, James F. 1972. *A Residence of Eleven Years in Holland and the Caroline Islands.* Ed. Saul H. Reisenberg. Honolulu: University Press of Hawaii. [Originally published in Boston in 1836.]

Osborne, Carolyn and Douglas. 1969. "Construction of the *Bai.*" In *Palau Museum "Bai."* Dedication Brochure, Koror, Palau.

Osborne, Douglas. 1966. *The Archaeology of the Palau Islands: An Intensive Survey.* Bernice P. Bishop Museum Bulletin, no. 230. Honolulu.

———. 1979. "Archaeological Test Excavations, Palau Islands, 1968–1969." *Micronesia* (University of Guam) Suppl. 1: 1–353.

Owen, Hera Ware. 1969. "Decorative Detail in the *Bai.*" In *Palau Museum "Bai."* Dedication Brochure, Koror, Palau.

Pacific Studies Institute. 1980. *Archaeological and Ethnographic Investigations, Alignment 5B Airport Historical Area, Yap, Western Caroline Islands.* 4 vols. Agana, Guam: Pacific Studies Institute.

Palau, Republic of. 1981. *Beluu Era Belau.* Koror, Palau.

Parker, P. L., and T. F. King. 1982. "The East End of Moen: Ethnographic and Archaeological Studies in Sapwuuk Village." Manuscript on file, Micronesian Archaeological Survey, Trust Territory Historic Preservation Office, Saipan.

Peebles, Christopher S., and Susan M. Kus. 1977. "Some Archaeological Correlates of Ranked Societies." *American Antiquity* 42(3):421–448.

Pigafetta, Antonio. 1969. *Magellan's Voyage: A Narrative Account of the First Circumnavigation.* Trans. and ed. R. A. Skelton. 2 vols. New Haven: Yale University Press. [First published in Paris in 1525.]

Plaza, Sr. Felicia. 1973. "The *Lattes* of the Marianas." *Guam Recorder* (University of Guam) January–March:6–9.

Prescott, William H. 1961. *History of the Conquest of Peru* (1847). Abr. and rev. Victor W. von Hagen. New York: Mentor Books, New American Library of World Literature.

Price, Willard. 1944. *Japan's Islands of Mystery.* New York: John Day Co.

Reinman, Fred R. 1973. "Guam Prehistory: The First Systematic Survey of Guam Latte Sites." *Guam Recorder* (University of Guam) January–March:10–14.

———. 1977. *An Archaeological Survey and Preliminary Test Excavations on the Island of Guam, Marianas Islands, 1965–1966.* Mangilao: Micronesia Area Research Center, University of Guam.

Riesenberg, Saul H. 1968. *The Native Polity of Ponape.* Smithsonian Contributions to Anthropology, vol. 10. Washington, D.C.: Smithsonian Institution Press.

Ritter, Lynn Takata, and Phillip L. Ritter. 1982. *The European Discovery of Kosrae Island: Accounts by Louis Isidore Duperrey, Jules Sébastien César Dumont D'Urville, René-Primevere Lesson, Fyedor Lütke, and Friedrich Heinrich von Kittlitz.* Micronesian Archaeological Survey Report, no. 13. Saipan: Office of Historic Preservation, Trust Territory of the Pacific Islands.

Rudolph, Paul M. Observation on vernacular architecture. *See* Warfield, 1983.

Rykwert, Joseph. 1983. *The First Moderns: The Architects of the Eighteenth Century.* Cambridge, Mass.: MIT Press.

———. 1984. *On Adam's House in Paradise.* 2d ed. Cambridge, Mass.: MIT Press.

Sam, Moses [Palau Historic Preservation Officer]. 1984. Personal communications incident to the author's visit to Palau.

Sarfert, Ernst G. 1919. "Kusae." In *Ergebnisse der Sudsee Expedition, 1908–1910,* ed. G. Thilenius. Hamburg: Friederichson and Co.

Saxe, Arthur A., Richard Allenson, and Susan R. Loughridge. 1980a. "Archaeological Survey of sections of the Circumferential Road on Ponape Island." Manuscript on file, Office of Historic Preservation, Trust Territory of the Pacific Islands, Saipan.

———. 1980b. *The Nan Madol Area of Ponape: Researched into Bounding and Stabilizing an Ancient Administrative Center.* Saipan: Office of Historic Preservation, Trust Territory of the Pacific Islands.

Schneider, David M. 1949. "The Kinship System and Village Orientation of Yap." Ph.D. dissertation, Harvard University.

———. 1984. *A Critique of the Study of Kinship.* Ann Arbor: University of Michigan Press.

Semper, Karl. 1873. *Die Palau-Inseln im Stillen Ozeane.* Leipzig: F. A. Brockhaus. [For an English translation, *see* Berg, 1982.]

Sengebau, Valentine N., P. F. Kluge, Carolyn and Douglas Osborne, and Hera Ware Owen. 1969. *Palau Museum "Bai."* Dedication Brochure, Koror, Palau.

Shutler, Richard, Jr., and M. E. Shutler. 1975. *Oceanic Prehistory.* Menlo Park, Calif.: Cummings.

Spoehr, Alexander. 1954. *Saipan: The Ethnology of a War-Devastated Island.* Chicago Natural History Museum, Fieldiana Anthropology, vol. 41. Chicago.

———. 1957. *Marianas Prehistory: Archaeological Survey and Testing on Saipan, Tinian, and Rota.* Chicago Natural History Museum, Fieldiana Anthropology, vol. 48. Chicago.

Spriggs, M. J. T. 1980. "Irrigation in Melanesia: Formative Adaptation and Intensification." Manuscript, Department of Prehistory, R. S. Pac. S., Australian National University, Canberra.

Stuart, George E., ed. 1983. *Peoples and Places of the Past.* Washington, D.C.: National Geographic Society.

Takayama, Jun. 1982. "A Brief Report on Archaeological Investigations of the Southern Part of Yap Island and Nearby Ngulu Atoll." In *Islanders and Their Outside World,* ed. M. Aoyagi, pp. 77–104. Tokyo: Committee for Micronesian Research, St. Paul's (Rikkyo) University.

Takayama, Jun, and Tomoko Egami. 1971. *Archaeology on Rota in the Mariana Islands: Preliminary Report on the "Latte" Site (M-1).* Reports of the Pacific Archaeological Survey, no. 1. Tokyo: Azuma Shuppan Co.

———. 1973. *Preliminary Archaeological Investigations on the Island of Tol in Truk.* Reports of

the Pacific Archaeological Survey, no. 11. Tokyo: Azuma Shuppan Co.

Takayama, Jun, and Michiko Intoh. 1976. *Archaeological Investigation of "Latte" Site M-13, Rota, in the Marianas.* Reports of the Pacific Archaeological Survey, no. 4. Tokyo: Azuma Shuppan Co.

Thilenius, George, ed. 1913–1938. *Ergebnisse der Sudsee Expedition, 1908–1910,* Part 2, B, *Mikronesien.* 12 vols. in 25 parts. Hamburg: Friederichson and Co.

Thompson, Laura Maud. 1932. *Archaeology of the Mariana Islands.* Bulletin 100. Honolulu: Bishop Museum Press.

———. 1940. "The Function of *Latte* in the Marianas." *Journal of the Polynesian Society* 49:447–465.

———. 1971. *The Native Culture of the Mariana Islands.* Bulletin no. 185. Honolulu: Bishop Museum Press. 1945. Reprint New York: Kraus Reprint Co.

Tillar, Debra. 1985. "The Ruins on Leluh, the Ancient Cities of Kosrae." *Glimpses of Micronesia* 25(4):28–31, 60–61.

von Hagen, Victor W. *History of the Conquest of Peru. See* Prescott, 1961.

Walter, Richard. 1974. *Anson's Voyage around the World in the Years 1740–1744.* New York: Dover Publications.

Ward, Graeme K., and John L. Craib. 1983. "Mochong Archaeological Research 1983." Preliminary Report of Archaeological Mapping and Excavations at Mochong on the Island of Rota, Mariana Islands, during June and July 1983. Report to the Historic Preservation Office, Commonwealth of the Northern Mariana Islands, Saipan.

Ward, R. Gerald, ed. 1967. *American Activities in the Central Pacific, 1790–1870.* Vol. 6 Ridgewood, N.J.: Gregg Press.

Warfield, James P., ed. 1983. *Paul Rudolph, 1983–84 Recipient of the Plym Distinguished Professorship.* Urbana-Champaign: School of Architecture, University of Illinois.

Wenkham, Robert, and Byron Baker. 1971. *Micronesia: The Breadfruit Revolution.* Honolulu: East-West Center Press.

Yawata, Ichiro. 1961. "On the Burial Methods of the Ancient Mariana Islanders." *Asian Perspectives* (Tokyo University) 5(2):164–165.

INDEX

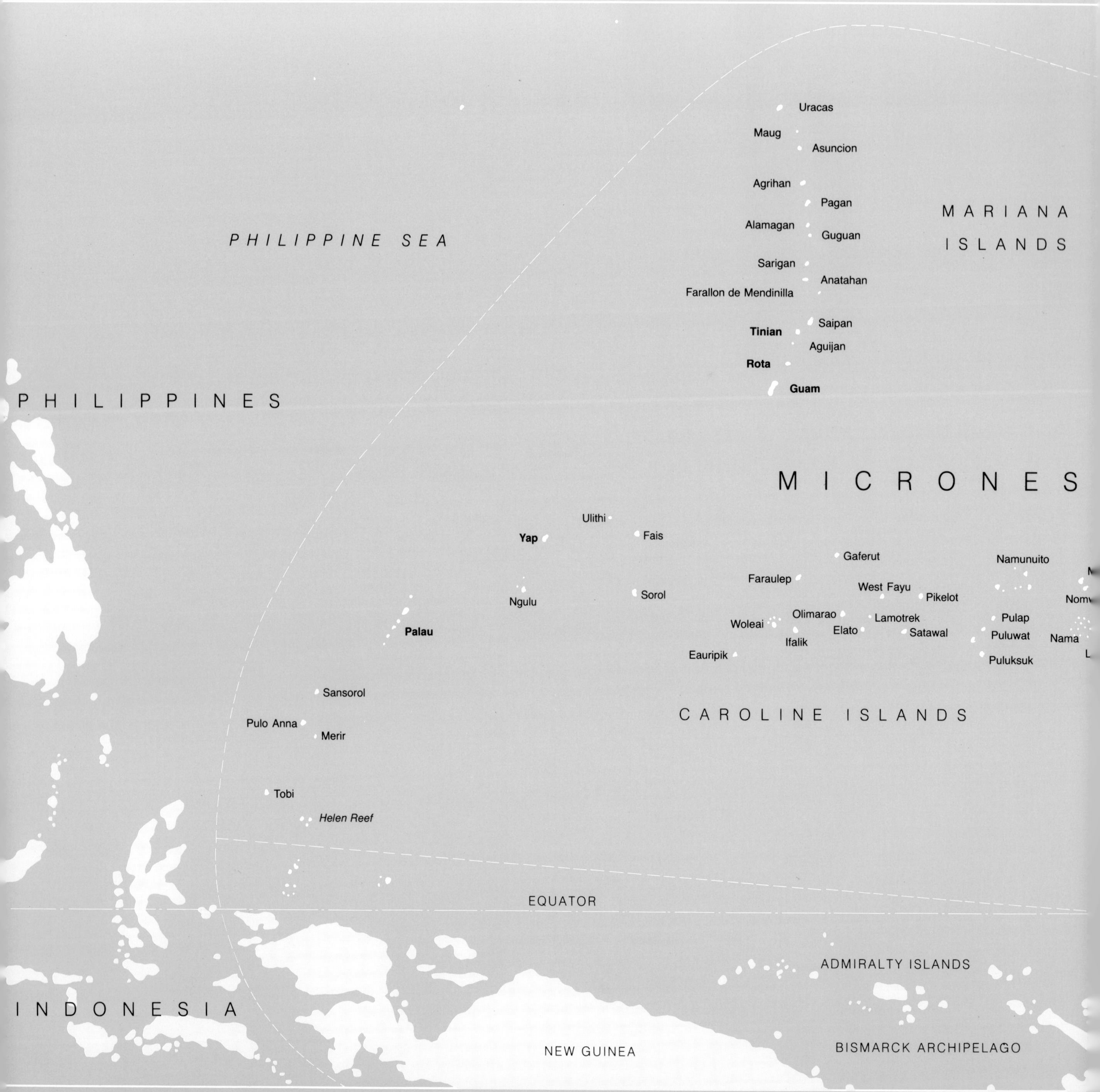

PHILIPPINE SEA

PHILIPPINES

INDONESIA

Island Groups of Micronesia

Uracas

Maug

Asuncion

Agrihan

Pagan

M A R I A N A

Alamagan

Guguan

I S L A N D S

Sarigan

Farallon de Mendinilla

Anatahan

Saipan

Tinian

Aguijan

Rota

Guam

M I C R O N E S

Ulithi

Fais

Yap

Gaferut

Namunuito

Faraulep

West Fayu

Pikelot

Sorol

Olimarao

Pulap

Ngulu

Lamotrek

Woleai

Elato

Satawal

Puluwat

Nama

Ifalik

Palau

Eauripik

Puluksuk

C A R O L I N E   I S L A N D S

Sansorol

Pulo Anna

Merir

Tobi

Helen Reef

EQUATOR

ADMIRALTY ISLANDS

NEW GUINEA

BISMARCK ARCHIPELAGO

PACIFIC OCEAN

Wake

Taongi

MARSHALL ISLANDS

Bikar

Bikini   Rongelap

Enewetak   Utirik
            Ailinginae   Rongrik   Taka

                                    Ailuk
            Wotho   Likiep   Mejit

Ujelang   Kwajalein   Wotje

        Ujae   Erikub
            Lae   Maloelap
                Lib   Aur
                        Namu

Orðluk   Jabwot
    Pakin   Alinglaplap   Majuro
                                              Arno
    Ant   **Pohnpei** Mokil
                                              Mili
amoluk   Pingelap   Jaluit   Knox
                              Namorik   Kili
    Satawan   Ngatik   **Kosrae**

                                    Ebon

    Nukuoru

                            Makin
                            Butaritari

                                    Marakei
                        Abaiang
                                Tarawa
    Kapingamarangi   KIRIBATI   Maiana
                                Kuria   Abemama

                                Aranuka

            Nàuru   Banaba   Nonouti
                                                Beru
                            Tabiteuea   Nukunau
                                        Onotoa
                                Tamana   Arorae

        0   STATUTE MILES   500

        0   KILOMETERS   800

NEW IRELAND

PHILIPPINE SEA

MARIANA
ISLANDS

Uracas

Maug
Asuncion

Agrihan
Pagan

Alamagan
Guguan

Sarigan
Anatahan

Farallon de Mendinilla

Saipan
Tinian
Aguijan

Rota

Guam

PHILIPPINES

MICRONES

Ulithi
Fais

Yap

Gaferut
Namunuito

Faraulep
West Fayu
Pikelot

Sorol

Ngulu
Olimarao
Lamotrek
Pulap

Woleai
Elato
Satawal
Puluwat
Nama

Ifalik

Eauripik

Puluksuk

Palau

CAROLINE ISLANDS

Sansorol

Pulo Anna

Merir

Tobi

Helen Reef

EQUATOR

ADMIRALTY ISLANDS

INDONESIA

NEW GUINEA

BISMARCK ARCHIPELAGO

Island Groups of Micronesia